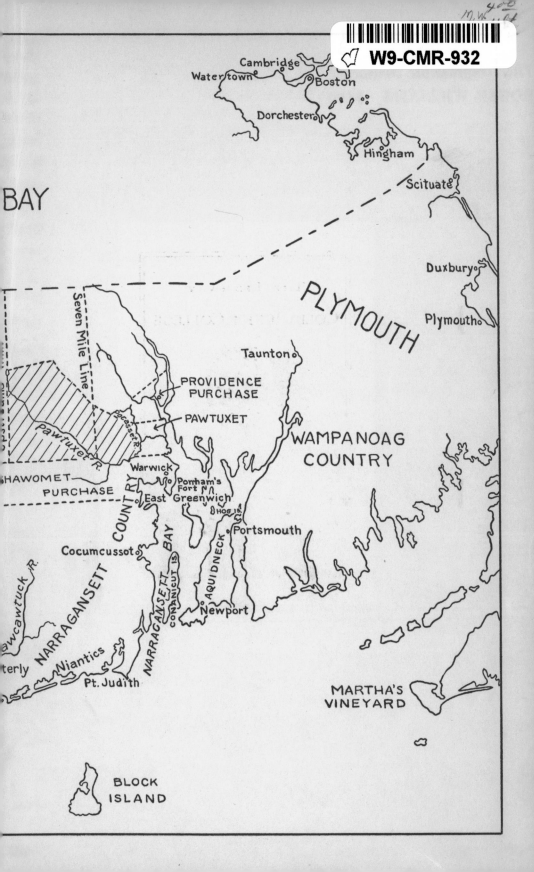

BAY

PLYMOUTH

Cambridge
Watertown
Boston
Dorchester
Hingham
Scituate
Duxbury
Plymouth

Seven Mile Line

Taunton

PROVIDENCE
PURCHASE

PAWTUXET

WAMPANOAG
COUNTRY

Pocasset R.

Pawtuxet R.

SHAWOMET
PURCHASE

Warwick

Pomham's
Fort

East Greenwich

Hog Is.

Portsmouth

Cocumcussot

COUNTRY

NARRAGANSETT

NARRAGANSETT BAY

CONANICUT IS.

AQUIDNECK

Newport

Pawcawtuck R.

Westerly

Niantics

Pt. Judith

MARTHA'S
VINEYARD

BLOCK
ISLAND

The
IRREPRESSIBLE DEMOCRAT
⟩ Roger Williams

By

SAMUEL HUGH BROCKUNIER, Ph.D.

ASSISTANT PROFESSOR OF HISTORY
WESLEYAN UNIVERSITY

A volume of the
RONALD SERIES IN HISTORY
Edited by RALPH H. GABRIEL, Yale University

THE RONALD PRESS COMPANY ⟩ NEW YORK

20019

PRINTED IN THE UNITED STATES OF AMERICA

To

SAWYER REED BROCKUNIER

FOREWORD

THE STORY OF SOCIAL REVOLT in America begins with Roger Williams. More richly than in the case of any contemporary founder of an overseas colony, the pattern of Williams' restless life was woven of the warp and woof of the seventeenth century English rebellion against social injustice and outworn folkways. Conventional New England Puritans wrote him down as contentious and unsound in judgment and consigned him to oblivion; yet in the course of two centuries he was to be hailed as the most original and arresting English thinker thrown up on American shores in the fruitful era of Milton and Locke. Biographies of Williams eventually surpassed in total number those of any other American colonial born earlier than Benjamin Franklin. In 1777 Isaac Backus published the first comprehensive account of Williams, and this was followed successively by Knowles (1834), Gammell (1846), Elton (1852), Dexter (1876), Straus (1894), Carpenter (1909), Easton (1930), and Ernst (1932)—to name only the more important.

Recent portraits of Williams as a distinguished progenitor of American democracy may need careful inspection. The supposition that democracy of any sort ever entered the minds of Englishmen in the seventeenth century, either at home or abroad, has been sharply challenged. At the Harvard tercentenary so eminent an authority as Charles McLean Andrews declared that "American-mindedness" was a late eighteenth century development and that in the first hundred years the American environment was a negligible factor in molding the colonial mind. Professor Andrews charged historians with carrying the beginnings of American democracy "much too far back" and cited Roger Williams as an impractical utopian who brought turmoil and confusion rather than democracy.

With these strictures in mind, I have continually posed the question whether Williams and the colonists who rallied about him were engaged in a democratic agitation for popular government; or whether they owed any debt to the American environment. When they were devising and modifying the institutions of Rhode Island, did these men find any arguments for equalitarianism or logic for democracy in frontier conditions? Or did they erect social and

political fences against the dynamics of open land? Did they in true
English fashion hedge themselves in with property rights, privileged
classes, and political inequalities much as they had known them in
the homeland they had left?

The evidence does not indicate that Williams was impractical and
visionary; nor that democratic ideas were unknown to or beyond the
comprehension of the average man of the seventeenth century.
Monographs on the political ideas of Cromwell's Army, English
Levellers, and contemporary writers on religious toleration abun-
dantly reveal that "American-mindedness" on vital social questions
had sturdy roots on both sides of the Atlantic. The dissenters and
democrats of the seventeenth century did not win the struggle for
religious liberty or popular government either in England or the
colonies; but they counted in their ranks some vigorous champions
of political equalitarianism and a host of exponents of religious
equalitarianism.

The controversies in which Williams participated were not simply
episodes in the struggle of individuals to obtain greater rights and
privileges for themselves. Williams and those who ranged themselves with him in the battle for a wider franchise and popular government justified their cause by a radical theory of the rights of
man. American-mindedness is inevitably a relative term, but one can
trace the appearance in Rhode Island of certain germinal principles
associated with later Americanism. When Williams and his colonial
associates toiled over the specifications of their "humble experiment,"
they drafted a plan much in the manner of the English middle class;
but their finished work likewise bore a functional relationship to the
free spaces of the American wilderness. The social freedom for the
common man in early Rhode Island had a far more marked resemblance to the individualistic character of the later American frontier
than to the traditional restraints in contemporary England imposed
by notions of place and privilege. The Rhode Island suffrage, open
to all freeholders, merely enlarged on English precedent; but the ease
of acquiring land converted it into a broad franchise as it never could
be in a country of enclosures and lordly estates.

Roger Williams more than any other in the English colonies
epitomized the revolutionary forces of his age. I have intended not
to eulogize him as unique in his century but to demonstrate his relevance to his own times. That relevance is attested by the failures of

Williams as well as by his triumphs. His efforts to translate his theories into practice reveal certain limitations. Seventeenth century reformers and radicals, like their spiritual descendants in the nineteenth century, seldom gave adequate consideration to the extent to which social stratification and economic power complicated the problem of creating and maintaining a democratic society. Williams, one of the severest critics of the New England town land system, fought with only partial success against the rapid transformation of that system into speculative enterprises incongruous in a democracy based upon freeholds. The latter part of this book deals with these and similar changes which made Rhode Island less democratic in the eighteenth century than in the generation of the founders.

Although this study proceeds by the medium of biography, it does not pretend to be a portrait of a man's career in the conventional sense. Williams' ideas and public life are considered in their total social milieu. This has involved continuous reference to the contest of aristocratic and democratic factors in Rhode Island and other Puritan colonies and the mother country as well. Drawing the contrast between developments in Rhode Island and those in orthodox Puritan colonies produces sometimes a deadly parallel; but that such a contrast may be disturbing to complacency has seemed no good reason for not drawing it. The parallel, of course, works against Rhode Island as well as for it. The common man in Rhode Island had no such opportunity for education as the common man in Massachusetts. The secular principle of Rhode Island was never all gain. Some of Williams' bitterest controversies were with members of his own colony who represented the forces of intolerance and class ambition as distinctly as opponents in Massachusetts or elsewhere.

Evaluations of Puritan folkways will always differ. Out of the heat of controversy there emerges no common measure of the importance of economic motives and of the relation of class concepts to political domination. In treating religious ideas I have employed the genetic point of view. Approached in this way, Williams' differences with orthodox Puritans, and theirs with him, seem neither incomprehensible nor absurd. The genetic approach, as a key to the stream of ideas, must include consideration of economic and social factors. English middle-class motives and ideals reinforced the peculiarities of Puritanism. Puritanism was a powerful influence; but it has been treated too frequently as a phenomenon dissociated from its medieval

background and from the contemporary English social system. Both
by the "filiopietistic" fraternity and by the school of accusation, New
England Puritanism has been invested with an all-powerful deter-
minism. Yet as our knowledge of the background of the Puritans
widens, it becomes steadily clearer that they did many of the things
that they did, not essentially because they were Puritans, or because
they lived in New England, but because they were Englishmen and
men of the seventeenth century.

It can be shown that the Puritan leaders' conception of themselves
as stewards of a holy experiment led them sometimes to act with
magnanimity, and even on occasion to neglect their self-interest. Yet
on the whole, and certainly in the instances with which Williams and
Rhode Island had particular connection, the impulse toward liberty
and equality was generally more potent among the downtrodden
than among their masters. This struggle, however, existed in every
colony; comparisons between Rhode Island radicals and Puritan
oligarchs are not intended to suggest that a particular merit was
possessed by the people of one colony alone or that a strange obtuse-
ness was the invariable mark of all the rest of New England. The
purpose has been merely to reveal the essential ingredients of the
democratic upthrust in the seventeenth century as exemplified in the
career of Roger Williams; and to point out the social and economic
forces which retarded the growth of libertarianism and frequently
defeated it. The final chapter estimates the place of the living
Williams in the course of later American thought.

S. H. B.

Wesleyan University,
  August, 1940.

ACKNOWLEDGMENTS

IT IS A PLEASURE TO ACKNOWLEDGE the invaluable assistance of many friends. To Samuel Eliot Morison who first suggested this study I am deeply indebted for encouragement and stimulating criticism of the bulk of the manuscript. Grateful appreciation for generous financial aid is due the Committee on Research and Board of Trustees of Wesleyan University. In the later stages I have been especially indebted to Ralph Henry Gabriel for fruitful discussions of larger questions of interpretation and invaluable editorial advice. For kindness on various occasions I wish to thank Arthur Meier Schlesinger and Frederick Merk of Cambridge; Howard M. Chapin and Lawrence C. Wroth of Providence; Stewart Mitchell of Boston; and Elizabeth Brockunier and others of the Boston Public Library. To my colleagues, George M. Dutcher, H. C. F. Bell, and Alexander Thomson, I owe a special debt; as also to Madelyn Brown, Ruth Lind, and Eloise Brockunier for expert assistance.

CONTENTS

PRINCIPAL ABBREVIATIONS USED IN THE FOOTNOTES

Conn. Col. Recs. . . . The Public Records of the Colony of Connecticut.

D.A.B. . . . . Dictionary of American Biography.

D.N.B. . . . . Dictionary of National Biography.

Harris Papers . . Papers of William Harris, Coll. R.I.H.S., X (1902).

Mass. Bay Recs. . . Records of the Governor and Company of the Massachusetts Bay in New England.

M.H.S. . . . . Massachusetts Historical Society. *Coll. M.H.S.* are the printed *Collections* of this society. *Proc. M.H.S.* are the *Proceedings.* Numerical prefixes indicate numbers of series.

N.C.P. . . . . Narragansett Club Publications (Providence, 1866-1874). Contain most of correspondence and tracts of Roger Williams.

N.E.H.G.R. . . . New England Historical and Genealogical Register.

N.E.Q. . . . . New England Quarterly.

N. Y. Col. Docs. . . Documents Relative to the Colonial History of the State of New York.

Plymouth Col. Recs. . Records of the Colony of New Plymouth in New England.

Prov. Recs. . . . Early Records of the Town of Providence.

R.I. Col. Recs. . . Rhode Island Colonial Records.

R.I.H.S. . . . . Rhode Island Historical Society. *Coll. R.I.H.S.* are the printed *Collections* of this society. *Pub. R.I.H.S.* refers to the series entitled *Publications.*

R.I.H. Tracts . . Rhode Island Historical Tracts (S. S. Rider, ed., Providence, 1877-1896).

THE
IRREPRESSIBLE DEMOCRAT
⟋ ROGER WILLIAMS

THE
BLOVDY TENENT,
of Persecution, for cause of
Conscience, discussed, in

A Conference *betweene*
TRVTH and PEACE.

VVho,
In all tender Affection, present to the High
Court of *Parliament,* (as the *Result* of
their *Discourse*) these, (amongst other
Passages) of *highest consideration.*

Printed in the Year. 1644.

1

PORTENTS

IN THE YEAR 1603 THE LAST TUDOR died and the first Stuart
came to the throne. On that throne where even the great Elizabeth
was beset by difficulties in the face of a turbulent and changing England, James I was to sit uneasily. The mental and physical framework of the Old World was breaking up. In the disintegrations and
new formulations of the sixteenth century, the old economic system
had been slowly breached. The medieval church which frowned on
usury had toppled in England and the old communal forms of guild
and monastery had given way before the onrush of free private
enterprise. The middle class was surging upward and the motives
and morals of the market place were invading the upper reaches of
society. Calvin had sprinkled holy water on the taking of interest
for one's loan or investment. The private capitalist had come, and
many a magnate of the reformed religion concluded that his success
was the will of God.

To these forces of religion and business enterprise was joined the
new nationalism of the rising modern state. Commercial patriotism
was pushing aside the medieval concept of a united Christendom. A
new world in the West had been discovered and old civilizations in
the East rediscovered. A great trade had sprung up and the expansion of Europe had begun. Now, with the coming of the commercial
revolution, the rise of commerce and competition on the great scale,
England was at last awake. Her middle classes were shouldering
their way forward in the struggle for power in the state and pushing
their way outward in the contest for wealth and dominion in the far
corners of the world.

As the dynamic forces of capitalism, nationalism, and religion
were unleashed, so was the stage set in England for the great conflicts of the seventeenth century: the struggle of the Puritans against
bishops and king for a new reformation of the churches; the struggle of England's middle orders, merchants and gentry, for political
power and constitutional monarchy; and England's deepening con-

3

test with the new national states for colonies, commerce, and world supremacy.

Into "this realm, this England," swept with the mingled fires of nationalism and religious zeal and driven on with the expanding and explosive energy of the middle class, Roger Williams was born. It was these new forces which were to make him by turns a dissenter, an exile, a planter in the new England overseas, an Indian trader and frontier peacemaker, and a religious radical and champion of democracy in England's Civil War.

Until recent years little was known of the early life of the young Roger. Patient research has shown that he was born in London to James and Alice Williams.[1] On his mother's side he was connected with the Pembertons of St. Albans, who had emerged from obscurity in the days of Elizabeth to rank among the lesser landed gentry. On his father's side he came of merchant stock, of the growing business class which was then contending with its peers in France, Spain, Portugal, and the Netherlands for the profits of world power. London-born, city-bred, young Roger came of the same sort of people as many another leader of New England whose family had grown up with the Tudors and now aspired to gentility.

Roger's year of birth still remains uncertain. The date of baptism was probably recorded at St. Sepulchre's, the ancient church of his parish, but in the great fire of 1666 this church was gutted and the records destroyed. Several statements by Williams have been taken to indicate that he was born about 1603. In 1632 he spoke of himself as "nearer upwards of 30 than 25."[2] On February 7, 1678, he declared that he was "aged about seventie five years."[3] If the first statement meant that he was about twenty-eight or a little older, then the birth year would have been 1603 or 1604. The second statement would make 1603 more probable. The recent discovery of a deposition of November 15, 1662, makes the problem more difficult. In this document Williams declared that he was "aged about 56 yeares,"[4] indicating that he was born about 1606. Williams' state-

1 The parentage and family connections were first indicated by Henry F. Waters in *N.E.H.G.R.*, XLIII (1889), 290, XLVII (1893), 498, and substantiated by the researches of G. A. Moriarty, Jr., *ibid.*, LXVII (1913), 90, LXXV (1921), 234, LXXVIII (1924), 272, and Walter Angell, *Book Notes* (Providence), XXIX (1912), nos. 11 and 12.

2 *Letters*, N.C.P., VI, 2.

3 *Pub. R.I.H.S.*, VIII, 156.

4 *Coll. R.I.H.S.*, XXVIII, 112; see pp. 112-115 for some less trustworthy clues.

ments of 1662 and 1678 are contradictory and in each case he used
the word "about," which suggests they were only approximations. It
is accordingly not possible, unless further evidence comes to light, to
fix his date of birth more definitely than to place it between 1603
and 1606.

Roger's lineage on his father's side still remains unknown. His
mother, Alice Williams, was born in 1564 at St. Albans, daughter
of Robert Pemberton and Katherine Stokes.[5] Roger Stokes, uncle
of Alice Williams, was a mercer by trade. Although the greater
landed gentry ranked far above the tradesman class, social lines
between the smaller gentry and families engaged in trade were not
sharply drawn, if indeed they were drawn at all. In both the Pemberton and Stokes families there were members described as mercer,
draper, or grocer,[6] as well as others of landed estate who wrote themselves "gentlemen." Of the latter, Robert Stokes, styled in his will
Master of Art, possessed certain "customary and copyhold lands
within the manor of Park, Gorham, et cetera," which he willed to
Roger Pemberton, brother of Roger Williams' mother.[7] Roger
Pemberton ranked among the gentry and held office in 1618 as sheriff
of the county. It was presumably after this uncle, who called him
"Godsonne" in his will, that the infant Roger Williams was named.
The Pemberton family by the time of Williams' birth had established
a place among the lesser gentry of the county, but none of them had
been active in affairs of the nation or achieved the honor of service in
parliament.

Alice Pemberton, by her marriage to James Williams, "citizen
and merchant tailor of London,"[8] entered a circle somewhat lower
than that of the country gentry of St. Albans. James Williams was
apparently a self-made London shopkeeper. He served apprenticeship
to Nicholas Tresswell, merchant taylor, and on April 7, 1587, was
admitted "to the Freedom of the Company by Servitude."[9] At this
date Alice Pemberton was 23 years old. Her marriage to James
Williams presumably took place subsequently. In these early years
the Williams family was not sufficiently prosperous to own their

---

[5] *N.E.H.G.R.*, XLIII (1889), 294-295, 297; *Coll. R.I.H.S.*, XVI, 78.

[6] Roger Stokes, "draper"; John Pemberton, "grocer," [*N.E.H.G.R.*, XLIII
(1889), 294, 299].

[7] *Ibid.*, 294.

[8] *Ibid.*, 291.

[9] *Ibid.*, 427.

dwelling house, for in 1595 James Williams was recorded as renting a "messauge" in Long Lane, London, in the parish of St. Sepulchre's. Probably the older Williams children, Sydrach and Katherine, were born here, and perhaps also Roger and Robert. At a later date the family moved to a house in Cow Lane. It has frequently been assumed that Roger Williams was born here, but there is no positive proof.[10]

James Williams had the business standing and the social position of a local guild merchant. The burgher class in town and city, like the gentry in the country, was divided into different social groups determined roughly by pedigree, wealth, and style of living. In earlier centuries the Merchant Taylors had been one of the chief trading organizations of London, and English monarchs had once been pleased to accept membership as a sign of favor.[11] When Roger Williams was born, the prestige and position of the old guilds were declining in favor of the new joint-stock companies which exploited the advantages of large corporate capital, traded with distant parts, and grasped eagerly at grants of monopoly. There was still a field for smaller traders, but the heyday of the old independent guild merchant was slowly passing.

Few of James Williams' associates could rate themselves the equals of the Merchant Adventurers or of the promoters of joint-stock organizations like the thriving East India Company. Some of the merchant taylors, to be sure, were men of local prominence and considerable wealth. In the earlier years of James I the Company numbered 299 members. Of these only the more prosperous achieved distinction as wardens or rose to the more exalted office of Master of the Company. The Merchant Taylor records do not show James Williams ever to have attained to such posts of honor in the ancient guild.[12] Although he never became a man of wealth, he evidently prospered in a small way, set up his eldest son, Sydrach, as a member of the guild, provided his daughter Katherine with a dowry, and when he died in 1621 left his family comfortably situated. Thirteen

10 *Coll. R.I.H.S.*, XXIV, 60; XVI, 79. The earliest mention of the home in Cow Lane appears in the will of Alice Williams, proved in 1634.

11 John Stow lists as "brothers," Richard II, Henry IV, Henry V, Henry VI, Edward VI, Richard III, and Henry VII; *Survey of London* (Kingsford ed., London, 1908), I, 182.

12 C. M. Clode, *Early History of the Guild of Merchant Taylors* (London, 1888), vol. I, p. 264; vol. II, appendix i, p. 336 ff.

years later the will of Alice Williams showed that she held the house
in Cow Lane, derived income from leases on an inn or tavern called
the Harrow and "three several tenements," and lived in enough style
to afford a maid, to whom she bequeathed her "gown and kirtle with
the embroidered lace."[13]

For the most part young Roger's associations would have been
with families like his own. His father's will mentions friends such
as Henry Bryan, coachmaker, Robert Kinge, clothworker, Thomas
Nicholson, "citizen and currier," Ralph Wightman, "citizen and
merchant taylor," who had married his daughter Katherine, and "my
kinsman, Thomas Morse, Inholder." Men of moderate means these
were, guildsmen and citizens some of them, but not men accounted
among the class of wealthy merchants. Thus, though Roger Williams was not reared in pinched circumstances, his place in life had
sharp limitations. Society was highly stratified and opportunities
unequal. Few boys of the shopkeeper class ever had opportunity for
university training. Through his mother's connections Roger
undoubtedly knew something of the traditions and ways of the
smaller gentry. As a London boy he might have glimpses of the
munificence of wealthy merchants and the pomp of royalty and the
nobles of the realm. If on gala days he might wander with boyish
curiosity and awe through Blackfriars and the fashionable quarters
of the old city, or see from afar something of the gay life at court,
it was as one who had no entrée. In due course Roger Williams was
to rise above his early associations by virtue of a Cambridge education and holy orders and by the more solid claim of individual attainments. But it was perhaps fitting that he who was to proclaim the
gospel of democracy and to place his confidence in the common man
should have been neither born nor bred among the titled aristocracy,
landed gentry, or great merchant class.

Williams' few references to his childhood leave us in the dark as
to most of his experiences as a boy in London. He tells of witnessing civic ceremonies "in the publikle walks in Pauls."[14] There were
numerous activities of this sort which a London boy could see. The
Merchant Taylor Company sometimes participated in elaborate public functions. When clothiers and drapers gathered in London for

13 See the wills of James and Alice Williams, *N.E.H.G.R.*, XLIII (1889),
291 ff.
14 *Pub. R.I.H.S.*, VIII, 150.

the opening of the Cloth Fair, the Merchant Taylors, by ancient custom, inspected the measures and certified the quality of cloth. Sometimes there were more sumptuous affairs when the Merchant Taylors had the proud privilege of entertaining great lords and ladies. At a banquet of 1607, when Roger was a mere infant, the old Guildhall of the Company had been ablaze with glory and the king himself had graced the board.[15] In 1614 when Roger was just reaching his teens, the Merchant Taylors outdid themselves in another lavish function, a ball and masque given in honor of the Count Palatine and the Lady Elizabeth. A London ballad celebrates one of these entertainments for James I:

(To the tune of *Treason's Joy.*)

Then let all London Companies
    So highly in renown,
Give Merchant Taylors name and fame
    To wear the laurel crown:

For seven of England's royal Kings
    Thereof have all been free,
And with their loves and favours grac'd
    This worthy Company. [16]

With the open-eyed curiosity of a boy, Roger early became familiar with activities of the commercial section of London. The metropolis was fast growing and had already reached a population of several hundred thousand. Long Lane, where the Williams family lived in 1595, was in the western quarter without Newgate, where the commercial population was expanding beyond the walls of the old City. Long Lane ran down to Smithfield, a great open expanse long celebrated as a pleasure ground and market place. About the time Roger was born John Stow described Long Lane as "now lately builded on both the sides with tenements for brokers, tipplers, and such like." The great grove of elm trees at Smithfield had been cut down and its east side was "inclosed with Innes, Brewhouses and large tenements." On the west were enclosures where sheep were "penned up to be sold on the market days." Close by this part of Smithfield was Cow Lane where the Williams family lived in later

---

[15] C. M. Clode, *Memorials of the Guild of Merchant Taylors* (London, 1875), p. 147.

[16] J. M. Lambert, *Two Thousand Years of Gild Life* (Hull, 1891), p. 228.

years. Not as fashionable as Cheapside, where rich merchants lived, or Blackfriars, where lords and ladies had their town mansions, this new western quarter of London had "divers fair inns, and other comely buildings"[17]—although, when the wind was right, the Williams family may have found itself too close to the sheep pens and cattle market for comfort.

The open grounds of Smithfield, long popular for public functions, in older times had been the scene of lavish exhibitions of martial exercises and gallant joustings. In Roger's youth Smithfield was still celebrated for one of the great pleasure events of London— St. Bartholomew's Fair. On this occasion the London companies marched to the grounds resplendent in livery; drapers and clothiers displayed fine woolens and linens in booths; and—to the scandal of the godly—theatrical diversions and games of chance abounded, strong ale flowed freely, and catchpennies, pickpockets, and harlots plied their trades with brazen impudence. Smithfield had also a grimmer history as a place of execution. When Roger read Foxe's famous *Book of Martyrs* he found accounts of dissenters burned there at the stake in the days of Queen Mary, one of them a vicar of the local parish. Such executions were now infrequent; but when Roger was about eight years old Smithfield claimed one more victim who endured to the last for sake of conscience. There, not far from the Williams home, Bartholomew Legate was burned at the stake as as incorrigible heretic.[18]

In these impressionable years Roger witnessed other activities in London which were portentous of the future. Down by the waterfront he saw ships loading for far-off ports or returning with prized products from the East or tobacco from Virginia. The Virginia colony, established by the London Company soon after Williams was born, was the only outpost of the English in America during most of his younger years. As a London boy of alert mind and never-failing curiosity, Roger doubtless grasped the opportunity to wander by the docks and ships along the busy waterfront of the Thames and listen to the talk of sailors, seizing eagerly at every scrap of information about strange races in the far corners of Europe and the East or about copper-skinned savages in Virginia. Captain John Smith was back in England in 1610, recounting his half-fabu-

17 Stow, *Survey of London,* II, 28.
18 Daniel Neal, *History of the Puritans* (London, 1822), II, 84.

lous adventures, drumming up interest in the great new continent, and projecting new colonies for the English. In 1616 came Pocahontas, wife of John Rolfe, to be received at court and to give London its first sight of an Indian princess. Possibly among those who gazed upon her in wonder was the boy who in his own time was to know the formidable Narragansett confederation better than any other white man.

Early in his London years Roger fell under the influence of the spirit of religious reformation which was sweeping England. From his childhood, as he declared later, "the Father of lights and mercies touched my soul with a love to himself, to his only begotten, the true Lord Jesus, to his holy Scriptures."[19] This reference to Scriptures suggests an early Puritan influence. Puritan non-conformity may already have appeared in his parish church, old St. Sepulchre's, largest in London and noted for its chime of bells. Even in the heart of London, under the nose of king and archbishop, the Puritan influence was not to be denied. Before long Nathaniel Bernard, lecturer at St. Sepulchre's in Charles's reign, was to suffer persecution at the hands of Laud.[20]

The Puritans engaged in their first contest with the king at about the time of Roger's birth. Defied by James in 1603, they bided their time and grew in strength. The middle orders, merchants in the towns and a great body of the country gentry, eventually reinforced with a sprinkling of the nobility, slowly turned toward Puritan doctrine. Elizabethan England had brought a magnificence and abundance of life, and in Roger's earliest years the solemn Puritan had often been the subject of ridicule; but a reaction was setting in against ceremonies and bishops and the licentiousness of the court and higher aristocracy, and by the time Williams attained his majority, Puritan dissenters were accounted the greatest part of the king's subjects.[21] Middle-class gentry and London burghers were finding a stern moral code in the Scripture, and their power and purpose were growing. It was not enough to legalize simplified worship, as they had requested of James in 1603; they would make over society in the middle-class image and impose "a discipline out of the Word."

There was as yet no concerted movement among dissenters, nor

19 *George Fox Digged*, N.C.P., V, lxiv.
20 Neal, *History of the Puritans*, II, 179.
21 *Ibid.*, 118.

would there be till politics and religious zeal were driven into com-
bustible combination by Stuart maladroitness. For the moment even
among themselves Puritans were at variance. Most conservative
were the old-line Presbyterians, anti-clerical as opposed to bishops,
but following in the path of Cartwright toward a clericalism of the
Lord's brethren as absolute as Rome's. Less conspicuous was a new
group among the Puritans inspired by the teachings of Dr. William
Ames and known eventually as Congregationalists. Neither Presbyterian nor Separatist, this group remained conformist and sought a
less centralized national church through a system allowing a degree
of autonomy to local congregations. It was this group which was to
found Massachusetts and Connecticut and to form the right wing of
the Independents when the Puritans came to power under Cromwell.[22]

Although from his youth Roger Williams was inspired by the
rising spirit of religious reformation, there is nothing to indicate
whether he leaned either toward Presbyterianism or the new Congregationalism. Other dissenting groups may have drawn his notice.
Worshipping under cover in London were scattered Baptists who
sometimes made bold to plead liberty of conscience. There were also
those of the "rigid separation," many of whom had fled to Holland,
but who in years when the wrath of the king was relaxed found some
measure of toleration in England. Perhaps some chance acquaintance
with these more radical dissenters first turned Roger's interest toward
those principles of Separatism and religious liberty which were later
to cause him such trouble and bring him such fame. Whatever
Roger's early religious convictions, they were intense enough and
sufficiently suspect so that he soon came to know what dissent might
entail. In 1632 when alluding to his early trials, he declared that
"though in Christ called," yet had he been "persecuted even in and
out of my father's house these twenty years."[23] It might be surmised
from this that Williams leaned to the Puritan way and that his
father did not; or possibly that if the parents were Puritans, the son
was already inclining to a rigid Separation. The breach, if any,
between father and son could not have been serious; for when his
father died, Roger Williams received his portion with the others.

[22] See P. G. Miller, *Orthodoxy in Massachusetts, 1630-1650* (Cambridge, 1933),
chap. iv: "Non-Separatist Congregationalism."
[23] Williams to Winthrop, *N.C.P.,* VI, 2.

Of Williams' first schooling and youthful ambitions, little is known. His family probably had little thought of his attending the university. If he followed the example of the elder members of his family, he would look to marriage with one of his own station and a career in business in London. His sister, Katherine, married a merchant taylor and his brother, Sydrach, was admitted to the guild in 1620 and promptly married the widow of Francis Pinner, "grocer."[24] Whether or not Roger originally planned to become a clerk or scrivener or to go into trade, his family probably sent him first to one of the grammar schools of London. Not far off within Newgate was St. Paul's, one of the best, to which John Milton, scrivener's son, was soon to go. The Williams family may have inclined toward another school which, if less ancient than St. Paul's, was fast rivalling it and which already could claim an Edmund Spenser on its rolls. This was the "notable free Grammar Schoole" founded by the Merchant Taylor Company in 1561 and proudly mentioned by John Stow, himself one of the guild and an associate of James Williams.[25] Whatever his early instruction, Roger early mastered an art that was then new and none too common. He spoke long afterward of "knowing what short-hand could doe as well as most in England from my childhood";[26] and shorthand notes in his copy of John Eliot's Indian Bible show that Williams still retained his proficiency in later years.[27]

Very likely Roger learned shorthand with some early intention of becoming a clerk or scrivener. One John May, a neighbor and "loving friend" of the family, was a professional scrivener.[28] This command of shorthand by a boy scarcely in his teens was no mean accomplishment and because of it Williams put himself in the way of a fortunate stroke that was to change his whole career and send him to Charterhouse school and then to Cambridge. He attracted the attention of a patron among the great and powerful, none other than the famous jurist, Sir Edward Coke, who was then setting the whole realm agog with his championship of the common law in

24 *N.E.H.G.R.*, XLIII (1889), 293, 294.
25 Stow, *Survey of London*, I, 74.
26 *George Fox Digged*, N.C.P., V, 131.
27 See photostatic reproduction, *Coll. R.I.H.S.*, XXIX, 40.
28 *N.E.H.G.R.*, XLIII (1889), 293.

King's Bench and Common Pleas against the wrathful assertions
of divine right by James I.

Just how Roger Williams first encountered the great man is
uncertain. Local tradition in Providence, written down as late as
1775, places the acquaintance of Coke and Williams in church: "Sir
Edward, one day, at church, observing a youth taking notes from
the sermon, beckoned and received him into his pew. He obtained
a sight of the lad's minutes; which were exceedingly judicious. . . . "[29]
Sir Edward is alleged to have been so favorably impressed that he
approached Roger's parents and undertook to advance the career of
their son. This tradition may be reliable, for both Sir Edward Coke
and the Williams family were communicants of St. Sepulchre's; but
a statement of Coke's own daughter conveys the impression that
Roger Williams was employed in Star Chamber and there won the
favor of the great English jurist. Star Chamber sometimes served
as a court of appeal from rulings of the guilds. It also took cases
between guilds and foreign traders doing business in England.[30]
Roger, though still but a boy in his middle teens, may have been
employed to take shorthand notes on some such occasions involving
the Merchant Taylors.

Sir Edward Coke, indispensable though he was in the popular
cause against the king, was notorious for his irascible temper and
disagreeable manner. A redeeming side of his personal character lay
in his private philanthropy. To Roger Williams he proved a good
friend; and long after, Williams wrote Coke's daughter in affectionate remembrance: "My much honored friend, that man of honor, and
wisdom, and piety, your dear father, was often pleased to call me his
son."[31] Through this fortunate connection, Roger Williams gained
an opportunity all too infrequently the lot of a boy of the smaller
merchant class. If he had dreamed hitherto of an education at Cambridge, the question of finances must have discouraged him. James
Williams could not much longer contribute to his family's support.
On November 17, 1620, he made his will, and the will was proved
the following year. Meanwhile, just before his father's death, Roger
started preparation for the university through the assistance of Coke.

[29] Cited in David Benedict, *General History of the Baptist Denomination in America* (Boston, 1813), I, 474.
[30] Clode, *Early History of the Guild of Merchant Taylors*, I, 75 f.
[31] *Letters*, N.C.P., VI, 239.

In later days when Williams was sounding his blast on the side of parliament and democracy, he wrote to Anne Sadleir, the daughter of Coke, in graceful tribute to his old-time patron:

> ... how many thousand times since have I had honorable and precious remembrance of his person, and the life, the writings, the speeches, and the examples of that glorious light. And I may truly say, that beside my natural inclination to study and activity, his example, instruction, and encouragement, have spurred me on to a more than ordinary, industrious, and patient course in my whole course hitherto.[32]

Mrs. Sadleir was on the side of monarchy and prerogative. On the back of Williams' letter she noted:

> This Roger Williams, when he was a youth, would, in a short hand, take sermons and speeches in the Star Chamber and present them to my dear father. He, seeing so hopeful a youth, took such liking to him that he sent him in to Sutton's Hospital, and he was the second that was placed there; full little did he think that he would have proved such a rebel to God, the king, and his country. I leave his letters, that, if ever he has the face to return into his native country, Tyburn may give him welcome.[33]

Williams entered Sutton's Hospital, then recently established as Charterhouse School, on June 25, 1621.[34] It was near Smithfield and a short distance from Williams' home. Once a Carthusian monastery, Charterhouse had fallen prey to the looters under Henry VIII and had become the town house of the Howards. In 1611 it was purchased by Thomas Sutton, who ranked in his day as the richest commoner in the land. Possessing a fortune carved out of a virtual monopoly on the coal output of England and multiplied by an advantageous marriage and ventures in trade in the Indies and on the Guinea coast, Thomas Sutton in his old age turned philanthropist and endowed Charterhouse as a school for indigent scholars.

The board of governors stipulated that no children were to be placed at Charterhouse "whose parents have any Estate of Lands to leave unto them but onlie the Children of poore Men that want

[32] *Letters*, N.C.P., VI, 239 f.

[33] *Ibid.*, 252 f.

[34] Records of Charterhouse; cited in Romeo Elton, *Life of Roger Williams* (London, 1852), p. 10.

Meanes to bring them up."[35] Williams would not have qualified as the son of a genuinely poor man, but from the early days the governors, departing perhaps from the intention of the founder, applied the rule with a latitude which favored scholars somewhat better off than the sons of artisans or common workmen. With the backing of Coke, who was one of the governors, Williams was admitted and for the next two years immersed himself in his studies. Coke's confidence in him was vindicated. In due course the committee which annually preferred the most promising students to the universities pronounced in favor of Roger Williams. With this honor went an exhibition or scholarship, which entitled the holder to an annual income of £16. By 1623 Williams was knocking on the gates of Cambridge, where for five years he was recipient of the annual stipend of his Charterhouse exhibition. Nearly three centuries later a chronicler of Charterhouse was to single him out: "The earliest scholar of Charterhouse who came to fame was Roger Williams, the founder of the State of Rhode Island in America."[36]

[35] G. S. Davies, *Charterhouse in London: Monastery, Mansion, Hospital, School* (London, 1921), p. 201.
[36] W. F. Taylor, *The Charterhouse of London,* J. M. Dent & Sons (London, 1912), p. 256.

2

CAMBRIDGE AND THE PURITAN LEAVEN

ROGER WILLIAMS WAS ADMITTED TO Pembroke Hall, Cambridge, on June 29, 1623.[1] Pembroke, though an ancient foundation, was one of the smaller colleges, its faculty and students numbering in 1621 no more than 140.[2] Thomas Fuller, himself at Cambridge in Williams' time, saw in its size no grounds for apology: "Let Pembroke Hall be compared with any foundation in Europe not exceeding it in bigness, time, and number of members, and it will acquit itself not conquered in all learned and liberal capacities."[3] In years past, Pembroke had had her share of famous sons. Pride of the college in Elizabethan times had been Edmund Spenser. No less esteemed by Pembroke men in Williams' day were Bishop Ridley, once master of the college, and John Rogers, who had been burned at the stake in the days of Mary. It was in praise of Ridley that Williams wrote the only passage in his publications in which he refers to his *alma mater*. Ridley, he says, "had got most of the holy Epistles in Greek by heart, even before he left Pembroke Hall in Cambridge: and as the fire of persecution grew hotter, so did those blessed Witnesses . . . spend hours and nights in Prayer and holy Conference upon the Scriptures. . . . "[4]

Williams on admission to Pembroke was eighteen or twenty years old. His preparation for the university had begun late and he was above the average age, as he had been at Charterhouse where Coke must have stretched the regulations to cover his case. The lack of thorough early preparation may be indicated by the long interval between admission to Pembroke and formal matriculation in the university. Instead of the usual interval of a few months, Williams' matriculation was delayed until June 7, 1624, when he had been enrolled at Pembroke more than a year.[5] He entered as a pensioner.

1 *Coll. R.I.H.S.*, XVI, 80.
2 David Masson, *The Life of John Milton* (Boston, 1859), I, 77 f.
3 *History of the University of Cambridge* (London, 1840), p. 67.
4 *George Fox Digged*, N.C.P., V, 147.
5 *Coll. R.I.H.S.*, XVI, 80.

Pensioners, who formed the largest class of students, paid the regular fees for board and tuition, whereas sons of the aristocracy were admitted as fellow-commoners and were entitled to special privileges, including that of paying double fees. At the bottom of the social scale were indigent students known as sizars who paid reduced fees and usually performed menial work such as waiting on table in college hall.

Two days after matriculation Roger Williams was awarded his exhibition from Charterhouse. This, though carrying a stipend of £16, was insufficient to pay for the usual college expenses. Williams' contemporary, Sir Simonds D'Ewes, complained that on the £50 his father allowed him at Cambridge he could barely get along.[6] But D'Ewes was a fellow-commoner, and a more humble pensioner like Williams could stretch £16 with less sacrifice of personal pride. The fact that Williams was not forced down into the ranks of the sizars would seem to mean he had enough to scrape through, possibly with some private assistance from his old patron in London. Toward the end of his years at Cambridge, when he was twenty-two or -four, he received also the small inheritance his father left him.[7]

It was a new Cambridge to which Williams had come. In earlier centuries the English universities trained scholars for the church and for the law, and opportunity for education was based on merit and not social rank. In those days when opportunity elsewhere was negligible, promising sons of the peasantry found welcome at the universities and could hope to rise in church and state. By the sixteenth century, society was changing and the universities followed. The new aristocracy, springing up on the basis of capitalist enterprise, were displacing clerics from offices of state and were beginning to send their sons to the university. When Roger Williams arrived at Cambridge, the older clerical ideals were on the wane. Most of the colleges dedicated themselves to a liberal education of "young gentlemen"; education was already a mark of rank.

The university lost something by catering to gentility; but there had been a gain.[8] The curriculum had broadened. "Polite learning" had its value, and when Roger Williams attended Pembroke, human-

---

[6] Masson, *Milton*, I, 77 n.

[7] *N.E.H.G.R.*, XLIII (1889), 291.

[8] For an analysis of this change at Cambridge, see S. E. Morison, *The Founding of Harvard College* (Cambridge, 1935), pp. 50-57.

istic studies were not neglected. Scholastic philosophy had fallen in esteem and specialized training in theology was now relegated to candidates for higher degrees. The study of humane letters had broadened to include a considerable range of classical *belles lettres,* geography, and history. The time was still remote when a young gentleman was required to know Chaucer, Spenser, or Shakespeare, but he must read intensively in Cicero, Livy, Martial, Horace, Seneca, Virgil, and Homer. One of the besetting sins of scholarly writings of the time was the attempt to impress readers by an incessant parade of classical erudition. Williams in his later writings largely escaped this habit, but this very fact makes it difficult to judge which of the classics he studied at Cambridge. That his reading was wide is evident. In his subsequent writings he seldom referred to ancient authors by name, but he drew upon them in abundance for historical comparisons and occasional aphorisms to point an argument.[9]

Despite concessions to the ideal of a liberal education proper to young gentlemen, there survived a heavy heritage of medieval method and scholastic philosophy. Williams and his fellows were driven through the old painful drill in logic, ethics, and metaphysics, had the art of disputation hammered into them, and were taught to pursue Aristotle for terms on end with a host of quarreling commentators. There was benefit in these studies, no doubt, and they were more congenial to Williams and other students of Puritan leanings than to young bloods of the gentry with less on their minds, for they gave power and artifice to those who thrived on controversial theology. They gave training in oratory and disputation, but they also left their mark on the writings of men like Williams.

The Cambridge program no doubt was the best intellectual fare to be had in an English university at the time, but it was not without great limitations. These, it is important to note, Roger Williams, like so many of his classmates, was never able to escape. Although Cambridge was considerably ahead of her more ancient rival, Oxford, she was by no means abreast of the best thought of the times. There was too little encouragement of originality, profundity, or healthy skepticism. A good student might learn the art of turning

9 See in *Coll. R.I.H.S.,* XIII, 125-129, list of books with which Williams was presumably familiar. For detailed accounts of Cambridge studies of the time, see Morison, *Founding of Harvard,* pp. 62-78, and J. B. Mullinger, *Cambridge in the Seventeenth Century* (London, 1867), pp. 44-60.

an adversary's arguments by appeals to authority or by subtle casuistry, but one need only examine the tracts of the times to discover the defects of the method. Scholarship was timorous. There was too much subservience to inherited ideas, too little disposition to experiment and correct in the light of new knowledge. There was too little freedom of thought in the pure sense, too much compulsion to passive acceptance of the standing order. A university dedicated to "Protestantism, classical scholarship and a gentleman's education" could offer much; but such ideals represented a limited objective and narrowed the search for truth.[10]

The best minds of the day were sharp in their scorn. Bacon attacked the "contentious learning" and logical prestidigitation then current. Methodical treatment by appeal to authority he scorned as a feat of memory and not an exercise of human intellect. He pleaded in vain for experimental science and a broadening of the curriculum.[11] Abysmal disregard of the new knowledge and the new scientific thought was in fact the glaring weakness of the universities. Williams and his classmates might get a smattering of Aristotelian physics or a brief introduction to the speculations of Lucretius and Seneca, but they would know nothing from this of the revolutionary discoveries of the modern world. This was the age of Christopher Columbus, Copernicus, Galileo, and Descartes. The horizon of knowledge had infinitely broadened, yet Cambridge men still studied the ancients, who had known so little of the earth and who had conceived of that little as static.

Even a penetrating intellect like that of Roger Williams or of John Milton found it difficult to rise above such training. Far from European contacts in later life, Roger Williams never repaired to any great degree the signal lack of a grounding in science; nor did Milton. Neither entirely escaped the method in which they had been trained, the old reliance upon appeal to authority. Of some of the deficiencies of his education, Milton was fully aware, and Williams as well. In good time Milton was to speak out in famous phrases for

10 S. E. Morison, *The Founding of Harvard College*, Harvard University Press (Cambridge, 1935), p. 53. For a critical judgment of the curriculum, see the same work, pp. 76-78. Note especially the treatment of Dorislaus while Williams was still at Cambridge; *ibid.*, p. 49. See also Fuller, *University of Cambridge*, p. 229.

11 Mullinger, *Cambridge in the Seventeenth Century*, p. 46 f. Note also critical comment in Masson, *Milton*, I, 196-198.

intellectual freedom and for a vital scholarship and to castigate the diet of "sowthistles and brambles," the arid abstractions, which Cambridge had fed him.[12] During the same years of ferment in which Milton wrote, Roger Williams also levied heavy charges against the universities. "I honour Schooles for Tongues and Arts," he declared in 1644; but he protested the arrogant assumption that only a university man was capable of discerning the truths of religion. Universities were too much in subjection to the pressures for orthodoxy and too much the creatures of the will of the sovereign. "We count the Universities the Fountaines, the Seminaries or Seed-plots of all Pietie: but have not those Fountaines ever sent what streames the Times have liked? and ever changed their taste and colour to the Princes eye and Palate?"[13]

But, withal, there was much that men like Williams and Milton gained at Cambridge: respect for learning, a passion for books, the habit of study, command of ancient languages, the indispensable instrument of scholarship; and a proficiency in the art of disputation which would serve them in their time.

Undergraduate life did not revolve wholly about studies. With the influx of the sons of the upper classes, Cambridge had lost much of the monastic tone of earlier times, and many a young gentleman found the injunctions of his tutor less imperative than the call of sports, good companionship, or less innocent pleasures in town and tavern. Among students at Cambridge who took rather less to learning—if we may trust royalist writers—but right strenuously to football, cudgels, and boisterous sports was Oliver Cromwell. Williams, too, may have had his fling at college sports, though presumably not to the neglect of studies. Afterward in his Narragansett days he was to show himself a man of iron constitution with a zest for those arts of the wilderness which took a man's strength, courage, and skill.

College regulations were strict, even frowning upon bathing in the Cam or wandering about the streets of Cambridge.[14] Sons of the great and powerful were not bred to such sobriety and broke the bonds, as good Puritans complained. Denzil Holles in his Cambridge days received a paternal warning against the shame and misery of

---

[12]*Areopagitica* (1644); *College Exercises,* No. III; *Of Education* (1644).

[13] *The Bloudy Tenent,* N.C.P., III, 305, 306. See also *The Hireling Ministry none of Christs* (London, 1652), pp. 14-17.

[14] Masson, *Milton,* I, 96 ff.

an "ill spent youth"; for the father feared that the son too much "guzzled and goodfellowed it."[15] Nor were young gentlemen of rank the only delinquents. Roger Williams may have had his lapses, and even Thomas Shepard, model of New England piety in later times, confessed to one sad occasion at Cambridge when he became "dead drunke and that upon a Saturday night"—necessitating, one gathers, a Sunday morning recuperation with an aching head and lowly heart in the solitude of a field when he ought to have been at church.[16]

The healthy give and take of undergraduate life was marred by the intrusion of sharp distinctions in rank and class. Roger Williams, as a pensioner, was not so humble in rank as the sizars who lived in inferior quarters and performed menial tasks, but he and other pensioners might still find themselves less than welcome in the goodly company of fellow-commoners. This latter group, sons of the wealthy, dined at high table with the fellows. Such young sprigs of the aristocracy, decked ofttimes in boots and spurs, flush in pocket money, set the tone of student fashion. These "university tulips"[17] took pains on occasion to put pensioner or sizar in his proper place. Once even the younger son of a peer was chagrined to find that he was "tied up by quality from mixing" at football with the young bloods of this elevated order.[18] Such humiliations were not uncommon, and no doubt Williams' spirit rankled inwardly when he found himself patronized or openly snubbed.

In these years the intensifying religious struggle deepened the conflict of ideas and bred animosities among faculty and students. The influx of Puritan scholars brought the gentlemanly ideal and worldliness of upper-class Anglicans under hot fire. A year after Williams' matriculation, the Puritan forces in parliament protested the laxness of the universities and Cambridge responded with new regulations, among them a sharp injunction against tolerating "young maids" in students' chambers.[19] John Milton and Sir Simonds D'Ewes, bred to Puritan sobriety, found undergraduate life far from serene. D'Ewes wrote in 1620 of the "swearing, drinking, rioting, and hatred of all piety and virtue" at Cambridge and declared

[15] *Letter Book of Sir John Holles*, British Museum, Add. MSS., 32, 464, fo. 78b (p. 208).

[16] See S. E. Morison, *Builders of the Bay Colony* (Boston, 1930), p. 108.

[17] So dubbed by a Cambridge tutor of Williams' day; Masson, *Milton*, I, 89.

[18] G. M. Trevelyan, *England under the Stuarts* (New York, 1904), p. 16, n. 2.

[19] Masson, *Milton*, I, 113.

in bitterness that he was "fain to live almost a recluse's life, conversing chiefly in our own College with some of the honester fellows thereof."[20] Milton, scornful of those who boasted their feats with the bottle or prowess in the brothel, found himself written down a prig and nicknamed "the Lady."[21] Inevitably Williams, too, had his share of ridicule and moments of heartburning.

Though Puritanism was gaining in parliament, it was losing in the universities. As older heads and fellows of the colleges died, Anglicans of the new school of Laud took their places. Under Ridley, Grindel, and Whitgift, Pembroke had had a Calvinist cast, but the tide had turned. Successively, Lancelot Andrewes, forerunner of Laud, and Samuel Harsnett, high Anglican and hated of the Puritans, and Jerome Beale had served as Masters. Strong Anglicans like Beale availed themselves of royal favor and followed the rising star of Laud and Anglo-Catholicism. Anglican sacerdotalism and Stuart divine right were not part of the curriculum, but it is hardly to be doubted that Williams' teachers found ways in class or chapel to preach the doctrine dear to their hearts.[22] It was propaganda such as this which Williams recalled and heatedly denounced in the turbulent days of the Puritan revolution.

In this atmosphere of increasing struggle for control of opinion Williams rounded out his undergraduate course. Before he was graduated, he was forced to swear to what James I was pleased to call "his three darling articles." By subscribing to the Three Articles a student acknowledged the king's supremacy in spiritual affairs; swore that the Prayer Book was the word of God and pledged himself to accept it "and none other"; and, lastly, acknowledged the Thirty-nine Articles "to be agreeable to the word of God."[23] A Calvinist could swallow the Thirty-nine Articles, but the Prayer Book and the ecclesiastical supremacy of the king went hard with a tender conscience. Puritans execrated these tests and one of the first acts of the Long Parliament was to denounce them as "against law

---

[20] D'Ewes, *Autobiography*, I, 141-142; Mullinger, *Cambridge in the Seventeenth Century*, pp. 29-30.

[21] Masson, *Milton*, I, 235.

[22] Among the notable fellows of Pembroke in Williams' time were Ralph Brownrig, Benjamin Laney, and Matthew Wren, uncle of Sir Christopher Wren. All of these men won favor with Laud, rose to bishoprics, and were ejected by the Puritans during the Civil War. See *D.N.B.;* also G. Dyer, *History of the University and Colleges of Cambridge* (London, 1814), I, 118; II, 103, 106, 107.

[23] See Dyer, *Cambridge*, I, 99-101; Masson, *Milton*, I, 155 f.

and the liberty of the subject."[24] Such oaths had ever been suitable instruments for witch doctors and heresy-hunters, but they were worse than useless as guarantors of orthodoxy. Avowed Puritans subscribed to the Articles without conviction, or else in some cases refused to swear and forfeited the degree.[25]

Roger Williams in after years detested such oaths, yet his signature in his own hand appears as of January, 1627, in the subscription book of Cambridge. This is significant. In view of his later uncompromising opposition to tests of orthodoxy as a violation of conscience, it would imply only one thing—he had not yet burned his bridges. His Separatist principles were not yet settled convictions. If he was Puritan in his general outlook, he still placed reliance on the Calvinism of the Thirty-nine Articles and hoped for reform of the church on Non-separatist principles. This is the simplest explanation of the decision he now made to continue at Cambridge, studying divinity to prepare himself for a place in the church.

At the commencement of 1627 Williams received his bachelor's degree, and on October 10 when Cambridge re-opened he returned for graduate study in the mysteries of theology. But Cambridge was to see him for scarcely two years more and apparently he never completed requirements for a higher degree. In 1629 the records of Charterhouse noted that "Roger Williams who hath exhibition and so for about five years past, has forsaken the university and is become discontinuer of his studies there. Exhibition suspended until order to the contrary."[26]

Why did Williams leave the university? A probable explanation is not far to seek. Two factors discouraged him from hope of preferment in the English church: Laud was in the ascendant; and Williams could no longer reconcile himself to service in the church.[27] He had come to a more radical non-conformist position, possibly already inclining toward Separatist principles. His tender conscience had mastered him and he was never again to be free of it.

[24] Neal, *Puritans*, II, 343.

[25] Morison, *Founding of Harvard*, 48 n., 339-341, 409. It is notable that for nearly three hundred years Harvard College had no such test, religious or otherwise—until the Massachusetts legislature saw fit to impose a Teachers' Oath, *anno domini* 1935.

[26] Quoted in O. S. Straus, *Roger Williams: the Pioneer of Religious Liberty* (New York, 1894), pp. 8-9.

[27] *Letters*, N.C.P., VI, 356.

"The way to rise in the church," says Neal, "was to preach up the absolute power of the King, to declaim against the rigours of Calvinism, and to speak favourably of Popery."[28] Such time-serving Roger Williams could not do. The "popery" of Laud and Andrewes he abominated, the "rigours" of Calvinism he approved, and the divinity that "doth hedge a king" inspired no awe in the future democrat of Rhode Island. The cruelties of Charles and his "blasphemous" father, he declared later, cried out for vengeance. He had once "spoke with" James—possibly in Star Chamber. To the sharp eyes of the youthful Puritan, James, garbed in his padded clothes, mean and undignified in appearance, ridiculed in his own court, was not a king to win respect. Nor was his son Charles. "I knew his person," Williams declared, "vicious, a swearer from his youth, and an oppressor and persecutor of good men. . . ."[29] Not a favorable portrait—and one drawn, it might be noted, when Charles was safely dead and a Puritan Caesar sat the throne without the crown.

Williams' picture of Charles was colored no doubt by religious animus, for Charles, as king, looked a king. Aloof, dignified, pure in personal life, and cherishing his own conception of honor, Charles nevertheless steadily alienated any loyal affection of his Puritan subjects. Like James he angered parliament with doctrinaire professions of the divine right of kings. Unlike his father, he showed complete disrespect for Calvinist theology. Horrified Puritans and moderate Anglicans noted his warm support of the Anglo-Catholics and the introduction of their "blasphemous" ceremonies. When his first parliament assembled, Charles hurled defiance at it, saving the hated Montague from its wrath and making him his own chaplain. Manwaring, also favored of Charles, attacked parliament's power over taxes and justified royal exactions on the provocative basis of divine right. In June, 1628, parliament impeached and imprisoned him, but royal Charles, in the teeth of parliament, pardoned him and presented him with a living. In July the king made Laud the dean of the Royal Chapel, and in December Charles issued his famous declaration intended to stamp out Puritan interpretations of the Thirty-nine Articles: "We will, that all further curious search be laid aside. . . . And that no man hereafter shall either print, or preach,

28 Neal, *Puritans*, II, 118.
29 *Letters*, N.C.P., VI, 246, 345.

to draw the Article aside any way. . . ." He who dared "put his own sense or comment to be the meaning of the Article" did so at his peril.[30] The day of Laud had come.

Toward the end of this year Williams reached his decision and quit the university. He had reached the point where he could no longer compromise with his dearest convictions. His inner turmoil, the sense of frustrated ambition, the proud, hard choice of the path of personal integrity may be conveyed by the words of his fellow Cantabridgian, John Milton, who likewise soon reached the same decision: ". . . perceiving what tyranny had invaded in the Church—that he who would take orders must subscribe slave, and take an oath withal, which unless he took with a conscience that would retch, he must either perjure or split his faith—I thought it better to prefer a blameless silence before the sacred office of speaking, bought and begun with servitude and forswearing."[31]

[30] S. R. Gardiner, *The Constitutional Documents of the Puritan Revolution, 1624-1660* (Oxford, 1906), p. 76.

[31] *The Reason of Church-Government* (1641) ; quoted in Masson, *Milton,* I, 246.

3

FRUSTRATION AND FLIGHT

SOMETIME BEFORE FEBRUARY 20, 1629, Roger Williams was settled at Otes, in the parish of High Laver, as chaplain in the household of Sir William Masham.[1] Through his new position Williams found himself for a year and more in the circle of newer wealthy families which had gained prominence in Tudor times and which were now reaching out for power in the state. His connection with these families was of crucial importance in his later career, for among those who gathered at the pretentious county seats of the great families of Essex were men who held in their hands the destiny of England. Scarcely, indeed, had Williams taken his place at the old manor house at Otes than he heard the first mutterings of the storm which was to sweep the king from a tottering throne.

Sir William Masham, although a comparatively young man, had risen rapidly to a substantial position among the great Puritan families in the broad lands of Essex. Admitted to the Inner Temple in 1610, he advanced himself by marriage and politics, in 1621 successfully contriving to have himself created baronet[2] and in 1624 managing to win a seat in parliament through the influence of the family into which he had married. Lady Elizabeth Masham, Sir William's wife, was the daughter of Sir Francis Barrington who had been one of the earliest members of the Virginia Company, represented Essex in parliament from 1601 to his death, and as early as 1604 had been remarked as "a man of note" by no less a personage than Sir Thomas Lake.[3]

When Roger Williams came to Otes, Sir Francis Barrington and

---

[1] *Coll. R.I.H.S.,* XXII, 98 f.

[2] Sir John Oglander wrote contemptuously of the usual procedure for elevation to rank: "All honour in those days of the great Duke being at sale"; Francis Bamford, editor, *A Royalist's Notebook,* Constable & Co., Ltd. (London, 1936), p. 32. Buckingham sold forty baronetcies for £150 and £200 apiece, to the great indignation of Sir John, who said they should sell for £1,000! *Ibid.,* p. 45.

[3] Hist. MSS. Report, *Calendar of the MSS. of the Marquess of Salisbury,* Part XVI (1933), p. 368. See also A. P. Newton, *The Colonising Activities of the English Puritans* (New Haven, 1914), p. 64 f.

Sir William Masham had already felt the wrath of the king. In Essex Sir Francis and Sir William led the resistance to the forced loan and late in 1626 both were imprisoned.[4] Resistance to the arbitrary royal levy subsided after the jails were filled, but the prisoners did not lie forgotten. A squire of Groton, county Suffolk, whom Roger Williams would soon know well, wrote his son, John Winthrop, Jr., urging him "to remember my love and service to Sir Francis Barrington" and to acquaint him "how thinges have gone in our countrye, but you must doe it in private."[5] Roger Williams was never to see Sir Francis. In June, 1627, word spread that Barrington was ill from the effects of incarceration. He, as well as Sir William Masham, was released the following January, but though immediately back in parliament, he was unable to take effective part and survived only a few weeks the triumph over Charles in the Petition of Right.[6]

Roger Williams came to know well the other members of the Barrington family. Lady Joan, widow of Sir Francis, lived a few miles west of Otes at Hatfield Priory, Broad Oaks, one of the former monastic estates which had swelled the fortune of Chancellor Rich in the bountiful days of the great confiscations. With the aid of their connection with the Rich family, the Barringtons had risen in the political scale, and Sir William Masham had become the close associate of Sir Nathaniel Rich, of the manor of Stondon, Essex, and Robert Rich, second Earl of Warwick, lord lieutenant of the county. Lady Joan Barrington's two sons, Sir Thomas and Robert, sat in parliament for Newtown, Isle of Wight,[7] one of the pocket boroughs which the Rich family had made its private preserve. The sharp electioneering methods of this group were not always relished, and a dour old royalist in the Isle of Wight wrote down bitterly: "Sir Thomas Barrington is Honour of Swainston, the best manor in our Island. He liveth in Essex, doth no service here and skimmeth away the cream of our country."[8] There were other prominent connec-

[4] R. F. Williams, editor, *The Court and Times of Charles I* (London, 1848), I, 161 f. Also *Cal. State Papers, Domestic, 1625-1626*, p. 469.

[5] *Winthrop Papers, 1498-1628* (Boston, 1929), I, 337.

[6] See news letters in *The Court and Times of Charles I*, I, 243, 323, 327, 329; also *Winthrop Papers, 1623-1630* (Boston, 1931), II, 69.

[7] *Return of Members of Parliament, Part One*, p. 477.

[8] Sir John Oglander, *A Royalist's Notebook*, Constable & Co., Ltd. (London, 1936), p. 137. For election methods of the Barrington and Rich families, see M. E. Bohannan, "The Essex election of 1604," *Eng. Hist. Rev.* (July, 1933), pp. 385-413.

tions of the Barrington family with whom there is every reason to believe Williams gained some acquaintance. Lady Barrington was the daughter of the "Golden Knight," Sir Henry Cromwell, and aunt of John Hampden and Oliver Cromwell. Another nephew of hers was Edward Whalley, later famed as a regicide and destined to the strange life of a fugitive in the remote fastness of the upper Connecticut valley.[9]

In such a circle Williams was in a position to witness at close hand the portentous events which were now taking place. In parliament Sir William Masham and Sir Thomas and Robert Barrington were opposing strongly with Coke, Warwick, Hampden, and Pym the detested policies of Charles and Laud. In February, 1629, Williams visited London and brought back the news. Robert Barrington sent a letter in his charge to Lady Joan:

> Madam, it was very late before I knew of Mr. Williams going down, yet I cannot let him pass without troubling you with a few lines. . . . Mr. Williams who walks the City will be able to say more than I can who have not the least time to be from the business of this house, which, if ever than now doth require all possible diligence; he can partly tell you what late rubs we have met with to our great distraction. . . .[10]

The next few weeks in parliament were the occasion of the momentous contest with Charles, ending in the historic resolutions of March 2, 1629. As the king's messenger pounded on the door, Denzil Holles held the speaker in his chair to prevent him from lifting the mace from the table to terminate the session. Meanwhile, amidst the uproar, the Commons passed the three resolutions of Eliot: the first aimed at Laud, condemning innovations of "Popery or arminianism," the other two declaring that any who advised or assisted in levy of tunnage and poundage without grant of parliament, or who should pay such a tax, was a betrayer of the liberties of England and a capital enemy of the commonwealth.

That day Sir Thomas Barrington wrote at white heat to Lady Joan:

> I love not to be a messenger of evell tideings, nor a relator of evells, yet my desyres are so greate to inform you with the occureunts of the times. . . . This daye in Parliament was like

[9] *N.E.H.G.R.*, XLIII (1889), 340; L (1896), 65.
[10] *Coll. R.I.H.S.*, XXIX, 71.

the generall of the times, such as hardly ever [illegible] no man allmost knowing what to doe; the distraction was so sodaine, and so greate. . . . In the generall I must saye, we have a verie greate cause to bless God, that we concluded the daye with oute any greater business, the consequences whareof no man can say what it would have ben; . . . 'tis farr more easy to speake bravely, then to be magnanimous in suffring yet he whose hart bleedes not, at the threates of theise times, is soe stupid; I pray God send us better grounds of comfort, and with all to be armed for the worst that can befall us.[11]

In a short time Sir William Masham and the Barringtons were back in Essex. Parliament was dissolved and the king was exacting his vengeance. Eliot was in the Tower, where he was to die like Francis Barrington, from the evil effects of prison life. Meanwhile, among the Essex gentry Williams heard sober talk, whispers of royal vengeance yet to come, and fear for English liberties and for the church. But there was to be time enough ere the final conflict. For eleven long years Puritan squires were to talk thus and to whisper, and the young nephews of Lady Barrington, Pym and Hampden, were quietly to perfect their organization and prepare for their stroke for power. For those eleven years "popery" and Arminianism and arbitrary taxation were to have their day, and parliament was to be stilled.

Charles's rule without parliaments began with the dissolution of March 2. Taking heed of the rising storm, a small group of Puritan leaders had already prepared an escape. In 1628 they purchased land from the Council for New England and Endecott embarked for Salem; and on March 4, 1629, in the name of the Governor and Company of the Massachusetts Bay, they obtained a royal charter— the notable document which Massachusetts rulers were to put to strange uses and which Laud was to attack and Williams also to impugn, although for very different reasons.

Before long Williams was to take deep interest in this Puritan project. Sir William Masham was not a member of the Massachusetts Bay Company,[12] but he and Sir Thomas Barrington both

11 British Museum, Egerton MSS., 2645, f. 21. Yale University Library now possesses a film of the Barrington letters in this collection.

12 Neither Barrington nor Masham appears in the list of adventurers. See Frances Rose-Troup, *The Massachusetts Bay Company and Its Predecessors* (New York, 1930) ; also S. F. Haven's list, *Archaeologica Americana*, III, cxxxiv-cxxxvi.

had interest in overseas plantations and doubtless had many a long talk with Williams about the new Zion to spring from the American wilderness. By May, 1629, Williams indeed received a "New England call," but it was yet awhile before he could persuade himself to cut so far adrift from home and country. Life was pleasant at his patron's old manor house with its ancient moat and formal grounds —and the bright eyes of one of the young women in Essex had ensnared the young chaplain.

When Williams came to Otes, Lady Elizabeth Masham and her mother, Lady Barrington, were busy considering a match for "Jug" Altham, daughter of Lady Elizabeth by her first marriage. The new chaplain was much in the company of two other young women: Joan Masham, daughter of Lady Masham and Sir William; and Jane Whalley, sister of the regicide, who was living with her aunt, Lady Joan, at Barrington Broad Oaks. For these young women Lady Barrington and her daughter had ambitious plans. It never occurred to them that a young chaplain, after five years of monastic plodding at the university, might succumb to the charms of one of their charges.

Lady Elizabeth and Lady Joan corresponded with friends and kin, prosecuting the search for unattached gentlemen with suitable prospects. The greater gentry weighed marriages carefully in terms of rank and pounds sterling, and the letters concerning prospective bridegrooms for Jug Altham turned much on dower rights, income, and social position. One offer ran to large figures, including a settlement of twelve hundred pounds a year; another would total several thousand when the gentleman came into his inheritance.[13] But these bargains were not closed and Roger Williams was to take a wife before a suitable catch had been found for Jug.

No portrait of Roger Williams exists, nor did contemporaries leave record of his personal appearance. But it is clear from the affectionate regard expressed in the letters of Sir William Masham and his wife that they were struck by the qualities of impetuous zeal, keenness of mind, and personal charm which won Williams friends throughout his life. Roger Williams also fluttered the hearts of two of the young women at Otes and Broad Oaks. The niece of Lady Barrington was first to be smitten.

[13] *Coll. R.I.H.S.*, XXIX, 74, 76.

Roger Williams and Jane Whalley precipitately fell in love. But the path of young love ran anything but smoothly. Williams, as confessed in a letter, had fears both of Jane's temper and her piety! Gossip soon circulated of his sudden infatuation, and Lady Barrington warned him that it gave her no pleasure. "I have hearkened after your Ladiship's mind," Williams informed her. "Your Laddiship may wonder at this unwonted absence and also aske what meanes this paper deputie! Give me leave (deare Madam) to say with David, to his brothers in the field: is there not a cause? . . . Many and often speeches have long fluttered or floune abroad concerning your Ladiships neere kinswoman and my unworthy selfe." For a time he had endeavored to hold himself aloof, in deference to Lady Barrington's request. "Yet like a royling snow-ball or some flowing streame the report extends and gathers stronger. . . ." Unable to conquer his attachment, he obtained "good Testimonialls" about Jane's "Godlines." She had been "much accused for passionate and hastie, rash and unconstant . . ."; but he desired to marry her, and Lady Elizabeth and Sir William had advised him "to open" to Lady Joan "the whole Anatomie of this business."

He had qualms on the point of social rank, "it being some Indecorum," he wrote, for Jane "to condescend to my low Ebb there I somewhat stick; but were all this cleared, there is one barr not likely to be broken and that is the present Estate of us both." Jane Whalley, he had heard, was not to receive her inheritance at any time in the near future and possibly her portion "as things stand now ir England shall never be by us enjoyed." Nor was he sanguine about his own prospects. A "tender conscience . . . hath kept me back from honour and preferment Besides many former offers and that late New England call, I have since had 2 severall livings proffered to me each of them £100 per annum. . . ." If he remained at Otes as he desired, he could hope for little beyond his small income as chaplain. After the death of his "aged loving mother" he expected—"though for the present she be close and will not promise"!—a humble inheritance of twenty pounds a year. Williams added with pride, he had "a little (yet costlie) studie of books."

Poor as he was, Williams gravely assured her Ladyship, he had prospects of marriage elsewhere, one offer at the moment in hand, "person and present portion worthy." But he hoped that the Lord would smile on his suit for Jane Whalley.

> To wrong your precious name and answer her kind love with want would be like gall to all the honey of my life, and marr my marriage joys. The kind affection of your deare Ladiship and worthy neice is of better merit and desert. I shall add for the present I know none in the world I more affect and (had the Lord been pleased to say amen to those other regards) should doubtles have answered (if not exceeded) her affection.

There is no record of Lady Barrington's answer to this plea, but a second letter of Williams' speaks for itself.[14] With courteous restraint Williams made only one swift allusion to what was uppermost in his mind. "I doubt not but your good wisdome and love have fairely interpreted my carriage in the late treatie, and I allso trust, quieted and still'd the loving affections of your worthy neice. We hope to live together in the heavens though the Lord have denied that union on Earth."

The main body of the letter dealt with "a business of more waight and consequence." The young chaplain confessed to Lady Barrington that he was greatly troubled by the state of her conscience. "What I shall now expresse to your Ladiship hath long lyen like fire in my bones Jer 20:9." In short, "(Madam) the Lord hath a quarrell against you." Thus, with understandable fervor, Williams turned from frustration in love to the good work of saving an unregenerate soul. While previously he had agreed to refrain from mentioning the Lord to her in this wise, now he was "weary with forbearing." He would be candid: "I know not one professor amongst all I know whose truth and faythfullness to Jesus Christ is more suspected, doubted, feared, by all or most of those that know the Lord." In fact, he had been astonished that "not only inferiour Christians but ministers, eagle eyed, faithful and observant" had been driven to sigh for her. Her Ladyship, it appeared, had allowed "the world" to choke in her the blessed seeds of redemption. With this interesting information Williams also submitted six considerations, the third indicating that the Lord "owes you no mercy" and the sixth concluding with a solemn warning: "Remember I beseech you your candle is twinkling and glasse neare run the Lord only knows how few minutes are left behind."

[14] Williams' two letters to Lady Barrington are printed in *N.E.H.G.R.*, XLIII (1889), 315-320; also E. J. Carpenter, *Roger Williams, a Political Pioneer* (New York, 1909), pp. 16-21.

It is perhaps extraordinary that Lady Barrington did not destroy this letter—a piece of restraint for which posterity is grateful. But she did not take kindly to Williams' pious endeavors for the good of her soul. The redoubtable guardian of Jane Whalley peremptorily excluded him from the hospitality of her home.

Up to this time Williams had taken the social order as he found it, but Lady Barrington's rebuke and the defeat of his hope for a marriage above his class stung him to the quick. His retort in his "six considerations" tartly referred her Ladyship to Job 34:19: "He with whome we deale excepteth not the persons of princes nor regardeth the rich more than the poore for they are all the worcke of his hands." His second proposition reminded her of Luke 12: "When birth greater, maintenance, more ample time longer and means of grace more plentifull, then a great account of the Lord is expected." There was more than a hint here that Williams was weighing social rank in the scales of religion and finding it of no pertinence. Along that course might lie the road to democracy.

Jane Whalley soon found solace elsewhere. Lady Joan arranged a match which she held more suitable and Jane married William Hooke, who had matriculated as a gentleman's son at Oxford and who was now rector of Upper Clatford, Hants, and a man of more substance than the young chaplain of Otes. Following her marriage Jane fell seriously ill, but recovering, she wrote Lady Barrington of the comfort her husband had been to her and thanked God for him, "not forgetting my thanks to your Ladyship."[15] One of her later letters cast an interesting sidelight upon her new helpmeet. She and Mr. Hooke had been alarmed by noises in the night, she wrote Lady Joan, caused as they supposed from burglars, and they had taken such fright that Mistress Hooke kept to her bed for two days and "Mr. Hooke lost his voyce that I thought would never com againe."[16] In this emergency the rector of Clatford found himself incapable of immediate investigation. Two days later they discovered the real cause of their fright: their maid had let "young fellowes into the house at unseasonable howers to riot with them both with our beare and bread." The maid's services were promptly terminated.

This marriage of Jane Whalley closed one of the episodes in Williams' life. Had his suit been successful he might well have been

15 *Coll. R.I.H.S.*, XXIX, 77.
16 *N.E.H.G.R.*, L (1896), 67.

marked for a different destiny, not founder of Rhode Island but chaplain of the Lord Protector, as William Hooke was later to be, and possibly not an American but an English apostle of liberalism, associated with Pym, Hampden, Cromwell, and other leading spirits in the Puritan revolution.

In the months following, Williams may well have felt despondent and rebellious. Lacking powerful connections, disappointed in love, and torn increasingly by his "tender conscience," he had cause to look with clear eyes upon a society which denied him recognition of his talents. But a new hope began to spring. Even now a project was forming for another England across the seas dedicated to a church out of the Word and holding the promise of opportunity to him who had the strength to endure and the will to endeavor. Williams had turned a deaf ear to a New England call, but events were now forcing him to hearken. In the summer of 1629 he attended a meeting of persons interested in the Massachusetts Bay enterprise. To this meeting, held at the house of the Earl of Lincoln at Sempringham, came John Winthrop from Suffolk with Emmanuel Downey. From Essex came Thomas Hooker and with him Roger Williams. Journeying northward to Boston in Lincolnshire they joined company with John Cotton; and so proceeded together three men in whom the future of New England lay fatefully intertwined.

Hooker, now in the prime of life, was an outstanding Puritan leader in Essex and already attracting the sharp eyes of Bishop Laud. Cotton, older, urbane, and portly, had gained renown as a Puritan lecturer at St. Botolph's and, like Hooker, was soon to find Laud on his back. These two men were moving in the direction of dissent; but Williams found at once that he had gone beyond them. Possibly, wrote Williams later, Cotton remembered riding with him "and one other of precious memorie (Master Hooker) to and from Sempringham" in the course of which Williams presented "Arguments from Scripture, why he durst not joyn with them in their use of Common prayer." The great lecturer of St. Botolph's replied that he "selected the good and best prayers in his use of that Book, as the Author of the Councel of Trent was used to do, in his using of the Massebook."[17] Williams found to his discomfiture that his objections to religious conformity "seemed sandie" to his companions. He could

[17] *Bloody Tenent More Bloody*, N.C.P., IV, 65.

not have met with two more formidable theologians; and Hooker and Cotton, schooled in the Non-separatist doctrine of William Ames, expounded to him the divine plan of one omnipotent church and the expediency of conformity. In after years Williams could claim that Cotton eventually found his objections not sandy but "rockie," and even published a tract of his own "against set Forms of Prayer."[18] But it was not until they had put themselves on the safe side of the Atlantic that Cotton and the Non-separatist brethren discovered the straddle by which they could repudiate the church and still not leave it. For Williams, his thoughts already turning toward Separatism, there could be no such stratagem.

Following the meeting at Sempringham, plans for the new plantations matured rapidly. The Massachusetts Bay Company was anxious to attract "persons of worth and quality," and Governor Cradock proposed a bold concession: to transfer the charter to the colony itself and grant to the freemen of the plantation a larger measure of self-government. At Cambridge on August 26, 1629, John Winthrop and five other future leaders of New England signed an agreement to transplant themselves and their families—if the charter went with them. Three days later at London the Company voted to transfer the government and in a little over six weeks Winthrop was named governor, replacing Cradock, and preparations were made for the departure of the great fleet of 1630.

Williams heard much of these developments. Sir Nathaniel Rich and Robert, Earl of Warwick, had long been active in overseas ventures and maintained close correspondence with the leaders of the Massachusetts enterprise.[19] Numerous Puritans in Essex and the eastern counties were members of the Massachusetts Bay Company, and Sir William Masham, though not a member, counted as an esteemed acquaintance his "worthye good frend" John Winthrop who had served as his attorney in a recent case in the Court of Wards.[20] As Williams learned more of Massachusetts affairs, he began to resolve in his mind the question of his own departure, but it was more than a year before he reached a decision. Meanwhile at Otes he fell desperately ill. In a letter to Lady Barrington, to whom news of Roger Williams was none too welcome, Lady Masham

18 *Mr. Cotton's Letter Examined*, N.C.P., I, 323, 324.
19 Newton, *Colonising Activities*, pp. 80-81, 84.
20 *Winthrop Papers*, I, 367; II, 33-35.

appended a postscript: "Mr. Williams hath bin very weak of a burning feavor and so continueth, but I hope there is some amendment."[21] A little later Sir William wrote that the stricken man, "god be praysed," was "on the mending." Lady Joan's daughter and Sir William, in their affection for their young chaplain, interceded in his behalf. "In the depth of his sickness," wrote Sir William, "when he and we all tooke him for a man of another world, he desired me to remember his humble and affectionate service to you." Williams had requested that Lady Barrington be told "that what he wrote to your Ladiship was out of depth of conscience and desire of your spiritual good, which is most pretious to him." Since these "might have bene his last words," Sir William reported himself "now much more confirmed in my former mind, that what he did proceeded out of love and conscience; so I doubt not but you are well persuaded of him, and will receive him into your former favor, and good opinion: A kind word from you would much refresh him in this his weake estate."

Lady Barrington did not come easily by the spirit of charity. Not for ten months longer did she relent. Meanwhile in harvest time, 1629, she received from Lady Masham another piece of information in regard to the young cleric: "Mr. Willyams is to marrye mary barnard Jug Altham's made."[22] Her Ladyship may have permitted herself a sardonic smile. The bumptious young man had discovered his proper place. Failing with the mistress, he had turned to the maid.

In December, 1629, when Mistress Jane Hooke was writing Lady Joan of her happiness in marriage, a new entry was made in the parish register of High Laver: "Roger Williams clarke and Mary Barnard were married the 15th day of Decem: anno dom 1629."[23] Little is known of Roger Williams' wife and nothing of her family. The fact that she was the maid of Joan Altham does not necessarily indicate that she came of humble stock. Joan was a young lady of rank and fortune, daughter of Sir James Altham of Mark Hall, Latton, Essex, who had been Lady Masham's first husband,[24] and it was not unusual for middle-class folk of moderate means to place

---

21 For extracts from this letter and those following see James Ernst, "New Light on Roger Williams' Life in England," *Coll. R.I.H.S.*, XXII, 97-103.

22 *Coll. R.I.H.S.*, XI, 122.

23 *Ibid.*, XV, 64.

24 *Ibid.*, XI, 123.

their daughters as maids in families of rank. Mary Barnard may have been of much the same class as Williams himself.[25]

Dowry and social advancement did not enter into Williams' marriage with Jug Altham's maid; and in Mary Barnard he found a good wife. A woman "of a meek and modest spirit," as John Cotton observed,[26] she had also qualities of steadfastness and quiet courage. Of these she had need, for in time of rigorous orthodoxy it would not be easy to follow a companion like Williams and brave the scorn of friends and kin; nor would it be easy to plunge suddenly into the unaccustomed and arduous tasks demanded of a pioneer mother in a far-off wilderness. Mary Barnard had no great store of education —"Thy holy and humble desires are strong, but I know thy writing is slow," Williams wrote to her; but their marriage was a happy one, and in years to come Williams expressed his devotion to her in a tract on spiritual improvement written especially for her comfort.[27]

Following his marriage Williams continued as chaplain at Otes. Lady Barrington eventually overcame her spite, and in the late spring or summer of 1630 Sir William wrote heartily, "I am right glad to heare of your inclinations to Mr. Williams."[28] Meanwhile at Otes there was preparation for a marriage far more conspicuous than that of Sir William's chaplain. Lady Masham wrote her mother of a "match for Jug" suggested by no less a personage than Sir Nathaniel Rich: "The gentleman's name is Mr. St. John that was lately in prison in the Tower."[29] Oliver St. John was winning his spurs as a young lawyer, but Lady Masham was troubled. In her letter to Lady Joan, materialistic ambitions and class considerations mixed agreeably with good Puritan doctrine: "I know God commands me," she wrote, to have a care "of outward conveniences"; and there was also the matter of keeping up with the Joneses. She would be "much taxed" by friends of her daughter if she did not assure herself of the young man's "competency of outward estate." To such as Roger Williams and Mary Barnard the estate might have seemed princely, five hundred pounds yearly, but Lady Masham feared it would "be

---

[25] For attempts to identify Barnard connections, see Emily Easton, "Mary Barnard," *Coll. R.I.H.S.*, XXIX, 66-79.

[26] *A Reply to Mr. Williams*, N.C.P., II, 20.

[27] See Williams, *Experiments of Spiritual Life and Health* (Providence, 1863), p. 2.

[28] *Coll. R.I.H.S.*, XXII, 101-102.

[29] *Ibid.*, XXIX, 74.

but little to pay house rent and maintain housekeeping."[30] Nevertheless, before the year was out Mistress Altham and Oliver St. John
were married; and in the interim Roger Williams made in the rising
young barrister one more friend who would be a powerful ally when
Williams, and Rhode Island, had need of friends.

There was another eminent member of the energetic Rich family
whom Williams knew at Otes and whose favorable support would be
of momentous importance when he had need of it. This was Robert
Rich, second Earl of Warwick. In 1643 Warwick was Lord President of the Council of State and Roger Williams was no stranger to
him when he petitioned the Council for a Rhode Island patent. The
Earl of Warwick had long played a leading part in promoting English plantations, and even now, in 1630, he was joining with Sir
Nathaniel Rich in launching the Providence Company for a bold
venture in the West Indies in defiance of Spain. Sir Thomas Barrington and Oliver St. John became members of the Company and
John Pym the treasurer.[31] Conceivably, had Williams remained in
England a little longer, the influence of men such as these might have
turned him to Old Providence Island where there was place for
Puritan clerics as well as in New England. But in 1630 the Providence venture was merely beginning, and Williams' thoughts
reverted to his New England call and to the great project of Indian
conversion which had been discussed at Sempringham.

As the weeks passed, in 1630, hundreds of Puritans began to settle their estates and pack their belongings, preparatory to embarking
on the great adventure. The strong resolutions of Eliot in the last
parliament had proved a failure and Puritanism as a political force
had been driven underground. Archbishop Laud and Sir Thomas
Wentworth—"Black Tom Tyrant"—were having it their own way
now, and multitudes in England, some even of the gentry, bethought
themselves of migration. Puritan families of greater wealth had
other things at stake besides religion; it was well to bide one's time
and to submit where one must. But for thousands of less conspicuous Puritans the die was cast and the great migration began.

The ambassador from Venice remarked in wonder at the lordly
riches and fine houses of great merchants and nobles, but there was

[30] Coll. R.I.H.S., XXIX, 74-75.
[31] Newton, Colonising Activities, pp. 64-65; C. E. Wade, John Pym (London,
1912), pp. 151, 153.

another England in sharp contrast: a country of poverty, scarcity, and unequal opportunity. To remove across the seas might bring something in addition to gospel purity. Reports had come of boundless opportunities in a land not yet despoiled. Impatient to be gone, Winthrop set down one of the crucial considerations through which he had reached a decision: England was growing "weary of her inhabitants, soe as man, whoe is the most pretious of all creatures, is here more vile and base than the earth we treade on." Winthrop, as a Puritan, was out of favor and had been deprived of his practice in the Court of Wards and Liveries. Not least among his reasons for migration was his ambition for wider scope for his undoubted talents.

Following his marriage Roger Williams likewise resolved on departure. While never summoned and silenced, he lived always under the shadow of Laud. For him as for Winthrop the way to honor lay closed. God, he declared, "knows what gains and preferments I have refused in universities, city, country, and court . . . to keep my soul undefiled in this point, and not to act with a doubting conscience."[32] Already he had been offered "2 severall livings," each of £100 per annum—not to be sneezed at by an impecunious chaplain, but Williams had refused them. Incapable of violating his innermost convictions, he was turning not simply against the Prayer Book but against the church in conformity with the logic of an avowed Separatist.

Although all these reasons operated to draw Williams to New England, it was a choice hard to come by. This was more than migration; it was exile. Of the decision on severance from kin and native soil, Williams afterwards wrote the daughter of Sir Edward Coke, in words poignantly suggestive of the inner torture of many a colonist: "and truly it was as bitter as death to me when Bishop Laud pursued me out of this land, and my conscience was persuaded against the national church and ceremonies, and bishops, beyond the conscience of your dear Father. I say it was as bitter as death to me, when I rode Windsor way, to take ship at Bristow and saw Stoke House, where the blessed man was; and I then durst not acquaint him with my conscience and my flight."[33]

When Roger and Mary Williams arrived at the thriving west

---

[32] Williams to John Cotton, Jr., 1671, *N.C.P.*, VI, 356.
[33] *Letters*, N.C.P., VI, 239.

coast port, they encountered a young Puritan who was to become a lifelong friend. Years later, in a letter to John Winthrop, Jr., Williams harkened back to this early meeting: "Your loving lines in this cold, dead season, were as a cup of your Connecticut cider, which we are glad to hear abounds with you, or that western metheglin, which you and I have drunk at Bristol together. . . ."[34] Genial, tolerant, well traveled, and endowed with indefatigable interest in books, people, science, and public affairs, the younger Winthrop found a kindred spirit in Williams. Within a year he, too, was to embark from Bristol. Meanwhile, over their western metheglin, the two men struck up a bond which was to grow closer with the years.

On December 1, 1630, the ship *Lyon* weighed anchor and for more than two months thereafter Roger Williams and his wife knew the taste of salt spray, the tedium of day upon day of endless vistas of open water, and the keen anxieties of a winter's passage amid icy winds and angry seas.[35] Mary Williams was never to see England again. Her husband, leaving in bitterness and in fear of Laud, perhaps little dreamed that he would make the Atlantic passage four times more.

[34] *Letters*, N.C.P., VI, 306 f.
[35] John Winthrop, *History of New England* (Boston, 1853), I, 51; hereafter cited as Winthrop's *Journal*.

4

TROUBLER OF ISRAEL

ON FEBRUARY 5, 1631, Roger and Mary Williams first set foot
on New World soil. Governor Winthrop, welcoming the *Lyon,* made
a note of some of her passengers: "She brought Mr. Williams (a
godly minister) with his wife, Mr. Throgmorton," and some others.[1]
Winthrop had met the young chaplain at Sempringham, and it is
apparent that Williams' zeal and ability brought him a ready welcome at Boston. The way to preferment in New England opened
before him. Hooker, Stone, Cotton, Shepard, Eliot, Nathaniel
Ward, and other great lights of New England churches had not yet
come. Boston was even now temporarily deprived of the services of
John Wilson, and before long the "godly" young minister from the
Lyon was offered the place as teacher of the leading church in the
colony. In 1631 the magistrates and ministers of Massachusetts
expected Roger Williams to become one of them.

It was not to be Williams' destiny to become one of that charmed
inner circle. His first action was a portent of much that was to follow. "Being unanimously chosen teacher at Boston," he wrote, he
conscientiously refused "because I durst not officiate to an unsepa-
rated people, as upon examination and conference I found them to
be."[2] Williams was not insensible of the opportunity for advancement and certainly he desired a church, but not at the price of his
convictions. He might, he declared later, "have run the rode of
preferment, as well as in Old as New England. . . ."[3] He now
exhibited that characteristic belief in "coming out," separating from
a corrupt church, which was to denote him as spiritual kin of the
Independent sects and not of the Non-separatists of England and
Massachusetts. He could not become teacher, he told them in Boston, unless the congregation would repent its former communion
in the Church of England and discourage its members from com-
muning with that church when they visited the homeland.

---

[1] Winthrop, *Journal,* I, 49-51.
[2] Williams to John Cotton, Jr., 1671, *N.C.P.,* VI, 356.
[3] *Bloody Tenent More Bloody,* N.C.P., IV, 104.

Non-separatists of the Ames persuasion could not accede to this, and Williams soon departed for Salem where the Ames doctrine was not yet so firmly rooted. Before leaving Boston he declared his adherence to another principle which caused equal shock to those of the Bay. The civil magistrate, he declared, might not punish "breach of the Sabbath" nor any other violations of "the first table."[4] Since the first table, comprising the first four of the Ten Commandments, consisted of the Mosaic injunctions against idolatry, blasphemy, and heresy, Williams in effect was denying the power of the government to compel conformity in matters of faith. Already he was bolstering his Separatism with something which looked dangerously akin to condonement of schism.

Williams departed to Salem without a summons or warning, but trouble was brewing. By April 12 word came to Governor Winthrop "that they of Salem had called Mr. Williams to the office of a teacher." Coddington, Ludlow, Bradstreet, and other nearby assistants deliberated at Boston and determined on the first in a long series of actions against Williams. They sent a letter to John Endecott, assistant at Salem, charging that "Mr. Williams had refused to join with the congregation at Boston" because they would not make public repentance "for having communion with the churches of England, while they lived there." The newly chosen teacher of Salem had also "declared his opinion, that the magistrate might not punish the breach of the Sabbath, nor any other offence, as it was a breach of the first table; therefore, they marvelled they would choose him without advising with the council; and withal desiring him, that they would forbear to proceed till they had conferred about it."[5]

No law existed which authorized interference with the right of a congregation to elect its officers, but this was neither the first nor the last time that the magistrates relied upon their claim of discretionary authority and effectively overrode a congregation. Williams found himself without a church and removed southward to Plymouth. For the moment, the magistrates had freed themselves of the threat of Separatism.

Williams' Separatism and the issue it presented frequently has been misunderstood. Because Williams urged renunciation of the Church of England, New England Puritans who rejected this step

4 Winthrop, *Journal,* I, 63.
5 *Ibid.*

have been upheld as more tolerant. "It is a surprising fact," remarked Goodwin, "that any person should have left Boston of 1631 because he found there religious liberality which amounted to a sin; but the surprise is increased manyfold when the person so departing is found to have been Roger Williams."[6] The real issue was the conflict between the sectarian principle which tended toward a free church system and toleration and the ideal of one authoritarian church which included the whole society.[7] Even as early as 1631 Williams aligned himself in support of the sectarian ideal and affirmed the right and the necessity of separating from false and idolatrous worship and of setting up an independent church.

Five years later, after Williams departed for Rhode Island, he and Cotton exchanged letters on this subject and Williams charged that Non-separatism attempted to "walke betwixt Christ and Anti-Christ"; to which Cotton replied that "the Lord hath guided us to walk with an even foote between two extremes."[8] Between these two positions there was an irreconcilable difference. Williams in the years to come unerringly exposed the lack of logic in "witnessing against a national Church and yet holding fellowship with it";[9] but there lay a subtle harmony in Non-separatism which outwitted logic. Those of the school of Ames might witness against the church of Laud—and did—but they must not separate. They must give no sanction to Separatism because they must give no sanction to schism. They must uphold the divine right of the church of the prelates because they must uphold their own claim of divine authority, as hopeful heirs apparent next in the line of succession. Laud might hold sway for the moment, but the Non-separatist trusted to the Massachusetts example and the growing might of numbers in England to conquer the church itself. Trained in the school of Ames, Governor Winthrop and the Bay leaders would not quarrel with the absolutist principle of the Church of England, nor separate from it while they hoped to capture it. Meanwhile behind the bulwark of

[6] J. A. Goodwin, *The Pilgrim Republic* (Boston, 1888), p. 348. See also J. T. Adams, "John Cotton," *D.A.B.*

[7] See Miller, *Orthodoxy in Massachusetts,* pp. 127-163, and *passim;* Ernst Troeltsch, *The Social Teaching of the Christian Churches* (New York, 1931), II, 656-661, 670-673, and especially 997-998; J. M. Mecklin, *The Story of American Dissent* (New York, 1934), p. 24 ff.

[8] See Cotton's *Letter to Mr. Williams,* N.C.P., I, 308.

[9] *Mr. Cotton's Letter Examined,* N.C.P., I, 371.

three thousand miles of ocean they proceeded to set up a new
clericalism in place of the one they had left and to substitute the uniformity of Ames for the uniformity of Laud. Roger Williams in
1631 betook himself to Plymouth with different ideas, and if for the
moment he merely asserted the right and necessity of Separatism
against the English church, it would not be long before he would
assert the same right against the churches of Massachusetts.

There are few records of Williams' life in Plymouth colony.
According to Governor Bradford, he was kindly "entertained,
according to their poore abilitie" and became a member of the
church. Since Plymouth people stemmed from the Separatists who
had once fled to Holland, Williams' doctrine was less suspect than in
Massachusetts and he "exercised his gifts amongst them" as assistant to the Reverend Ralph Smith who also had been ordered from
Salem on the grounds of Separatism.[10]

In October, 1632, Winthrop and other worthies from the Bay
were entertained at the older colony of the Pilgrims. On the afternoon
of the sabbath "Mr. Roger Williams (according to their custom)
propounded a question, to which the pastor, Mr. Smith, spake briefly;
then Mr. Williams prophesied." After Bradford and several others
of Plymouth had spoken to the question, they desired Winthrop and
John Wilson, minister at Boston, to speak to it, "which they did."[11]
Perhaps the question presented at these exercises related to the
"goodman" controversy. Williams and Smith, according to Cotton
Mather, were "leavened so far with the humors of the rigid separation, that they insisted vehemently upon the unlawfulness of calling
any unregenerate man by the name of 'good-man such an one,' until
by their indiscreet urging of this whimsey, the place began to be dis-
quieted."[12] When this question was propounded during the visit of
Winthrop, the Massachusetts governor gave his opinion that such
salutations were a mere "civil custom"; which, Mather declared,
"put a stop to the little, idle, whimsical conceits, then beginning to
grow obstreperous." Winthrop's own account of his Plymouth visit
does not mention such an incident, nor does Bradford, and the story
may be apocryphal. Yet Williams on occasion exhibited religious

10 *Mass. Bay Recs.*, I, 390; Frances Rose-Troup, *John White* (New York,
1930), p. 143 f.; William Bradford, *History of Plimoth Plantation* (Commonwealth ed., Boston, 1898), pp. 369-370.
11 Winthrop, *Journal*, I, 109.
12 *Magnalia Christi Americana* (Hartford, 1820), I, 117.

scruples which he spun to airy flimsiness, and the anecdote of Cotton
Mather does not seem improbable. In after years at Providence, the
records spoke often of "neighbor" so and so, but seldom made use
of the appellation "goodman."

Such an episode, if it occurred, was of minor consequence, and in
his two years at Plymouth Williams gained the high regard of the
congregation by his services in the church and his labors among the
Indians. Governor Bradford acknowledged him "a man godly and
zealous, having many precious parts." His account of Williams,
written after the latter's banishment from Massachusetts, was colored by that event. Williams was "very unsettled in judgment"; yet
his teaching was

> well approoved, for the benefite wherof I still blese God, and
> am thankfull to him, even for his sharpest admonitions and
> reproufs, so farr as they agreed with truth. He this year begane
> to fall into some strang oppīions, and from opinion to practise;
> which caused some controversie betweene the church and him,
> and in the end some discontente on his parte, by occasion wherof
> he left them some thing abruptly. Yet after wards sued for his
> dismission to the church of Salem, which was granted, with some
> caution to them concerning him, and what care they ought to
> have of him.[13]

The unnamed bone of contention was probably Williams'
advanced views of Separatism. Although sired by the earlier school
of Separatists, Plymouth was swinging back to views like those of
Ames, and "rigid separation" was becoming suspect at Plymouth as
well as in the Bay.[14] Bradford seems to have approved of the subsequent banishment of Williams by Massachusetts. In the course of
time the conventional Plymouth estimate of Williams' ministry
became considerably less kindly than Bradford's. Nathaniel Morton's account, published in 1669, reflected the glacial drift of later
Puritan days and marked the development of the scathing or satirical portrayal of the celebrated Rhode Islander which, repeated by
Hubbard, was embellished and perpetuated by Cotton Mather. Morton's version depicted Williams as "well accepted" on his first arrival

[13] Bradford, *History*, pp. 369-370. Bradford's account refers to the year 1633,
but internal evidence shows that it was written or rephrased after Williams'
banishment.

[14] Miller, *Orthodoxy in Massachusetts*, pp. 127-136.

at Plymouth, but as gradually venting "singular opinions"—not specified—and seeking to "impose" them on the congregation; "not finding such a concurrence as he expected," he requested "dismission to the church of Salem, which though some were unwilling to, yet through the prudent counsel of Mr. Brewster, the ruling elder there, fearing that his continuance amongst them might cause divisions, and there being many abler men in the bay, they would better deal with him than themselves could. . . ."[15] At the time of its publication years later Williams wrote laughingly of this account to John Winthrop, Jr.: "Sir, since I saw you I have read Morton's Memorial, and rejoice at the encomiums upon your father and other precious worthies, though I be a reprobate, *contemptâ vitior algâ.*"[16]

Some time between July and November, 1633, Williams removed to Salem and became assistant to the pastor of the church, Samuel Skelton, "but not in any office," noted Winthrop, "though he exercised by way of prophecy. . . ."[17] In this capacity Williams was soon in opposition to one of the new ecclesiastical practices by which the clergy were consolidating their control of the churches. The ministers had begun to hold periodical meetings at which "some question of moment was debated." Skelton and Williams "took some exception against it, as fearing it might grow in time to a presbytery or superintendency, to the prejudice of the churches' liberties." Williams, as in 1631 when he questioned the disciplinary power of magistrates, was fearful of a new hierarchy and a national church and seized upon a defense of congregational independence as the surest way to combat compulsory uniformity and clerical absolutism. Winthrop understood the point but he derided such fears as "without cause; for they were all clear in that point, that no church or person can have power over another church; neither did they in their meetings exercise any such jurisdiction. . . ."[18] Only four years later the first synod in Massachusetts was to belie Winthrop's words. The system of synods, consociation, ministerial advice to the magistrates, and magisterial enforcement of the first table was presently to establish a "superintendency" over the churches and shackle local

[15] *New England's Memorial* (Boston, 1855), p. 102.

[16] *Letters,* N.C.P., VI, 333.

[17] *Journal,* I, 139; *Plymouth Col. Recs.,* I, 15.

[18] *Journal,* I, 139. The bitterness of Hubbard on this subject is revealing; see 2 *Coll. M.H.S.,* V, 189-190.

congregations in the iron clasp of the centralized uniformity that Williams had feared.

In December, 1633, Governor Winthrop made a notation of another protest by Williams:

> The governour and assistants met at Boston and took into consideration a treatise, which Mr. Williams (then of Salem) had sent to them, and which he had formerly written to the governour and council of Plimouth, wherein, among other things, he disputes their right to the lands they possessed here, and concluded that, claiming by the king's grant, they could have no title, nor otherwise, except they compounded with the natives.[19]

This striking criticism of the practice of European monarchs of granting vast tracts inhabited by Indians arose out of Williams' friendship with the natives and concern for their rights. From Plymouth he wrote Winthrop, "I am no Elder in any church . . . nor ever shall be, if the Lord please to grant my desires that I may intend what I long after, the natives souls. . . ." From the first, Williams had a keen desire to "dive into the Indian language." He and Massasoit, sachem of the Wampanoags, became "great friends at Plymouth"; he spared no cost in tokens and presents to him and "all his," and had friendly relations also with Canonicus, great sachem of the Narragansetts.[20] The description of New England by William Wood, published in 1634, spoke in warm praise: "One of the English Preachers in a speciall good intent of doing good to their soules, hath spent much time in attaining to their Language, wherein he is so good a proficient, that he can speake to their understanding, and they to his; much loving and respecting him for his love and counsell. It is hoped that he may be an instrument of good amongst them."[21] Eliot had not begun his notable labors; the unnamed missionary was Roger Williams.

Williams' manuscript on Plymouth patent has not survived, but it is clear that he called on the planters to make amends for the "sinne of unjust usurpation upon others possessions."[22] The Indians

---

[19] *Journal*, I, 145.

[20] *Letters*, N.C.P., VI, 2, 317; Williams' Plea, 1677, printed in E. J. Carpenter, *Roger Williams, a Political Pioneer* (New York, 1909), p. 224.

[21] *New England's Prospect* (Boston, 1865), p. 103.

[22] See Winthrop to Endecott, January 3, 1634, *Proc. M.H.S., 1871-1873*, pp. 343-345.

alone were lords of the soil and no grant by the king could alienate their title. The "great sin" of New England's patents lay in their provisions respecting "Donation of the Land"—"wherein Christian Kings (so calld) are invested with Right by virtue of their Christianitie, to take and give away the Lands and Countries of other men. . . ."[23]

The action of the authorities on this issue revealed forcibly to Williams the increasingly close association of leading clerics and magistrates. The court sounded out "some of the most judicious ministers," doubtless among them John Cotton, the great new light of Boston church, and the ministers promptly brought in a verdict which "much condemned Mr. Williams's error and presumption. . . ." The magistrates thereupon summoned Williams "to be censured." By private intervention Winthrop averted immediate disciplinary action. He wrote Endecott to confer with Williams and secure a retraction; and in response to this overture, the young Salem cleric stated the simple truth of the question without rancor. His treatise had not been aimed specifically against the Massachusetts patent but had been written at Plymouth "for the private satisfaction" of the authorities there. The Bay magistrates would have heard nothing of the matter if Winthrop had not asked him for a copy of the tract; and if they desired, they might burn the manuscript or the parts objectionable.[24]

The "offensive passages" in Williams' manuscript turned on certain allegations which reflected upon royalty. Williams had charged James with "a solemn public lie" in acclaiming himself the first Christian prince to discover "this land." The magistrates knew as well as Williams that James had no title as discoverer of the continent; but they were not prepared to contradict the royal word. Nor was it expedient to attack James' patent for calling Europe "Christendom." True, the infidel Turk held much of Europe, and all Puritans knew that "Anti-Christ" ruled over much of the rest. Still more impolitic was Williams' citation of three uncomplimentary passages from *Revelations* which he "did personally apply to our present king, Charles." Nevertheless on January 24 the authorities found the offensive passages "obscure" and matters not "so evil as

---

[23] *Bloody Tenent More Bloody*, N.C.P., IV, 461.
[24] Winthrop, *Journal*, I, 145-146.

at first they seemed," and with the concurrence of Cotton and Wilson, the court withheld its censure.[25]

This affair of the patent, while indicative of Williams' tendency to scruple over trivia, first revealed his stature as one of the few Englishmen who demanded equal justice for the natives. According to Cotton, Williams contended that the Indians "hunted all the Countrey over" and on their big hunts once or twice a year burnt out the underbrush—a sufficient proof of their "Propriety of the Countrey"; an evidence of title at least as good as that of English nobles to their "great Parkes" or of the king to his "great Forrests."[26] The Massachusetts retort to Williams on this point was subtle and revealing. Although admitting the Indian title by generally paying "purchase money" for lands, the Bay authorities did not relish a defense of the "Propriety" of the natives. Land-hungry Puritans were not disposed to treat the heathen as the equals of "Saints." The fat lands of nobles and king in the mother country, they said, were earned by great services to church and state. As for the aborigines and their hunting grounds: "We did not conceive that it is a just Title to so vast a Continent, to make no other improvement of millions of Acres in it. . . ."[27]

Governor Winthrop, to confound Williams with good European legalism, declared bluntly that "these parts" were *"vacuum Domicilium."*[28] Even before embarking from the homeland, Winthrop had dug into the Old Testament for the warrant of Higher Law. The cases of Ephron the Hittite, Jacob and Hamor's land, and the relations of Abimelech's servants with Isaac's readily came to hand, and Winthrop concluded that the Indians had only a "natural right" to the soil, the right of occupancy. Land that lay in common and had never been replenished or subdued was "free to any that possesse and improve it. . . . Soe if we leave them sufficient for their use, we may lawfully take the rest, there being more than enough for them and us. . . ."[29] Along this road lay hidden the sentiment that the heathen had no rights which a white man was bound to respect. If

---

25 *Ibid.*, 145, 147. The passages from *Revelations* are printed in H. M. Dexter, *As To Roger Williams* (Boston, 1876), p. 28.

26 *Reply to Mr. Williams*, N.C.P., II, 46-47.

27 *Ibid.*

28 See his letter on the controversy, *Proc. M.H.S., 1871-1873*, pp. 343-345.

29 "Reasons for the Plantation," printed in R. C. Winthrop, *Life and Letters of John Winthrop*, I, 309-310.

for the moment the English "bought" the land with coats and trinkets, before long they were to dispose by fraud of claims of the natives. In later years Roger Williams was to be shocked to see the saints dispense even with coats and trinkets and extort rich lands from the Indians in the guise of judicial punishments or through forcible persuasion by military expeditions.

The significance of Williams' attack on royal patents, in the long view of history, springs from its honorable position as the first American attack on the white man's imperialism. Modern critics of the dogma of the white man's burden would doubtless believe that Williams, although obscure in his statements, was on the right track. He insisted upon equitable treatment of the Indians in purchasing their lands and attacked the current practice of "Christian Kings" in blandly appropriating new countries by right of discovery. Williams, however, was speaking out of turn in an age when backward races were not understood to have any particular rights as independent nations. How far imperial arrogance was then carried may be seen in the charter which Charles I granted to Lord Baltimore, which contained a provision that no one should recognize claims of the Indians to any part of the lands assigned in the grant. International law of the seventeenth century, created by world powers and designed for their ends, sanctioned the practice which Williams protested.

During the nine months following the affair of the patent, Williams reputedly was involved in two minor controversies centering in Salem. One concerned scriptural warrant for the appearance of women in church without wearing veils; the other, the Puritan scruple against the cross in the English ensign as a popish superstition. Neither episode brought Williams into direct conflict with the authorities, but each furnished the later Puritan chroniclers, Hubbard and Cotton Mather, with rich materials for ridicule of Williams' tender conscience.

Holy Writ revealed that no woman should prophesy or pray with her head "uncovered."[30] The question whether this enjoined veils had been agitated in England, and in March, 1634, it reappeared in Massachusetts. William Hubbard's anecdotes of the celebrated exile from Massachusetts included an account of Williams as the ludicrous champion of the wearing of veils.[31] Williams had, indeed, the full

[30] I *Corinthians*, 11:5.
[31] *General History of New England*, 2 Coll. M.H.S., V, 204.

measure of Puritan literalness and, as Hubbard alleged, may have drawn instances from the Bible to sanction the practice in Salem church. Other than this fallible tradition, recorded nearly five decades after the event, there is little to show that Williams figured largely in this curious and typical Puritan controversy. The real agitator in the affair was John Endecott, and the dispute began in Boston and not Salem. On March 7, 1634, during the regular Thursday lectures John Cotton spoke upon the question of veils and denied their necessity. The magistrate of Salem happened to be present and had his own ideas. Endecott spoke his mind, a wrangle followed, good fellowship seemed on the point of being forgotten, and the meeting reached the point of "some earnestness" when Governor Winthrop intervened and induced the fire-eaters to "brake-off."[32] Sometime afterwards Cotton preached a sermon at Salem which immediately put an end to the wearing of veils. His most effective persuasion was the example of Tamar the Harlot whose reason for wearing a veil did not commend itself to Puritan maids and goodwives. It is an interesting sidelight on the little comedy that John Cotton himself, while still in the mother country, seems to have thought favorably of veiling the charms of the ladies when they were engaged in divine worship.[33]

The controversy precipitated in November, 1634, when the cross was cut from the flag was more crucial and, with the help of the later great novelist of Salem, was to become celebrated. Nathaniel Hawthorne in the nineteenth century worked it into a dramatic story in which Endecott was the hero. William Hubbard in the seventeenth century worked it into a satirical attack in which Williams was the villain. Hubbard was official historian of the Bay and knew both Winthrop's account and the records of the colony. Neither Winthrop nor the colony records mention any responsibility of Williams. By contrast, Hubbard's account is illuminating:

> Another notion diffused by him occasioned more disturbance, for in his zeal for advancing the purity of reformation, and abolishing all badges of superstition, he inspired some persons of great interest in that place, that the cross in the King's colors ought to be taken away as a relic of antichristian superstition.

[32] Winthrop, *Journal*, I, 149.
[33] Hubbard, *History*, 2 Coll. M.H.S., V, 205; Thomas Hutchinson, *History of Massachusetts* (Boston, 1795), I, 379 n.

What that good man would have done with the cross upon his
coin, (if he had any left,) that bore that sign of superstition, is
uncertain. But this notion about the King's colors prevailed with
some so far, that it was taken out of the ensign at Salem by one
in place. . . . In this manner did overheated zeal vent itself in
the said Mr. Williams, of whom they were wont to say in Essex,
where he lived, that he was divinely mad; as if his too much zeal,
as Festus said of Paul's too much learning, had made him beside
himself.[34]

The "one in place" was Endecott, although neither Hubbard nor
Cotton Mather, who repeats the story, felt it necessary at that point
to mention his name.[35] Since enemies in England might seize on it
as "a kind of rebellion to deface the King's colors," the magistrates
decided to bring the culprits to book. They levied no accusation
against Williams. Richard Davenport who had carried the defaced
colors received a summons; and at the general court on May 6, 1634,
Endecott was deprived for a year of all public offices. The magistrates were not more severe on the Salem assistant because they were
all "persuaded he did it out of tenderness of conscience."[36]

Williams was one of those who disliked the red cross of St.
George as a relic of popery, but as in the controversy over the veils
his responsibility was secondary. Hubbard, in 1680, constrained to
make the most of the "dangerous opinions" of the exile from Massachusetts, described Endecott as "bewitched" by Williams. John
Endecott, however, was a man who generally could stand stoutly on
his own legs and take responsibility for his own actions. He was a
distinguished founder of the colony, long an assistant and for some
years governor, and a man of wealth with a considerable investment
in the Massachusetts Bay Company. It is understandable why Williams was saddled by Cotton, Hubbard, Morton, and others with
"singular opinions" while little was said of the identical scruples of
Endecott and the saints. The outcome of the controversy was to
show still more clearly that not Roger Williams alone, nor Endecott,
but magistrates, ministers, and a large part of the population were
capable of singular opinions and "over-heated zeal." Throughout the

[34] *History,* 2 Coll. M.H.S., V, 205-206. See also Coddington's letter of 1677,
printed in George Fox and John Burnyeat, *A New-England Fire-Brand Quenched*
(London, 1679), p. 246.

[35] See *Magnalia*, II, 433.

[36] Hubbard, *History,* 2 Coll. M.H.S., V, 164-165; Winthrop, *Journal*, I, 175,
188-189.

year of 1635 the agitation against the cross in the flag steadily mounted, so that court and colony became divided; and although these were the months when Laud's attack on the Massachusetts charter roused grave fear, the magistrates finally gave leave for display of the ensign without the cross. Hooker wrote a treatise in defense of the cross, but Cotton threw his weight on the other side, being for this once of the same conscience as Roger Williams. For years to come the hated symbol was seen no more, and even at the end of the century Sewall and Mather "judged it a Sin" to have the cross put in again.[37]

Williams' scruples sprang out of Puritanism. Governor Winthrop, on his visit to Plymouth in 1632, when passing a place named Hue's Cross, renamed it Hue's Folly lest the Papists take credit for it.[38] Literalness, magnification of the trivial, absence of a sense of humor went with the age and with the doctrine of purity out of the Word. The notions of wearing veils and cutting out the cross were born of the selfsame logic that ensnared John Cotton in *Moses, His Judicialls.*

Although nothing Williams had done since his return from Plymouth had brought him into serious conflict with the ruling order, the trend of affairs must have filled him with misgivings. In the Bay colony by curious cross-breeding, the Holy Commonwealth beloved by the Puritans had sprung from the loins of an English company organized for trade. A government with plenary power over the life and liberty of English subjects was being fashioned from the patent of a business corporation. In conjunction with their Puritan lords spiritual, the transmigrated patentees of the company were making themselves holy stewards of a wilderness Zion, deriving, as they imagined, mediately from God a design for the winnowing of souls, the wooing of profits, and the elevation of the righteous to the seats of the mighty. The pattern of life and government in the Bay as it stood revealed in 1634 offered little peace of mind to men like Williams and boded ill for the high cause of a generous freedom. An English opposition had become a New England oligarchy. The patentees who came with the charter had made themselves omnip-

---

[37] Samuel Sewall, *Diary,* 5 Coll. M.H.S., V, 147. For a careful study, see H. M. Chapin, "Roger Williams and the King's Colors," *Coll. R.I.H.S.,* XXI (1928).

[38] *Journal,* I, 110-111.

otent through the court of assistants, and in violation of their patent did not propose to share their supremacy. The landed interest and the clergy were in the saddle, and the process had already begun by which in forty-five years the ruling group manipulated the general court, successfully obtaining special grants of land for thirty-two of their circle for a munificent total of 57,214 acres,[39] this in addition to large estates obtained through the channel of town allotments.

The bulwark of power lay in the suffrage, and in May, 1631, the court of assistants ordered that none should be freemen unless they were church members. This limitation on the suffrage was decisive and insured domination by the close alliance of ministers and magistrates; for "church members" were not the whole body of the congregation but only those who had received admission into the select inner circle of "Visible Saints." Puritan clergy of theocratic bent took care to admit only men zealous in orthodoxy and well affected to the dominant order; and before long, English Puritans were startled to hear that in the new Zion over the seas three-fourths of the people had been shut out from membership in the church.[40]

Yet already a rising protest warned the magistrates of the need of circumspection. To attract settlers and win their subjection to rule by the saints, the colony was making grants of small farms through the agency of the towns. So was formed a growing body of property owners, men who as freeholders would have enjoyed wider liberties in the mother country they had left; and in the face of these, "very jealous of their liberties,"[41] the magistrates were compelled to make concessions more in conformity with the charter. The men of Watertown in 1632 expressed fear that the assistants would bring "themselves and posterity into bondage";[42] before the year was out the freemen of the colony wrested from the assistants their proper right to elect the governor and deputy-governor. In 1634 they demanded and obtained a look at the charter, the terms of which had been concealed from the public. The result was that the freemen won the right to elect their own members as deputies to sit in the general court. But the victory was inconclusive. The body of freemen were restricted in number and their deputies subservient. When Deputy

---

[39] *Mass. Bay. Recs.*, I-IV, *passim*.
[40] Thomas Lechford, *Plain Dealing*, 3 Coll. M.H.S., III, 73.
[41] Hubbard, *History*, 2 Coll. M.H.S., V, 165.
[42] Winthrop, *Journal*, I, 84.

Stoughton in 1634 dared protest the irregular arrogation by the assistants of a veto on decisions made by the deputies, he was deprived for three years of public office. Men like Williams were to find virtually no protection for themselves against arbitrary rule and rigorous orthodoxy.

With a suffrage linked to sanctification, and clerical influence over the people employed as a stout crutch to support magisterial statecraft, oligarchy served well the dual purpose of keeping democracy out and orthodoxy in. Believing in wealth and power in the hands of the few, and dressing up magistracy as a divine stewardship, the assistants sanctioned their conduct by Higher Law when charter or English precedent would have tied their hands, and parried the popular clamor for a code of "known laws." The Massachusetts squirearchy, intrenched in the ranks of assistants, clung to ultimate judicial authority, including a loose, irregular prerogative power, the executive authority, and the bulk of the legislative authority, and saw to it in the elections that these sinews of power did not change hands.[43] Only the husks of political rights had been conceded to the rank and file of the "Saints"; the vast body of yeoman farmers and common folk remained unenfranchised, and any movement for redress faced insuperable odds.

It was inevitable that such overweening authority should meet with challenge, and that challenge when made might not be fruitless. Before the end of 1634 Roger Williams ran afoul of the rising oligarchy in good earnest. In November he received a summons from the court on the grounds that he had again impugned charters by challenging the king's title to the lands of the Indians and had also termed the churches of England "antichristian." Five months later, on April 8, 1635, he was likewise accused of teaching that "a magistrate ought not to tender an oath to an unregenerate man." Events were taking a more serious turn. Williams was no longer merely one of those whom Winthrop castigated as "troublers of Israel." He was, from the magisterial view, on the road to rebellion.

---

[43] For the best appraisals of the devices of the Massachusetts oligarchy, see Morison, *Builders of the Bay Colony*, pp. 83-95, 225-230; and C. M. Andrews, *The Colonial Period of American History* (New Haven, 1934-), I, 430-519.

5

THE SALEM REBELLION

THE PROCEEDINGS WHICH LED up to the banishment of Williams really began in November, 1634. Prior to that time nothing had occurred which foreshadowed his expulsion. It was true that some of the "offenses" which were later cited as grounds for banishment had made their appearance. Williams had already questioned the authority of magistrates to enforce penalties for breach of the first table, and he had been dealt with by the magistrates in connection with his treatise against the patent. These difficulties had been ironed out. It was the series of events from November, 1634, to October of the following year which made the final break inevitable.

At this fateful November meeting the general court brought up two counts against Williams. One was his unquenchable Separatism: he was preaching that the churches of England were false churches; the other and more serious was that Williams "had broken his promise to us, in teaching publickly against the king's patent, and our great sin in claiming right thereby to this country."[1] The breach of promise alleged by Winthrop was probably not a breach of any formal oath, since at the time of his previous summons about the patent Williams simply gave "satisfaction of his intention and loyalty."[2] Interpreting Williams' conciliatory spirit on that occasion as substantially a pledge of silence, the magistrates were the more irate because this was not a case of a mere manuscript shown to authorities in private. Williams was now "teaching publickly." Taking prompt action, the magistrates summoned him to the next court.

The reason why Williams had raised the issue of the patent in public can only be surmised. In 1647 Cotton charged that he "pressed upon the Magistrates and People" to repent in "dayes of solemne Humilitation" and return the patent to the king. Williams' version, in answer to Cotton, was that he proposed an address to the king to secure modification "of that part of the Pattent which respects the

[1] Winthrop, *Journal,* I, 180.
[2] *Ibid.,* 146.

Donation of Land." Otherwise the sin "could not be Expiated" except by returning to England again, leaving the land to its native owners and making public acknowledgment and confession of the "Evill."[3] This latter suggestion was sheer idealistic fantasy, though of interest as showing that Williams was thinking strongly of human rights irrespective of race. The other alternative was obviously imprudent, for to invite the king to reconsider the patent would strengthen its enemies. To hold days of humiliation was more thinkable and well in accord with the Puritan practice of bewailing public sins to appease the wrath of a just God. Yet to clergy and magistrates there was no need for humiliation; New England was the promised land of God's chosen people.[4]

At the meeting of March 3, 1635, the court took no action either on Williams' Separatist indictment of English churches or his views on the patent, probably because of the intervention of John Cotton and the brethren who felt that Williams' "violent course" sprang from scruples of conscience rather than "seditious" intent. Cotton's account throws a shaft of light on the dual authority of church and state: "I presented (with the consent of my fellow-Elders and Brethren) a serious Request to the Magistrates, that they would be pleased to forbeare all civill prosecution against him, till our selves (with our Churches) had dealt with him in a Church way, to convince him of sinne." The governor, presumably Thomas Dudley, warned Cotton that the clergy were deceived in Roger Williams, if they thought that he would "condescend to learne of any of us," but in spite of this pessimism Cotton's request was approved and the brethren undertook to labor with the recalcitrant of Salem.[5]

The device of dealing with offenders through consociation already had proved a formidable weapon of social pressure.[6] A battery of confident and capable Puritan priests was generally an irresistible answer to a doubting Thomas; nor were such advice and admonition unavailing with Williams. Although there is no evidence that he yielded his Separatist position as to the churches of England, the brethren won him to silence on the score of the patent. On none of

[3] Cotton, *Reply to Mr. Williams,* N.C.P., II, 46. Williams, *Bloody Tenent More Bloody,* N.C.P., IV, 461-462.

[4] See Winthrop's letter to Endecott, Jan. 3, 1634, *Proc. M.H.S., 1871-1873,* esp. p. 345.

[5] Cotton, *Reply to Mr. Williams,* N.C.P., II, 62.

[6] Miller, *Orthodoxy in Massachusetts,* p. 188 and *passim.*

the three subsequent occasions when Williams appeared before the court was the charge renewed that he was agitating against the charter.[7] "Councells from Flesh and Bloud supprest" his intended letter to the king, Williams confessed later, although, as he shrewdly pointed out, this did not prevent the rulers of the colony from seizing the stratagem of "Worldly policy" and making his earlier activities against the patent a "cause" of banishment.[8]

The tortuous uses which the assistants were making of the charter which they defended so carefully from the attack of Williams are not without pertinence. On April 1, 1634, these magistrates sat for the last time as the general court of the colony. Two months later the freemen discovered the flagrant violation of the charter by which the inner oligarchy had defrauded them of legislative power and in consequence rejected Winthrop for governor for a number of years. Meanwhile, on April 1, Winthrop, Dudley, Coddington, Endecott, Ludlow, Bradstreet, Nowell, and Pynchon voted themselves and their group special colonial grants of lands apart from their allotments from the towns where they lived. Among the *douceurs* voted privileged dignitaries, 200 acres of choice land went to John Wilson, minister of Boston; 200 to Assistant Nowell; 500 to Dudley, Deputy-Governor; and to the wealthy newcomer, John Haynes, Esq., soon to be governor, a full thousand acres.[9] In preceding years they had already granted Winthrop 650 acres; Dudley 200, bringing his new total to 700 acres; Endecott 300; and smaller allotments to the assistants Bradstreet and Ludlow.[10]

At this same meeting of April 1, 1634, the ruling clique in the colony adopted a measure which eventually induced Williams to take the road of opposition. The magistrates entrenched themselves behind a new requirement compelling inhabitants who were not freemen to take a "resident's oath" in which they swore to submit to the laws and authority of the governor and magistrates and to "give speedy notice" of any sedition "plotted or intended against the . . . government. Soe helpe mee God."[11] The occasion of the oath, John Cotton affirmed, was "Intelligence of some Episcopall, and malignant practices against the Countrey" on the part of their enemies in Eng-

7 See Winthrop, *Journal*, I, 188, 193, 204; *Mass. Bay Recs.*, I, 151-152, 160-161.
8 *Bloody Tenent More Bloody*, N.C.P., IV, 462.
9 *Mass. Bay Recs.*, I, 114.
10 *Ibid.*, 91, 96, 97, 100, 102.
11 *Ibid.*, 115, 116.

land.[12] But John Cotton did not explain the full significance of the oath. "Let men only look over to the fruits of their principles in New England," wrote Robert Baillie of Scotland, who had heard Roger Williams' version. To Baillie, the Massachusetts oath smacked of disloyalty to England. Upon "suspition," he said, that the king might have their patent altered, "they did quickly purchase and distribute Armes among all their people, and exact of every one an Oath for the defence of their Patent against all impugners whosoever."[13] John Cotton in 1647 passed lightly over the damaging fact that the magistrates secretly determined to resist recall of the charter and stooped to the gentle prevarication that the court was not "imposing" the oath but merely "offering" it.[14] According to the actual records, the oath was to be tendered twice; residents who refused it a second time were to be banished.[15]

This dire penalty did not deter Roger Williams. The ideas that had already led him to impugn the patent virtually obligated him on the same grounds to attack the oath. "This Oath when it came abroad," wrote Cotton, "he vehemently withstood it, and disswaded sundry from it. . . ."[16] As a non-freeman, Williams would be required to take the new oath and by its terms he would be forced to give a pledge to be "obedient and conformeable" and "submitt" to the "lawes and constitucions" of the colony.[17] In substance, if the future democrat of Rhode Island had sworn to this, he would have taken oath to uphold the patent and to submit without opposition to the dictates of the oligarchy.

Williams objected to the oath because it mixed the things of Caesar with the things that belonged to God. A magistrate made a mockery of religion if he tendered an oath to an unregenerate person. This was taking the name of God in vain—making an irreligious person swear and call God to witness.[18] An oath was "a part of God's worship, and God's worship was not to be put upon carnall persons."[19] Nor was it proper to employ an oath to cast a halo of

[12] Reply to Mr. Williams, N.C.P., II, 47-49.
[13] Robert Baillie, Dissuasive from the Errours of the Time (London, 1645), p. 126.
[14] Reply to Mr. Williams, N.C.P., II, 13.
[15] Mass. Bay Recs., I, 115.
[16] Reply to Mr. Williams, N.C.P., II, 48.
[17] Mass. Bay Recs., I, 115.
[18] Winthrop, Journal, I, 188.
[19] Cotton, Reply to Mr. Williams, N.C.P., II, 48.

sanctification over the officers and fiat of the civil authority. Williams harked back to his assertion of 1630 that enforcement of the first table was not the business of civil magistrates. As his ideas clarified, he felt it an abomination to invoke the name of God in swearing allegiance to a mere government of men. Later Williams was to state bluntly his belief that the magistrates and clergy of Massachusetts utilized the combined agency of church and state to bolster their privileged position. How far his thoughts had progressed by April, 1635, when he was summoned for opposing the oath, is a matter of surmise. We can at least be certain of his suspicion that the rulers of the Bay were employing an act of worship for political ends. As Cotton noted, Williams affirmed that an oath or covenant was "Christs Prerogative" alone. "So by his Tenent," lamented Cotton, neither Visible Saints nor other godly men might take the oath, "because it was the establishment not of Christ, but of mortall men in their office."[20] This to Roger Williams smacked too strongly of oligarchy by divine right.

Williams' attack on the oath appeared to the founders of the Bay more obstreperous and menacing than any of his earlier actions and, as Baillie surmised, loomed large in his final trial. "Mr. Williams opposition to this Oath, as he alledgeth, was the cheife cause of his banishment."[21] Summoned before the court on April 30, "he was heard," wrote Winthrop, "before all the ministers, and very clearly confuted." Endecott likewise opposed the oath, but presently "gave place to the truth."[22] Confuting Williams consisted of a one-way debate in which the authorities simply expounded their side of the case and then voted that they had won. This process convinced neither Williams nor the people at large, and in the following months so many inhabitants joined Williams in refusing to take the oath that "the Court was forced to desist from that proceeding."[23] On this issue Williams had won.

On July 8, 1635, the young Salem cleric was again hailed to court, charged with contending that magistrates had no power to punish breaches of the first table except in cases disturbing "the civil peace." This return to his old Separatist heresy grew out of a recent action

20 Cotton, *Reply to Mr. Williams*, N.C.P., II, 48.
21 *Dissuasive*, p. 126.
22 Winthrop, *Journal*, I, 188.
23 Cotton, *Reply to Mr. Williams*, N.C.P., II, 13, 48-49.

of the magistrates. On March 4 they called for a "uniforme" church discipline and clarification of the civil power to make it compulsory.[24] Since this conception of church and state struck fundamentally at any idea of independent congregationalism, Williams openly challenged it. Summoned to account for this bold opposition, Williams was also charged with continued opposition to the oath and with certain annoying scruples that one ought not to pray with an unregenerate person or give thanks after sacraments or after meals.[25]

Williams' opposition to civil enforcement of religious commandments struck at the vital spot in the armour of magistrates and clergy. When he faced his accusers on July 8, he discovered that leading ministers were there by special request. Their faces were hostile. Cotton and the brethren who had been laboring with Williams had finally determined to write Salem church to "admonish" him, and when, in the course of the lengthy proceeding, the magistrates called for advice, the clergy replied that by Williams' principles "a church might run into heresy, apostasy, or tyranny, and yet the civil magistrate could not intermeddle." Seeing clearly that the great recalcitrant of Salem had come close to stretching the old Separatist doctrine of Robert Browne into religious liberty, they told the court that such a man should "be removed."[26]

Another matter highly prejudicial to Williams' case was a recent action of the Salem congregation in calling Williams as minister in place of Skelton, who had died the year before. This warm approval of one who was "under question" evoked the phantom of a free pulpit and a democratic congregationalism. Consulting together, the vigilant clerics and magistrates unanimously condemned Williams' opinions as "erroneous, and very dangerous" and censured Salem's action in making him minister as "a great contempt of authority." The magistrates granted "time" to Williams and his church "to consider of these things," but at the next general court Salem's minister must give satisfaction or else "expect the sentence."[27]

As Williams heard these words, his thoughts may have flitted back to his earlier fears of a national church under strict "superintendency." The brethren had replied all too readily that "no church

24 *Mass. Bay Recs.*, I, 142-143.
25 Winthrop, *Journal*, I, 193-194.
26 *Ibid.*
27 *Ibid.*

or person" could have power over another church. The falsity of those assurances now stood naked.

Before Williams left the court that day he was to see any pretense of a free church abandoned. Unwittingly the town of Salem played into the hands of the magistrates and clergy by petitioning for land in Marblehead Neck to which it had claim. The magistrates were delighted; here was an opportunity for a brilliant stratagem to force Salem church to reconsider its contempt. They rejected the petition "because they had chosen Mr. Williams" while he stood under question.[28] The Salem representatives endeavored to submit proof of the town's title to the land which, Salem alleged later, "would have given satisfaction might they have had leave to speak. . . ."[29] The frankness of the court was admirable. No trial of legal right of the town to the land would be permitted. It was a warning that the oligarchy held all the cards.

The sentiments of Williams and Endecott and the congregation, following this threat of sentence upon Salem's minister and the peremptory dismissal of the town petition, may well be imagined. Salem church held an indignation meeting at which Williams and his followers drove further in the direction of democratic congregationalism. The ministers and magistrates who had intended the other churches to advise Salem church to admonish Roger Williams found the tables turned. Salem wrote to the other churches "to admonish the magistrates" for their "heinous sin, and likewise the deputies."[30]

In the Massachusetts of 1635 this was an extraordinary procedure. Williams and Salem, resorting to something of a modern democratic device, were appealing over the heads of the politicians to their constituents. Since only Visible Saints or church members were freemen, they alone could normally bring pressure on the general court. The letters from Salem, criticising not simply the inner oligarchy of the assistants but the deputies as well, constituted an appeal not only to the small body of the enfranchised but to the whole people in their separate congregations.

The magistrates and clergy dared not risk a backfire from their constituents and were prompt to scotch such a democratic precedent. Through their connivance, the elders quietly pocketed the letters and

28 Winthrop, *Journal,* I, 195.
29 Letter from Salem Church, 1635, *N.C.P.,* VI, 75.
30 Winthrop, *Journal,* I, 195.

they never were read to the people in the congregations. Oligarchy must rule in church as well as state and the common man in the congregation must not be heard.[31]

Salem church was incensed. The authorities not only challenged its clear right to choose its teacher but now assailed its right to communicate with other churches. The congregation met for a heated discussion and Williams and the lay elder, Samuel Sharpe, drafted a letter of protest to the elders at Boston. Boston magistrates, reading this letter, could no longer doubt Williams' heresy as to civil authority: to punish Salem church by refusing land to the town was "to deal with a church out of a church way." Nor could Cotton and Wilson mistake Williams' radical demand for a democratic church: "We have not yet apprehended it to be the choice of the officers of a church, when public letters are sent from sister Churches, to deliver or not to deliver the letters unto the body. . . ." Affairs of the congregation belonged "to the whole body" rather "than to one or all the elders." Salem did not hold with the belief that "the people are weak . . . giddy and rash, and therefore should not enjoy such liberties."[32]

This plea for free government and a free church fell on deaf ears. During August and September the magistrates and clergy joined forces to wean Salem from Williams, hoping thereby to maneuver him into a position where they could deal with him without embarrassment. Hooker, Cotton, and the elders brought pressure on the saints of Salem to repudiate the "offensive" opinions and practices of their pastor.[33] Their labors were aided by a fortuitous event which they triumphantly hailed as a judgment of God. Because Williams continued to dispute the holy testimony of the brethren, "it pleased the Lord," said Cotton, "to stop his mouth, by a sodaine disease."[34] While stricken "neare unto death," Williams engaged in painful self-searching and found no cause for remorse.[35] Magistrates and clergy, he now knew, would relent only upon his retraction and submission. His only rightful course as a Separatist was to

[31] See Miller, *Orthodoxy in Massachusetts*, pp. 182-186.

[32] *Letters*, N.C.P., VI, 72, 73, 74-75.

[33] See abstract of letter from Boston to Salem, printed in Morton, *Memorial*, p. 106.

[34] *Letter to Mr. Williams*, N.C.P., I, 298; *Reply to Mr. Williams*, N.C.P., II, 50, 63, 92.

[35] *Mr. Cotton's Letter Examined*, N.C.P., I, 340.

strike for the independence of his church. A majority of his congregation had already joined him in professing the necessity of separating from the false churches of England.[36] It was now equally necessary to "come out" from the churches of the Bay. Williams rallied himself on his sickbed and composed a letter to his congregation. The Massachusetts churches, he contended, had stumbled from the way, and Salem must free itself of such spiritual jurisdiction. For his own part, he could not walk betwixt Christ and Antichrist. To submit without faith was sin; he could not continue as pastor unless the church purged itself by a separation.[37]

Meanwhile a committee of ministers drew up a "Model of Church and Civil Power" which they sent to Salem. It was a sober warning that if a church grew schismatical or corrupt, the civil magistrates could strike down those who corrupted it. Toleration of other religions, it said, would dissolve the state as well as the church. The civil authorities could therefore compel church attendance, coerce an offensive church, and forbid any independent churches.[38]

Not without reason did the little oligarchy speak of its members as "Gods upon earth"; nor did the magistrates shrink from the course of narrow repression which the committee of ministers outlined. On September 3, to put an end once for all to the opposition in Salem, the oligarchy struck and struck hard. The general court unseated the deputies of the town and sent them home; the freemen, or Visible Saints of Salem, were to have no representation until they disclaimed the church letters,[39] nor would the court hear their claim to land in the Neck until the church repented of its choice of Williams. This stern action showed clearly enough how far the oligarchy would go in coercing a church and in beating down any public criticism of magisterial policy. Dismayed, yet furious, John Endecott appeared defiantly before the authorities and attempted to justify the Salem letters. This was *lèse-majesté*. Peremptorily refusing him a hearing, the court ordered Endecott imprisoned for contempt. There had been no more vigorous and independent figure in the ruling class of

[36] Cotton, *Reply to Mr. Williams*, N.C.P., II, 106.

[37] Winthrop, *Journal*, I, 198. For the Separatist ideas upon which this letter was based, see Williams' tracts, *N.C.P.*, I, 299, 308, 369-370, 378; II, 196-198; III, 258.

[38] See excerpts from the "Model," printed in *The Bloudy Tenent*, N.C.P., III, vii, 226-227, 278-279, 311-312.

[39] *Mass. Bay Recs.*, I, 156, 158.

the Bay than John Endecott, but it was now shown him that he would reap little if he opposed his fellow-dignitaries. In a little while his head cooled, and "he came and acknowledged his fault, and was discharged."[40]

The tide had begun to turn. Salem had moved surprisingly far, and a part of the congregation were ready to follow their pastor into absolute separation, even if it meant exile; but if the majority had to make choice between Roger Williams and the Puritan oligarchy, the choice was not to be Williams. The greater part of the church, declared Williams, "was swayed and bowed (whether for feare of persecution or otherwise) to say and practise what, to my knowledge, . . . many of them mourned under."[41] The oligarchy had more to offer in the way of tangible persuasions, and slowly during the month of September Williams witnessed the town inclining toward submission. It remained only for the magistrates to deal with the great leader of the remonstrants. The back of the Salem rebellion was broken.

[40] Winthrop, *Journal*, I, 199; *Mass. Bay Recs.*, I, 157.
[41] *Mr. Cotton's Letter Examined* (London, 1644), p. 2.

6

OLIGARCHY IN THE JUDGMENT SEAT

ALTHOUGH THE MAGISTRATES WARNED Williams on July 8 to give satisfaction at the next court or "expect the sentence," they shrewdly held their hand until they had pressed Salem down into the ruts of orthodoxy. By the time of his trial Williams was isolated, his cause lost, and the sentence of the court a foregone conclusion. On his way to the trial Cotton told a friend that the magistrates were so "incensed" that the verdict was certain.[1]

The general court of October 8, 1635, was not an ordinary assemblage. Because of the importance of Williams' case, all the ministers of the Bay had been requested to attend. Cotton and other worthies who believed in severity against those who questioned the ways of the oligarchy had the support of the wealthy John Haynes, now governor, and of two new arrivals, the energetic Hugh Peter who was soon to succeed Williams as minister of Salem, and narrow-minded John Wilson, just back from England. Williams soon had clear indication of the judgment he could expect from men of such stamp. The court found John Smith of Dorchester guilty of broaching "dyvers dangerous opinions" and sentenced him to banishment.[2]

Later in the day came the celebrated trial of Salem's pastor. Williams' heresy in denying the coercive power of the state in matters of religion and the other charges of July 8 were again presented. The court added new charges concerning the offensive Salem letters and Williams' plea to Salem church to separate from the churches of the Bay. Given leave to speak, Salem's fiery Separatist stood up stoutly, justified the letters, and "maintained all his opinions."[3]

Magistrates like Winthrop knew Williams' sterling qualities of mind and heart and they valued them too well not to offer him one final chance. After hesitation the court granted him a month's respite. But the accused man knew he was offered no final escape;

[1] *Reply to Mr. Williams*, N.C.P., II, 64.
[2] *Mass. Bay Recs.*, I, 159.
[3] Winthrop, *Journal*, I, 204.

for he could save himself only by retraction and submission. Since there was no point in delay, he requested "to dispute presently."

Hooker, of whom it was said that so great was his majesty he could put a king in his pocket, was selected to confute the heretic. During the disputation Williams complained "he was wronged by a slanderous report up and downe the Countrey, as if he did hold it to be unlawfull for a Father to call upon his childe to eate his meate." Hooker, a skilled dialectician, thereupon set a trap for his young opponent. "Why, saith he, you will say as much againe, (if you stand to your own Principles) or be forced to say nothing." Williams was "confident he should never say it." Hooker then seized on Williams' contention that it was unlawful to call on an unregenerate person to take an oath or pray. If a child was unregenerate, he could not properly pray God to bless his meat. But according to the Bible it was improper to eat meat unsanctified by prayer. Thus, concluded Hooker, "it is unlawful for you to call upon him to eate it." This confutation, according to Cotton, forced Williams into silence. Winthrop, however, recorded after the trial that not even Hooker could reduce him from his errors.[4]

The modern mind is not so impressed by ingenious dialectics as Hooker and Cotton. What Hooker demonstrated was the intellectual confusion which could flow from the Puritan effort to join systematic logic with scriptural literalness. Wedded to the dogma of Non-separatism, Cotton and his associates could see in Williams' obduracy merely proof that he was "sinning against the light of his own Conscience."[5] If a man stood to his principles after the elders reasoned with him, then that was not his conscience but his obstinacy. Williams, on the other hand, was groping toward a more scientific understanding of the mind of mankind. As an authentic Separatist, he was not committed to the dogma that all must agree, none should oppose, and any who criticized the lords temporal or lords spiritual must be silenced or banished. It was a courageous man who could be a good man and still differ with his fellows. But Williams was not chained by the rigid compulsions which dominated the Puritan minds that passed judgment upon him. He did not believe that his opinions must be wrong because authority said so. Unlike John Cot-

[4] Cotton, *Reply to Mr. Williams,* N.C.P., II, 52-53; Winthrop, *Journal,* I, 204.
[5] *Reply to Mr. Williams,* N.C.P., II, 185.

ton in 1637, he could not argue himself into a sense of error merely because the magistrates demanded it.

As the formality of "confuting" Williams proceeded, the sun slowly sank over the horizon. Williams knew that his voice was lost in that place of gathering darkness. The magistrates were now ready to give sentence; "yet night being come, the Court arose and enjoyned him to appeare the next morning."[6] Williams still had a night to sleep on it, a respite granted presumably in the hope that he might lose his nerve. It was not a peaceful night for the great recalcitrant of Salem, but no still small voice whispered to him that he was wrong.

Unshaken and unflinching, he appeared before the court in the morning to receive sentence. Governor Haynes, who within a few months was to criticize Winthrop for too great leniency, stood up and summarized the formal charges. Then, to identify the will of the court with the will of God, the governor pronounced the words of St. Paul: "Mark them which cause divisions and offences, contrary to the doctrine which ye have learned, and avoid them." The way to avoid such, as Haynes interpreted it, was "by banishment."[7]

With this divine sanction—favorite of persecutors—ringing in his ears, Roger Williams heard the oligarchy pronounce the famous sentence to exile:

> Whereas Mr. Roger Williams . . . hath broached and divulged dyvers newe and dangerous opinions, against the aucthoritie of magistrates, as also writt letters of defamaĉon, both of the magistrates and churches here, and that before any convicĉon, and yet mainetaineth the same without retracĉon, it is therefore ordered, that the said Mr. Williams shall departe out of this jurisdicĉon . . .[8]

There have been so many contradictory statements about the banishment that it seems worth while to review the chief points at issue. No other incident in Williams' life has aroused more protracted controversy. Almost from the date of the trial, the banishment became a *cause célèbre*. In the eyes of the law the issue may now be considered officially settled by the slightly ridiculous gesture of the

[6] Winthrop and Weld, *A Short Story of the Antinomians* (London, 1644), p. 26.
[7] *Romans*, XVI:17. See *Bloody Tenent More Bloody*, N.C.P., IV, 106, 240.
[8] *Mass. Bay Recs.*, I, 160-161. For the date of sentence, see H. M. Dexter, *As to Roger Williams* (Boston, 1876), pp. 58, 222 n.

Massachusetts general court in repealing the act of banishment in the year of Rhode Island's tercentenary. Yet in most discussions of the banishment certain elements have been overlooked; and moreover the banishment itself still has meaning in its reflection of profound and recurrent conflicts between the impulse toward freedom and the forces of repression.

The chief controversy has centered upon the disagreement as to the principal causes of Williams' banishment, the motives of the magistrates and ministers, and the necessity or justice of their decision. Since there has been little disposition to contest the legality of the banishment, the issue has been largely whether Williams was sentenced for political reasons or for religious beliefs. The classical view in Rhode Island has been that Williams espoused the cause of religious liberty in Massachusetts and that the persecuting Puritans banished him because of it. The opposing view has made the attack on the charter the chief cause of banishment and has presented Williams' trial as a case of sedition.[9]

Cotton and Williams had their first exchange on the subject soon after the latter's flight to Rhode Island.[10] It was but natural for that sharp-tongued son of Rhode Island, Samuel Gorton, to assert bluntly that Williams was banished "for dissenting in some points about church government"; and for John Clarke, himself expelled as an Antinomian, to cry persecution and to publicize the case of Williams as another expulsion "for matter of conscience."[11] Within a decade the banishment became celebrated on both sides of the Atlantic as one of many instances of severity charged against Massachusetts. New England Puritans, who had long groaned under persecution in England and who had cried out against it as persecution of God's people, smarted under the accusation that they had become persecutors in turn. Disconcerted and indignant, they undertook to place the onus on Williams, on the Antinomians, on the Baptists, the Quakers, and the long train of persons, men and women, who

---

[9] See Cotton, *Reply to Mr. Williams*, N.C.P., II, 44-50; Edward Winslow, *Hypocrisie Unmasked* (Chapin ed., Providence, 1916), pp. 65-66; J. G. Palfrey, *History of New England* (Boston, 1858-1890), I, 414; Dexter, *As to Roger Williams*, p. 79; H. C. Lodge, *The English Colonies* (rev. ed., New York, 1902), p. 348.

[10] See Cotton, *A Letter to Mr. Williams*, N.C.P., I, 299 ff.

[11] Samuel Gorton, *Simplicities Defence against Seven-headed Policy*, Coll. R.I.H.S., II, 42; John Clarke, *Ill Newes from New-England*, 4 Coll. M.H.S., II, 24.

suffered the lash, the halter, or the sentence of banishment at the hands of the godly in New England. "Persecutours," remarked Williams drily, "endure not so to be called."[12]

In this long, acrimonious debate, Massachusetts Puritans strove to rebut the accusation that they had become Separatists. To this they gave the pat answer that Separatists or schismatics were banished from the state—for political reasons—and excommunicated from the church for sinning against conscience. In 1641 Cotton hit upon this interesting distinction in giving alarmed conservatives in England fervent assurance that New England had not sunk into Separatism: "I answer, God forbid, God forbid: It is true, one Sheba of Bickry blew a Trumpet of such a seditious Separation; I meane one Mr. Williams late Teacher of Salem"; but he and others of that ilk "were all excommunicated out of the Church and banished out of the Common-wealth." "See therefore," cried Cotton, "how unjustly we are slandered for renouncing communion with you."[13]

Cotton's *Letter to Mr. Williams,* appearing in London bookstalls in 1643, presented the expulsion of Williams as a "civill banishment." This was an invidious distinction, but it served the double purpose of disclaiming Separatism and at the same time disclaiming persecution. Edward Winslow of Plymouth colony similarly tried to clear Massachusetts of the charge of intolerance. In 1646 when representing the interests of the two colonies in London, he turned hotly on Gorton's reference to the persecution of Williams and declared "God cals mee at this time to take off these aspersions." He then followed Cotton's cue and by concentrating on the political causes of Williams' banishment, contrived to make Williams' expulsion a case of civil banishment.[14]

A year later, in his *Reply to Mr. Williams,* John Cotton made an elaborate disquisition on the same theme. He gave the flat lie to Williams, charging that his statement of the causes of banishment was "fraudulent." Williams' contention that the civil power extended "onely to the bodies, and goods, and outward state of men" and his Separatist objection to hearing ministers in English parishes, Cotton dismissed as "no causes at all." The real causes were Williams'

---

12 *The Bloudy Tenent,* N.C.P., III, 278, marginal note.
13 *A Coppy of a Letter of Mr. Cotton* (London, 1641), p. 1; cited in Dexter, *As to Roger Williams,* p. 70.
14 *Hypocrisie Unmasked* (Chapin ed.), pp. 65-66.

"seditious opposition against the Patent, and against the Oath of fidelitie." There were also two secondary factors: Williams' letters admonishing the magistrates; and his Separatism and "spreading of his Leaven to sundry that resorted to him." These last two counts, although incidental, "hastened" the sentence. The argument followed that the trial represented "prosecution," not persecution. Roger Williams was not banished at all but simply deported—for civil offenses. "I did never belieeve," affirmed Cotton, "that the sentence passed against him was an act of Persecution."[15] "Master Cotton," retorted Williams, "knows not his own desire."

The pages of Winthrop's *Journal* furnish a sufficient refutation of Cotton's charge that Williams had given a fraudulent explanation of his trial, and one may conclude that Williams, Clarke, and Gorton had good reason to consider that the banishment was not simply political. Precisely because church and state were so nicely dovetailed, the political and religious became nearly indistinguishable. "The frame or constitution" of the Bay churches, as Williams retorted to Cotton, was "implicitly National." "Otherwise," demanded Williams, "why was I not yet permitted to live in the world, or Common-weale, except for this reason, that the Common weale and Church is yet but one, and hee that is banished from the one, must necessarily bee banished from the other also." By contrast, "particular Churches,"—Separatists and other liberal sects which did not believe in a state church—expelled unworthy persons merely "from their particular societies," and heretics "may still live in the Countrey . . . unmolested by them."[16]

Contemporaries found the attempt to shift responsibility to Williams and absolve Massachusetts of persecution anything but convincing. Heresy and sedition in Massachusetts were inextricably joined, and only by artful casuistry could Cotton contrive to deny it. A little less than a decade after the banishment of Williams, the English divine, Thomas Edwards, thrust home through the Massachusetts defense: "They found out a pretty fine distinction to deceive themselves with, that the magistrate questioned and punished for

---

[15] *Reply to Mr. Williams*, N.C.P., II, 19, 43-51, 184. The distinction between prosecution and persecution was Nathaniel Ward's; see *The Simple Cobbler*, Force's Tracts, III, no. 8, p. 13.

[16] *Mr. Cotton's Letter Examined*, N.C.P., I, 326-327; *Bloody Tenent More Bloody*, N.C.P., IV, 390.

those opinions and errors not as heresies and such opinions, but as breaches of the civil peace and disturbance to the Common-wealth."[17]

Although it is sometimes contended that Williams' views on the first table were of little or no consequence among the causes of banishment, Winthrop's account, the public admonition to Salem written by Cotton and the Boston elders, and Governor Haynes' summary at the trial, all show that such a supposition is clearly wrong.[18] It is also questioned whether the heresies for which Williams was tried included a belief in religious liberty; his proposition about the first table, it is asserted, never meant such a large principle. In his later tracts Williams harked back to the question of the first table, saying repeatedly that magistrates could not punish religious offenses without exceeding their lawful authority. Though this position was necessarily pivotal in his whole later conception of the separate spheres of church and state, it is urged that Williams did not understand the point so clearly in 1635; there was a difference between the original intention and the final result.

To take this view is to strain at a gnat and swallow a camel. Obviously at the time of trial Williams demanded no less than toleration of dissent. The assembled ministers at the court on July 8 made no mistake when they pointed out in consternation that Williams' proposal would be fatal to their object of compulsory uniformity. By such a principle, as Cotton wrote Salem in 1635, the churches could do no more than admonish a wayward congregation; though a church dissented so abominably as to fall into "papism," the civil magistrate could not compel it.[19]

At the time of his trial Williams was taking the usual position of the extreme Separatists who attacked the whole system of national churches. Thence came his efforts at Salem to carry democratic congregationalism to its logical conclusion. More truly than Robert Browne before him, he was seeking a reformation without tarrying for any. An authentic Separatist, he attacked the consociation of ministers as leading to a national church system, insisted on the autonomy of local congregations, and, when the government interfered at Salem, held Separatist meetings in his own house. These

---

[17] *Antapologia* (London, 1644), p. 165.

[18] Winthrop, *Journal*, I, 193-194; Morton, *Memorial*, pp. 103, 105-106; *Mr. Cotton's Letter Examined*, N.C.P., I, 324-325. For the contrary view, see Dexter, *As to Roger Williams*, pp. 64-80.

[19] Morton, *Memorial*, pp. 105-106.

actions, coupled with his views on the first table, mark him already in 1635 a believer in radical Independency, an avowed advocate of free churches in a free state.[20]

Williams' belief as to the first table, as Cotton, Hooker, and Hugh Peter knew, was a cardinal doctrine of Separatists, Baptists, and the independent sects. Logical on its own premises, contending that truth could defend itself without the use of force, that regeneration was inward and individual and outward compulsion powerless to promote spirituality, Separatism could never be palatable to authoritarian Puritans. Non-separatists in New England well knew its consequences. Enraptured by the vision of the disciplined uniformity of the great church militant, they shrank from the schisms and brawls which divided the ranks of English Independents in the mother country and Holland. Cherishing the eternal hope of rising to power in the English church, orthodox saints could do no other than condemn Williams' denial of use of the civil sword to compel uniformity. Had the magistrates done otherwise, Massachusetts would have entered on the high road to toleration.

To contend that Williams' demand for the right to dissent played little part in his trial and sentence is to take the hazardous view that the ministers and magistrates were strangely unmindful of their dearest convictions. In 1635 Roger Williams had grasped the central point of his later famed theory of religious liberty as a natural right. Hubbard was not wide of the mark when he listed as a cause of banishment a demand for liberty of conscience and an "unlimited toleration of all religions."[21]

Although Williams spoke for the future, for the liberation of man, he has long had reputation as one who brought his sentence upon his own head. In the eyes of the magistrates and their later defenders, he was "a dangerous intruder and an agent of mischief."[22] He was accused of having an unsettled judgment and pride of opinion. He "had a zeal," declared Hubbard, and added subsequently, "too much zeal."[23] That celebrated nineteenth century Puritan, John Quincy Adams, adjudged him guilty of "conscientious

[20] For Williams' position on the first table, see *The Bloudy Tenent,* N.C.P., III, 151, 153, 155, 237 ff.

[21] *History,* 2 Coll. M.H.S., V, 206.

[22] G. E. Ellis, *Proc. M.H.S., 1873-1875,* pp. 22-23.

[23] *History,* 2 Coll. M.H.S., V, 202, 206.

contentiousness."[24] John Palfrey diagnosed his case as *certaminas gaudia,* the joy of quarrel.[25] But a contemporary of Palfrey and Adams, that ardent Jacksonian Democrat, George Bancroft, had a different understanding: "If he was charged with pride, it was only for the novelty of his opinions."[26]

Williams' scruples of conscience sometimes did and sometimes did not coincide with those of the rulers of the Bay, but his contentiousness and supposed self-pride were scarcely proper grounds for expulsion from the colony. There had been nothing scandalous in his conduct. He had committed no offense of the sort which he afterwards defined so accurately as violations of the civil peace; he had not offended against the "life, chastity, goods or good name" of any one in the colony.[27] He was "a man lovely in his carriage," declared Winslow.[28] Stewards of the Lord might tell themselves that opposition to their will could only spring from pride and self-conceit; yet magistrates and clergy alike admitted Williams' integrity and sincerity, the high order of his intellectual attainments, and the warm humanity of his character. If the banishment were to be defended, it should be on grounds other than the personal characteristics of Roger Williams.

The most frequent defense of the banishment has centered on the attack on the patent. Williams had all the effrontery of a belligerent democrat. By questioning the charter, he attacked the power of the king; by assailing the cross in the flag, he attacked the king's abuse of true religion; by advocating the rigid Separation, he attacked the royalist church. These agitations, coming precisely at the time when the royal government was actively hostile, would seem highly embarrassing to the men who had established a government of saints in the Wilderness Zion. Presented from this single point of view, the banishment becomes a justifiable action of self-defense.

This view, that Williams' criticism of the charter jeopardized the rights and liberty of the people of Massachusetts, leads to certain difficulties. As the simple facts of chronology show, John Cotton,

---

[24] Adams judged the founders of New England equally contentious; 3 *Coll. M.H.S.,* IX, 206.

[25] *History of New England* (Boston, 1858-1890), I, 417.

[26] *History of the United States* (13th ed., Boston, 1846), I, 372.

[27] *Mr. Cotton's Letter Examined,* N.C.P., I, 335; *The Bloudy Tenent,* N.C.P., III, 171.

[28] *Hypocrisie Unmasked* (Chapin ed.), p. 66.

who pounced on the affair of the charter as an easy rebuttal of the charge of persecution, strained the evidence. The last occasion on which Williams is known to have preached against the patent was in 1634. There is no record of new outbursts after the meeting of the court on November 27, when Williams was summoned. Williams still believed that the patent should be modified but he "supprest" his objections.[29] Ten months later at the trial, the oligarchy seized the opportunity to rake up this older charge, but if it entered into the judgment of the court, it was more as an added irritant and convenient excuse than as an immediate menace to Massachusetts' security.

From these facts of chronology it would appear that Cotton was guilty of distortion, and that the issue of the charter was scarcely preëminent at the time of the trial. No evidence has been found that Williams' conduct in Massachusetts in any way increased the royal animosity against Massachusetts or that Charles and Laud ever knew of his attack on the charter. Williams' "sedition" in the matter never reached the point of constituting a direct immediate threat to the state, whether one regards the imperial government at home as the state or whether one takes the highly irregular position of the Massachusetts oligarchy and views the colony as more or less an independent state.

Williams neither provoked the proceedings against the Massachusetts charter nor influenced their course. The responsibility for the writ of *quo warranto* must be placed squarely where it belongs, upon the rival colonial ambitions of the Massachusetts company and Gorges and Mason, and upon the conflict between the holy purposes of the Bay oligarchy and the no less holy purposes of Laud. In this conflict, the magistrates, by ignoring the call for the charter, were obstructing the course of English justice in proceedings which were undoubtedly legal; and, by preparing for armed resistance, they were involved in a far more flagrant defiance of lawful authority than any they could charge to Roger Williams. The actual danger of success in the *quo warranto* proceedings and of effective royal intervention is now known to have been remote.[30] That danger, such as it was, would not have diminished if the young agitator of Salem had been

[29] See Chapter 5.
[30] Andrews, *Colonial Period*, I, 419-424; see also Palfrey, *History*, I, 403-405.

ejected ten months sooner; nor, had the charter been vacated, would historians attribute its loss to Roger Williams.

The question of the charter has been often confused by the supposition that that document was the cornerstone of Massachusetts liberties. It was rather the cornerstone of power for the small and arbitrary group which sat in judgment on Williams. It was the bulwark behind which for more than a generation this group repressed the upthrust of the submerged population and established a system of ironclad rule. These men who resented Williams' scruples about the charter had embarked upon a course of flagrant and oppressive violations of that same charter.[31] It is not apparent, therefore, that any concern of the magistrates and clergy for the charter was actuated by the desire to defend Massachusetts liberties and the cause of free government.

There is strong evidence that it was not Williams' disrespectful remarks about royal authority but the disrespect which he showed for their own authority which infuriated the leaders of the Bay. This is indicated in the very phraseology of the sentence of banishment. That sentence contains no mention of seditious attack upon royal authority but charges Roger Williams with dangerous opinions "against the aucthoritie of magistrates."[32] The founders of Massachusetts, already thinking of themselves as rulers of a state virtually independent, were quick to resent attacks on magisterial power; and for the same reason, were prepared to flout even the prerogative of royal Charles, which was the real aspect of sedition in the eyes of English law.[33] This determination to rule in their own house, to suppress any possible threat to their own supremacy, dictated alike their resistance to the royal government and their severity toward dissidents in the Bible commonwealth.

For a larger understanding of Williams' banishment, one must turn to his attack on the oath of submission in 1635 and to the Salem rebellion, in which he appealed to public opinion and led an opposition to the governing class. He never placed in jeopardy the provisions for self-government in the Massachusetts charter. The

---

[31] For the disrespect shown by the magistrates for the plain provisions of the charter, see Andrews, *Colonial Period,* I, 436 and *passim.*

[32] *Mass. Bay Recs.,* I, 160.

[33] As eminent authority has properly objected, American historians, taking the cause of the colonies, have often forgotten historical perspective. See Andrews, *Colonial Period,* I, Preface, xi-xiv.

crime of Roger Williams was that he dared to oppose and to appeal to the people. If his agitations never struck at the right of home rule, they raised the forbidden question of who should rule at home.

Political and ecclesiastical expediency and the principle of religious intolerance dictated the expulsion. Chief responsibility for the banishment may be charged to two elements in the ethos of the Bay colony: the dogmatic requirements of the ecclesiastical establishment and the aristocratic requirements of magisterial domination. The magistrates and their clerical auxiliaries had combined to establish an authoritarian church and a government by oligarchy. Nor could the philosophy of men who made religious worship the monopoly of one church and political power the monopoly of a class allow them to consider that any could question that their sentence was just. In the very year of Williams' banishment, the clergy reported that it was not the will of the lawgiver but the divine purpose behind the law which made it binding.[34] "Judges are Gods upon earthe," maintained the magistrates. The Stuarts contended for divine right in England with never more confidence than the new pretenders in the colony of saints. Nor did the clergy of the Bay, preaching the famous Biblical injunction to be submissive, allow their flocks to conceive otherwise: ". . . the powers that be are ordained of God. Whosoever therefore resisteth the power, resisteth the ordinance of God: and they that resist shall receive to themselves damnation. . . . Wherefore *Ye* must needs be subject, not only for wrath, but also for conscience sake."[35] Intoxicated by this doctrine, John Cotton intimated to Williams that God himself had moved the court to pronounce the sentence.[36]

Formal charges in a case like Williams' seldom cover all considerations. The religious thinking of the magistrates of the Bay was not the single deterministic element in their social and political philosophy. No one can deny the factor of religious aspiration, but concentration of power, whether in Massachusetts of the Puritan epoch or in other communities and other times, had also its bearing upon class ambition and economic advantage. Middle-class Englishmen who had struggled against their monarch to control taxation,

[34] *Model of Church and Civil Power;* cited in *The Bloudy Tenent,* N.C.P., III, 255 f.
[35] *Romans,* XIII: 1, 2, 5.
[36] *Reply to Mr. Williams,* N.C.P., II, 75 f.

destroy the monopolies of royal favorites, and sway national policy to favor their interests, lost none of their zest for power and wealth in the act of passage over the Atlantic. If the builders of the Bay colony were Puritans as well as Englishmen, their sense of a sacred calling shook none of their faith in the concept of class which flourished in the homeland. Their aristocratic view of the many as vicious and the few as the wise made it logical to assume that the elect should rule and the unregenerate submit. If they translated this into practice through an exclusive church membership linked to the suffrage, making qualified voters of Visible Saints, such joining of the politically privileged with the spiritually elect was but a Puritan rephrasing of the ancient identification of the wealthy and powerful with the wise and the good.

The close control which the oligarchy maintained upon public office, political franchise, and upon press, pulpit, and election sermons, was not simply relevant to religious zeal. Zealous magistrates and dignified clericals were not insensible of the perquisites of power, and the first families in Massachusetts like those in other colonies obtained advantages for themselves in land and income. In 1634 the inhabitants of Boston feared that "the richer men would give the poorer sort no great proportions of land" and tried to elect town officers from the ranks of the plain people. Winthrop already had preempted eighteen hundred acres, Dudley seventeen hundred, and Saltonstall sixteen hundred.[37] The common people obtained small allotments, but the larger landed interests utilized the town land system to reward the saints, converting it gradually from a communal enterprise to a system of local land companies exclusive in membership and keen for speculation.

Discriminations which worked to the disadvantage of the common people dotted the records of the general court. Lest labor profit by its scarcity and bargain with employers, the court followed the venerable practice of English squires and kept down wages by fixing the rates through the fiat of the lawmaker. Men and women of humble station were restrained by law from aping the gentry in matters of dress. Laws which provided for ignominious punishments allowed lesser penalties if the culprit was a gentleman. The

[37] Winthrop, *Journal*, I, 180 f.; C. F. Adams, *Three Episodes of Massachusetts History* (Boston, 1892), I, 365.

concept of class, flavored with Puritanism, tinctured economic policy and permeated the statute book.

Neither awe of the magistrates nor injunctions of the clergy could prevent the people from resenting such discriminations. "The great questions that have troubled the country," admitted Winthrop in 1645, "are about the authority of the magistrates and the liberty of the people."[38] Even upon the clergy fell the suspicion of over-much worldliness and love of power. With the Bay clergy in mind as well as the English hierarchy, Roger Williams later attacked "hireling ministries" for love of "maintenance" and concern for self. John Cotton he suspected of "swimming with the streame of out-ward credit, and profit."[39] The more downright and class-conscious Samuel Gorton openly castigated the Massachusetts clergy for cruelty, arrogance, and worldly ambition.

Protests like that of Williams were generally fruitless, and occasional concessions of political privileges were limited in the main to the small class of freemen upon whose support the oligarchy depended. Criticism from individuals or petitions from groups outside the court brought quick retaliation. So Eliot discovered in 1634; and Endecott and the people of Salem in 1635; and so also Vane, Coddington, and even John Cotton in 1637. When Robert Child and his fellow-remonstrants rose to ask—in language milder than that used in the parliaments of James and Charles—for guarantees of their rights as Englishmen, they were not only silenced but heavily fined. When Winthrop made his "little speech" in 1645, he told those who complained of the "yoke" of authority, that if they would not "endure" but would "murmur, and oppose," they desired not liberty but only a corrupt license. By narrowing its definition, he emptied liberty of its essential content. "Sedition," he declared, "doth properly signifie a going aside to make a party."[40] The founders of New England conceived of liberty as the duty to submit. There was no right to oppose.

Only in this larger background can the suppression of the congregational movement in Salem and the banishment of its leader be seen in perspective. Roger Williams made no immediate frontal attack on

---

[38] *Journal*, II, 280.

[39] See Cotton, *Reply to Mr. Williams*, N.C.P., II, 91.

[40] *Journal*, II, 281; *A Short Story*, pp. 52-53. See Stanley Gray, "The Political Thought of John Winthrop," *N.E.Q.*, III (1930), pp. 687-691.

the class structure by which magistrates and clergy perpetuated their power; the full development of his democratic ideas was only to come later. But here was a man already too suspiciously democratic, too resolutely a believer in the value of untrammelled public discussion; a man who agitated against the oath of submission and whose powers of persuasion won wide popular support; a schismatic who cared nothing for the dogma of one authoritarian church; an inspired apostle of the left-wing sects who denied that magistrates could pluck forth men whose consciences turned them from the path of orthodoxy. For such a man, the ministers and magistrates, revolving in the narrow orbit of conservative Puritanism and mundane ambitions, could find no place in the commonwealth they had compounded from the charter of a trading company and the written word of God and William Ames.

In evaluating the importance of particular offenses of Williams one deals with imponderables. The crucial matter was not the affair of the charter in 1634 but the agitations of 1635 turning on the oath, the first table, Separatism, democratic congregationalism, and the Salem letters. The Salem rebellion was in substance a demand for the right of setting up a democratic opposition to those who had obtained power. Williams demonstrated, to the scandal of clergy and magistrates, the possibilities of use of the pulpit to awaken a popular resistance. At the end he reached the point of striking out for a full free-church system. Williams, concluded Cotton Mather, struck at "the whole political, as well as ecclesiastical constitution of the country."[41]

The vigorous liberalism of these agitations, the support they won from the people in Salem, and the penalty they brought show the subtle relevance of the system of banishments to the political purposes of the governing class. Thomas Shepard issued sober warning against a principle which figured in the case of Williams: "if the magistrate hath no power over his subjects in matters of the first table he may have also all his feathers pull'd from him."[42] It is scarcely conceivable that on October 9 when Williams stood before them, the magistrates were unmindful of Shepard's point.

"Liberty of searching out Truth," said Williams in a later great appeal for freedom, is "hardly got, and as hardly kept." For that

[41] *Magnalia*, II, 430.
[42] *Theses Sabbaticae*, 311; quoted by Andrews, *Colonial Period*, I, 473.

precious "Jewel," New England had run mighty hazards; but if New England forgot the nature of liberty, if it made it "a crime, humbly and peaceably to question even Lawes and Statutes, or what ever is even publickly taught and delivered," then it would find itself enslaved and in "Chains," a captive of ignorance and dark superstition.[43] Roger Williams' fear stemmed from an accurate perception of the historic transformation of overseas Puritanism. The founding of New England set the stage for a subtle sea change. From constitutional resistance to the absolutism of the Stuarts and the innovations of Laud, the Puritan fathers moved backward into the bleak pathway of arrogant domination.

In 1676 the general court thought sufficiently better of Williams to grant him a temporary suspension of banishment. Three centuries after the trial the proud commonwealth of Massachusetts did an intended honor to Rhode Island by officially rescinding the sentence against Williams—and in the same year passed a teachers' oath, backtracking toward 1600! For some years, by that time, the state of which Roger Williams was the original founder had had a red-hot teachers' oath of its own.

[43] *Bloody Tenent More Bloody,* N.C.P., IV, 30.

7

WILDERNESS EXILE

SENTENCE OF BANISHMENT being read against Mr. Williams, the whole Town of Salem was in an uproar; for such was the Popularity of the man, and such the Compassion of the People, occasioned by his Followers raising a Cry of Persecution against him, that he would have carried off the greatest part of the Inhabitants of the Town, if the Ministers of Boston had not interposed . . . .

So wrote Daniel Neal in 1720.[1] But the view of an English historian of the Puritans might be expected to differ from Massachusetts accounts from orthodox sources. After the court's sentence upon Roger Williams, says Winthrop, Salem church "openly disclaimed his errors, and wrote an humble submission to the magistrates."[2]

The collapse of Williams' influence in Salem was neither as spontaneous nor as complete as the reader of Winthrop might believe; and but for forceful action by the authorities Williams indeed might have "carried off" a considerable body of the townsfolk. On October 9, following the sentence of banishment, the magistrates solemnly warned the Salem elder, Samuel Sharpe, to answer at the next court for his part in the objectionable letters—"as also to bring the names of those what will justifie the same."[3] With his leader banished, Endecott cowed, and the body of the church divided and hesitant, Elder Sharpe bowed his head and made submission. The tide of authority was now running too strongly, and although some still adhered to Williams, none dared justify the Salem letters. Within five months after its submission, Salem had its reward. On March 5, the next year, appeared a cryptic entry in the records: "It was proved this Court that Marble Necke belongs to Salem."[4] Explanation was superfluous.

[1] *History of New England* (1720), I, 143; quoted in Dexter, *As to Roger Williams,* p. 63 n.
[2] *Journal,* I, 204.
[3] *Mass. Bay Recs.,* I, 161.
[4] *Ibid.,* p. 165.

If the hard choice of selling house and lands and departing to build a new plantation in the wilderness was more than most of the Salem remonstrants had bargained for, there remained a few in whose hearts Roger Williams had kindled a lasting flame. In the next two years Salem families, numbering with the wives and children about sixty persons, were to follow their banished pastor southward into exile. At least four of these, John Throckmorton, Thomas Olney, Robert Coles, and Francis Weston, were qualified freemen and Visible Saints, and one of them, Weston, had served as deputy in the general court.[5]

Before long these adherents of Williams were to be singled out for persecution in turn, but for the moment it was their leader who still proved a prickly thorn to the men who had sat in judgment on him. By the sentence of October 9, Williams had six weeks' grace before his final departure. The magistrates had banished him; it remained for the churches to admonish him—a process which was to end only in 1639, when he was excommunicated. "It pleased the Lord to open the hearts" of Salem church, wrote Cotton, "to assist us in dealing with him."[6] In sorrow, Williams now followed the thread of his logic to its end. Since Salem now stood with the Bay, committing itself thereby to communion with the church of Laud and to enforcement of the first table, he trod the path of many a Separatist before him. "Conscientiously and peaceably" he withdrew from Salem church.[7]

The rulers of New England never forgave him for this defiance, but Williams defended his action as a matter of keeping faith with himself:

> I confesse it was mine owne voluntary act; yea, I hope the act of the Lord Jesus sounding forth in me (a poore despised Rams horn) the blast which shall in his owne holy season cast down the strength and confidence of those inventions of men in the worshipping of the true and living God.[8]

[5] Others who migrated from Salem, most of them with families, were William Harris, Thomas Harris, Joshua Verin, John Greene, Richard Waterman, Ezekiel Holliman, "Widdo" Sweet and her grown sons, and Mrs. Alice Daniels.

[6] Reply to Mr. Williams, N.C.P., II, 63. Cotton inaccurately places this, and Williams' separation from Salem church, as prior to the banishment. See N.C.P., II, 64 n.

[7] Mr. Cotton's Letter Examined, N.C.P., I, 379.

[8] Ibid., p. 325.

In their later controversy John Cotton flayed Williams for separating from his own church and in the heat of contention stooped to a needless slander which is still repeated. He expressed "compassion" for Mary Williams,

> ... (a woman as then, of a meek and modest spirit) who a long time suffered in spirit, (as I was informed) for his offensive course: which occasioned him for a season to withdraw communion in spirituall duties, even from her also, till at length he drew her to partake with him in the errour of his way.[9]

By Cotton's own admission this was hearsay. Winthrop, who wrote contemporaneously of Williams' separation from Salem, mentions no such occurrence, and in referring to the episode again several years later he states that Williams had "refused communion with all, save his own wife."[10] In actuality, as the magistrates soon discovered, Roger Williams was holding communion with others as well as his wife.

Before Williams' six weeks of grace expired, the magistrates extended the deadline until the following spring. They had done as much for the notorious Ratcliffe, and there was good reason for treating Williams at least as well. He was still recovering from his recent illness and Mary Williams was soon to have a child. Years later Williams entered a record of the birth of this, his second child: "Freeborne the daughter of Roger Williams and Mary his wife was borne at Salem in the later end of October 1635."[11] She was born three weeks after her father's trial and banishment, and he named her *Freeborne*—a token of the future which he was planning and an epitome of his defiance of the past.

The court extended the deadline for Williams under the supposition that Salem Separatism had been crushed. It had not; it had been driven underground. The court, however, coupled its permission to remain over the winter with a stern command to Williams "not to go about to draw others to his opinions." Williams obeyed this to the extent of ceasing public agitations, which was probably the principal object of the injunction. But when close friends came to see him, Salem people who still clung to their affection and con-

9 *Reply to Mr. Williams,* N.C.P., II, 20.
10 *Journal,* I, 204, 369.
11 *Prov. Recs.,* I, 7.

fidence in him, he was naturally less cautious. These he did not seek to convert to his opinions, for they were already Separatists. Presently the magistrates in the Bay had word that they had but scotched the snake. It was reported that Mr. Williams "did use to entertain company in his house, and to preach to them, even of such points as he had been censured for"; many, especially "devout women," had separated from the church.[12] Here was the serpent at work again; a new church was in the making, independent of the Massachusetts order.

Early in January the magistrates met at Boston and decided to ship Williams immediately to England. As Cotton explained later, the increasing "concourse of people" who deserted Salem church to meet Williams for private services, thereby spreading "the Leaven of his corrupt imaginations, provoked the Magistrates rather then to breed a winters spirituall plague in the Countrey, to put upon him a winters journey out of the Countrey."[13] The court had another reason for issuing its warrant for Williams' arrest. Williams and his adherents were making plans for a daring experiment. Some twenty or thirty men and women, intent on placing themselves and their children beyond the reach of Massachusetts, determined to build a new plantation where uniformity by compulsion should never be accounted a test of health and truth in church and state. These Salem Separatists, noted Winthrop, "taken with the apprehension" of the "godliness" of Roger Williams, intended to erect their plantation near Narragansett bay; "from whence the infection would easily spread into these churches."[14]

There was land enough in New England waiting settlement beyond the Massachusetts bounds, and the magistrates of the Bay had no authority granted them in their patent to restrain those who wished to banish themselves. Yet now—ironically, with Governor Haynes presiding over the court—Massachusetts sought to nip the Salem migration in the bud and preserve New England for her own special sphere of influence. In later years, when Haynes had himself drawn off Massachusetts population to new plantations and was governor of Connecticut, he made an enlightening admission to the man upon whom he had pronounced banishment:

12 Winthrop, *Journal*, I, 209-210.
13 *Reply to Mr. Williams*, N.C.P., II, 93.
14 *Journal*, I, 209 f.

> I think, Mr. Williams, I must now confess to you, that the
> most wise God hath provided and cut out this part of his world
> for a refuge and receptacle for all sorts of consciences. I am
> now under a cloud, and my brother Hooker, with the Bay, as you
> have been, we have removed from them thus far, and yet they are
> not satisfied.[15]

To destroy simultaneously Separatism in Salem and Williams'
project for a Narragansett plantation, the magistrates dispatched
the marshal, James Penn, with a warrant to bring the culprit to Boston to be placed on a ship for England. Williams outwitted them.
Supported by "the mourning complaint" of some of his friends, he
pleaded his lingering illness and prevailed on the marshal to carry
back word that he could not come without hazard to his life.[16] Williams' fighting courage was up and he did not propose to submit to
deportation to the land of Laud. His heart was set on missionary
labors among the Narragansetts as well as on a plantation and he
knew that both projects might readily fall through if there was long
delay. If shipped off now, he would not be permitted to disembark
again at the Bay; and the delay and cost of a roundabout return to
New England, so be it Laud permitted him, was an obstacle he did
not intend to have placed in his way. Hastily he made what preparations he could. Meanwhile, in Boston the magistrates dispatched a
pinnace under Captain Underhill to apprehend him and carry him to
the ship then waiting at Nantasket. But the ship was fated to sail
without him, for when Underhill and his men "came at his house,
they found he had been gone three days before"; where, no one could
tell—or none would.[17]

Only a man of stout heart and sturdy body would have dared the
adventure to which Williams had set himself. Somewhere between
Salem in Massachusetts and Sowams in Plymouth colony he was
skirting the coastal fringe of settlements and steering his course
inland, south and west by compass in the white solitudes of winter
snow. Winthrop records that on a journey he once made afoot from
Boston to Salem, it took one day to make Saugus and the next to
reach his destination.[18] How many days longer it took Williams in

---

[15] Williams to Mason, 1670, N.C.P., VI, 345.
[16] Cotton, *Reply to Mr. Williams,* N.C.P., II, 93; Winthrop, *Journal,* I, 210.
Cotton denies Williams' sickness. Winthrop mentions testimony to the contrary.
[17] Winthrop, *Journal,* I, 210.
[18] *Ibid.,* p. 75.

mid-winter to reach Sowams, now Rehoboth, one can only guess. We may suppose him burdened with a small stock of provisions for food and blankets for warmth at night, trudging along sometimes knee-deep in drifted snow, or fording the ice-cold waters of inland streams, his clothes wet and stiffening with cold—and once wet never seeming again to dry, even by campfire if he was where he dared light one.

The rigors and bitter hardships of that "sorrowfull Winters flight" struck deep into Williams' bones. He was never to forget the experience and eight years afterward he recalled it to score heavily upon the Bay for persecution, writing with a bitterness which is not surprising. His hardships were severe; and though magnanimous in later relations with the Bay, he reminded Major Mason as late as 1670 that he had been "unkindly and unchristianly," as he believed, "driven from my house and land and wife and children," though in the midst of a New England winter and "in winter snow, which I feel yet."[19]

Williams, though in the prime of life, not over thirty, might well have perished had he not encountered friendly Indians who led him to Massasoit. In the winter quarters of his old Plymouth friends the weary fugitive had at last a rude shelter overhead, a fire to dry his clothes, and food and human friendliness, though nothing of civilized comfort. "I was sorely tossed," he said, "for one fourteen weeks, in a bitter winter season, not knowing what bread or bed did mean." [20] Three months Williams lodged with the Indians in their "filthy smoke holes"; ample time to test his missionary zeal—and to turn over in his mind arguments against persecution and to think out principles which might avert the supposed necessity of it.

Afterward when Williams had settled at Providence, John Cotton wrote him that if he had perished, his blood would have been on his own head.[21] More charitable than the great Puritan priest was the leading member of the Massachusetts squirearchy. Williams recalled long afterwards with gratitude that at the time of the flight from Salem "that ever honored" Mr. Winthrop privately wrote him "to steer my course to the Narragansett Bay and Indians, for many high

[19] Williams to Mason, *N.C.P.*, VI, 335.
[20] *Ibid.*, p. 336.
[21] *Mr. Cotton's Letter Examined*, N.C.P., I, 315.

and heavenly and public ends."[22] No doubt the high and public end
which Winthrop had in mind was the service Williams could render
in cultivating friendly relations with the Narragansetts and converting them to Christianity. Winthrop probably wrote before he knew
of the radical settlement for outcasts from the Bay, for he later
frowned on that project as sternly as his fellow magistrates.

In suggesting the Narragansett country as a field for labors with
the Indians, Winthrop had selected an area of great strategic importance; and there Roger Williams was soon to merit many times over
Winthrop's confidence in his abilities as a mediator. For more than
a decade the Narragansetts had loomed as the principal native threat
to English occupation and early had met with the blustering challenge
of doughty little Captain Miles Standish. Since that day relations
with the Narragansetts had been peaceful. In November, 1634, a
Massachusetts trader, John Oldham, brought back 500 bushels of
corn from Narragansett and described to Winthrop the "very fair
bay" where the Narragansetts lived, "above twelve leagues square,
with divers great islands in it, a deep channel close to the shore, being
rocky." The west shore was "full of Indians." Late in 1634 the
Narragansetts had friendly negotiations with the magistrates in the
Bay and "in all things showed themselves very ready to gratify us."[23]
Nevertheless, they were still the greatest tribe in southern New
England and must be kept peaceable. Winthrop knew that Williams
in exile might become a useful instrument to those who had cast him
off. So it was to prove.

Williams' first achievement as frontier peacemaker came not long
after he had found refuge at Sowams. The Wampanoags, under
Massasoit's shrewd leadership, had relied upon their entente with
Plymouth and the Bay to deliver themselves from allegiance to the
dominant Narragansetts. Following this precedent, the New England colonies formed the policy of making allies of tribes subject to
the Narragansetts, encouraging them to assert their independence.
Through the years this policy led the Narragansetts to chafe against
such interference and the English in turn began to fear a border war
and charge the Narragansetts with treachery and guile. Precisely
because of such complications, Williams in his first months of exile
found the Narragansetts and Wampanoags in "a great contest."

[22] Williams to Mason, *N.C.P.*, VI, 335.
[23] Winthrop, *Journal*, I, 175, 177.

Immediately he lent his efforts as mediator and succeeded in quieting both parties. He was known among the Wampanoags and Narragansetts as "public speaker" at Plymouth and Salem, he declared, "and, therefore with them held as a Sachem."[24]

By late spring four Englishmen joined the exile in the wilderness and with these few companions Williams proceeded westward to the northern tip of Narragansett bay, there to found a settlement at Seekonk. His companions were William Harris and Thomas Angell from Salem, the Dorchester miller, John Smith, banished at the same time as Williams, and "a poor young fellow," Francis Weeks, whom Smith had brought along. On April 20, 1636, came William Arnold and a large family, including a son-in-law, William Carpenter. Later in the year three more arrived from Salem: John Throckmorton, Joshua Verin, and John Greene. The Salem migration had begun.[25]

The plantation at Seekonk did not survive to the first harvest. Soon after Williams had "first pitched, and began to build and plant" at Seekonk, the bolt fell. Williams explained afterward that he received

> . . . a letter from my ancient friend, Mr. Winslow, then Governor of Plymouth, professing his own and others love and respect to me, yet lovingly advising me, since I was fallen into the edge of their bounds, and they were loath to displease the Bay, to remove but to the other side of the water.

The purchase of the land, the erection of a crude shelter, and the laborious task of clearing the ground, breaking the sod, and sowing for the first crop had gone for naught. The warning from Plymouth was only "their gentle advice," but Williams perceived what Bradford and others of the council at Plymouth admitted to him later, that he was "as good as banished from Plymouth as from the Massachusetts." This refusal to tolerate the outcasts in Plymouth territory cost the settlers the severe hardship of "loss of a harvest that year."[26]

From Plymouth Williams received word that if he would remove across the bay, then "I had the country free before me, and might be

24 *Letters*, N.C.P., VI, 316, 406; *Williams' Plea*, 1677, printed in Carpenter, *Roger Williams*, p. 224.

25 Howard M. Chapin, *Documentary History of Rhode Island* (Providence, 1916-1919), I, 5-7, 11-12.

26 Williams to Mason, *N.C.P.*, VI, 335, 336.

as free as themselves, and we should be loving neighbors together."[27]
Once more heading westward, Williams and his followers crossed
the Seekonk river to the peninsula jutting down into the upper
reaches of Narragansett bay. On the western side of the promontory
near the confluence of the Moshassuck and Woonasquetucket, they
picked a site bulwarked at the back by a towering hill. Again Williams purchased the land, this time from the Narragansett sachems.

Believing that at last he had found a safe refuge, Williams called
the place Providence—"in a Sence of Gods mercefull providence
unto me in my destresse."[28] The site was to prove well chosen. On
the west side lay a sheltered cove whence southward ran a tidal
waterway, broadening out into the upper expanse of the great bay
some twenty-eight miles from the open sea. Before Williams died he
was to see wharves appearing on the Providence shoreline; but tall-
masted Indiamen were not to cluster there until the eighteenth century and the hum and clatter of spindle and loom from the first
American factories were not to be heard in Providence until the thirteen colonies had formed a new nation.

A humble beginning in agriculture and the erection of houses
were the first and all-important tasks of the settlers. The gently
undulating sand-plain lowlands left by the retreating glacier had a
soil good for vegetables and light grains, but the region was heavily
timbered and the dense stands of evergreen and hardwood could
only be cleared gradually through the years. In the emergency the
settlers made haste to get seed from the natives and plant scattered
Indian fields around the town in corn, beans, pumpkins, and squash.
For meat, until they could bring in livestock, they bartered with the
natives or relied on their own skill in hunting game. To obtain hoes,
axes, and other tools and supplies for the settlers, Williams
mortgaged his house and land in Salem.[29] With neighborly helpful-
ness the settlers joined forces to erect houses for their families in
preparation for the blasts of the coming winter, such a house being
prepared for Mary Williams and her two small children sometime
before the next spring.[30] Besides Mary Williams and her two
youngsters, other wives and children made the hard journey to the

[27] Williams to Mason, *N.C.P.*, VI, 335.
[28] *Prov. Recs,* V, 307.
[29] Chapin, *Doc. Hist. R. I.,* I, 24.
[30] *Letters,* N.C.P., VI, 17, 22.

little wilderness outpost. All told, the plantation in the first year numbered eight householders who with their families made a total of thirty-two or more persons.

In the near vicinity Williams found an eccentric friend. William Blaxton, Anglican cleric and man of learning, Emmanuel bred, had lived on the site of Boston before the Puritans came and had migrated again to a point just north of Providence the year before Williams came. Blaxton declared that he left England to get from under the power of the lord bishops and left Boston because he had fallen under the power of the lord brethren. The proximity of Rhode Island heretics never seemed to disturb him. He built a house in the beautiful solitude of the valley of the Blackstone river and there at Study Hill gathered a fine library, cultivated the first apple orchard in the region, and preached Anglican doctrine to Rhode Island come-outers!

About twenty of the thirty odd persons at Providence came from Salem. Meanwhile the lord brethren in the Bay colony followed a course which was destined to send a swarm of refugees scurrying to Rhode Island. In April, 1636, Winthrop noted that most of the Salem congregation were "still infected" with Williams' heresies and some were reported as ready to separate. The elders rejected a proposal to grant "dismission" to Williams' followers "to be a church by themselves" and threatened to excommunicate any who withdrew from the church.[31] On May 30 the governor with Winthrop and Dudley signed a warrant in which sundry dissenters of Salem were charged with separating from the church and attempting to "seduce" others of "weak capacity." The magistrates feared that the town was "like to be deserted by many of the chief and most useful members, to the great dishonor of God," and the constable was ordered to serve notice that their conduct was "very offensive to the government here, and may no longer be suffered." He was to prevent any meetings of Separatists and to warn them plainly "that we shall by God's assistance" take some "strict and speedy course" against such disorders.[32]

It was under the propulsion of this fresh persecution that Greene, Throckmorton, and Verin migrated to Providence. Verin was the son of a prominent Salem citizen who was a deacon of the church and an officer of the town. Throckmorton and Greene were also men

[31] Winthrop, *Journal,* I, 221.
[32] *Ibid.,* II, 420.

of some consequence. The others who had made covenant with Williams to found the plantation lingered in Salem to endure persecution for another year or two before risking their all in the remoteness of Rhode Island. In the later history of the American frontier waves of pioneers with confidence born of experience and numbers plunged boldly into the wilderness. It was not so in 1636. "The air of the country is sharp," complained an early Puritan, "the rocks many, the trees innumerable, the grass little, the winter cold, the summer hot, the gnats in summer biting, the wolves at night howling."[33] Nostalgia for the trim English countryside drew many Puritans back to the homeland. Even Roger Williams, not a man to harbor any terror of the unfamiliar life of a frontier village, alluded more than once to the "miseries, poverties, necessities, wants, debts, hardships" which he and his family endured in their "banished condition."[34] Long afterward he recalled that in these hard first years at Providence "that great and pious soul, Mr. Winslow," visited the Williams family and graciously "put a piece of gold into the hands of my wife, for our supply."[35]

Dire events during the summer and fall of 1636 dissuaded all but the hardiest from risking removal to the isolated settlement at Providence; for this, as Williams phrased it, was the year in which "the Lord drew the bow of the Pequod war against the country."[36] The first outbreak of Indian trouble occurred almost immediately after Providence was founded. The Connecticut settlements were decimated. Lion Gardener of Saybrook, who protested against war at a time when the frontier settlements were newly formed and almost defenseless, declared to the Massachusetts men who had instigated hostilities: "You come hither to raise these wasps about my ears, and then you will take wing and flee away."[37] Providence, like the new Connecticut settlements, was a defenseless outpost and to make matters worse there were rumors in the Bay that the Narragansetts might join forces with the Pequots.

The Pequot war grew out of an incident at Block Island, off the south shore of the Narragansett country. On July 20, 1636, John Gallop brought news to Boston that a marauding band of Indians

---

[33] Quoted by Hutchinson, *History,* I, 427.
[34] Cited in Chapin, *Doc. Hist. R. I.,* I, 9.
[35] Williams to Mason, *N.C.P.,* VI, 337 f.
[36] *Ibid.,* p. 338.
[37] Gardener, *Pequot Warres,* 3 Coll. M.H.S., III, 140.

had attacked the island trading post of John Oldham, a Massachusetts man, and had murdered him. It was charged in Boston that
this was the work of the Narragansetts, but a letter from Williams
asserted that the Pequots had done it and that Canonicus and Miantonomu, the great sachems of the Narragansetts, had gone with 200
men to exact retribution from them. The magistrates disregarded
this information and Governor Vane wrote Williams to "look to
himself," for war with the Narragansetts might soon follow. Subsequently when the Pequots harbored the murderers of Oldham and
the peaceful intentions of the Narragansetts became clear, the authorities of the Bay veered about and laid new plans designed once for
all to impress the Pequots and all natives with the necessity of submission to Massachusetts' demands. Endecott, restored to favor and
appointed general, embarked with ninety men in three pinnaces to
seize the murderers of Oldham and wreak vengeance on those responsible for the earlier slaying of Captain Stone.[38]

The Pequots, most warlike tribe of southern Connecticut, were
the least disposed to tolerate advance of the English into the hunting
lands of the natives. The imperial march of the white man set English law above tribal custom and brought in the European system of
private ownership. Alone among the Indians at this time the Pequots
challenged this legal system by which the white man alienated the
red man's land. Roger Williams' earlier protest in defense of Indian
rights now proved its relevance. The Endecott expedition was
designed to establish the supremacy of English law in disregard of
Indian custom and in territory of the natives lying outside the
boundaries of Massachusetts. Like Williams, the Pequots perceived
no justice or sanctity in the white man's law which denied to the
Indian race more than the right of occupancy and which asserted that
the true lord of the soil was an absentee potentate in England who
had never seen it.

Trial by battle was the age-old method to terminate conflicts
between two opposing races and economic systems, and to this
arbitrament the magistrates of the Bay appealed with determination
and despatch. Under the command of Endecott, Massachusetts men
who had crossed the seas with high professions of ardor for Indian
missions and native conversion sailed to the Pequot country singing

[38] Winthrop, *Journal*, I, 225-230; John W. De Forest, *History of the Indians
of Connecticut* (Hartford, 1851), pp. 86-91.

battle psalms with Old Testament vindictiveness. Meanwhile Williams wrote Winthrop that the Pequots had been warned of the coming invasion. A "witch" in the tribe professed to be a human submarine and planned to sink the pinnaces "by diving under water and making holes."[39]

The Pequots discovered to their cost the immense superiority of the white man's armament. At Block Island the Massachusetts forces easily repulsed the Indians, burned their villages and corn, and destroyed their canoes. Thence the expedition re-embarked for Connecticut, only to encounter the heated protest of Gardener against precipitation of a general war. There was no deterring the fiery Endecott, and Gardener, an old soldier in the Low Countries, reluctantly but dutifully enlisted himself and his Saybrook men. In parleys with the Pequots, Endecott demanded immediate delivery of the culprits, indemnity of 1,000 fathoms of wampum, and, if they could not pay at once, surrender of twenty children of their chieftains as hostages.[40]

The Pequots, having no relish for peace on such terms, played for time. Endecott thereupon sounded the call to war, marched his troops to the Pequot town and with little resistance destroyed wigwams and canoes; after which he bravely marched his men back to the boats and set sail for home—returning with neither wampum nor murderers and leaving over all southern New England the heavy menace of a war of revenge. "Not a hair fell from the head" of any of the English, noted Winthrop.[41] The expedition, however, cost £200; and there was to be a heavier cost, paid by Connecticut. Before long the wasps were indeed about Gardener's ears. The Pequots killed three of his men, captured the brother of a minister and "roasted him alive," and surprised and cut down several more. Nine were slaughtered at Wethersfield and "two maids" were carried off captives, later rescued—stripped of their clothes.[42]

During the summer of 1636 Williams had been busy in the interests of peace, clearing the great sachems of the Narragansetts of complicity in the Oldham affair and averting the danger of further strained relations. He had the satisfaction at the end of July of

[39] *Letters*, N.C.P., VI, 6.
[40] Winthrop, *Journal*, I, 229-232; De Forest, *Indians of Connecticut*, pp. 91-98.
[41] *Journal*, I, 233.
[42] Gardener, *Pequot Warres*, 3 Coll. M.H.S., III, 143-147.

receiving instructions from Governor Vane and the council to inform Canonicus and Miantonomu that they were adjudged innocent; although some of their tributaries were still suspected. The following month Massachusetts agents, after conferring with Canonicus, gave the Narragansetts a clean bill of health and returned with high praise of the great sachem, reporting that they found in him "much state, great command over his men, and marvellous wisdom in his answers."[43] The Bay authorities on this occasion employed a Massachusetts Indian as interpreter, but they were soon to discover the indispensability in such negotiations of the man they had exiled. However strong his resentment of banishment, Williams willingly rendered all the services he could. Time after time he conferred with the Narragansetts and reported his findings to Winthrop and Vane.[44]

Then in the fall of 1636 came the great crisis. The Pequots, exasperated rather than intimidated by the Massachusetts expedition, were bent on revenge. Conferring with the Narragansetts, their old enemies and chief rivals for supremacy among the tribes of southern New England, they quickly concluded a peace and sought to consolidate it into a formidable combination which would place the English in dire peril. Late in September ominous news reached the Bay. Canonicus sent word that some of Gardener's men had been killed at Saybrook and simultaneously Roger Williams wrote that the Pequots, now negotiating for an alliance, were endeavoring to persuade the Narragansetts "that the English were minded to destroy all Indians."[45]

Awake at last to the crisis they had provoked, the Bay authorities sent word for Miantonomu to come to Boston, and to Williams the governor and council sent an urgent request to employ his "utmost and speediest endeavors to break and hinder" the Indian league. Because of the pressing "haste of the business" they regretted that they could not assist with a military escort and supplies. The man whom the oligarchy had cast out now paid them back but not in their own coin. "Scarce acquainting" Mary Williams of the danger, Williams set forth "all alone, in a poor canoe" and managed "to cut through a stormy wind, with great seas, every minute in hazard of

[43] Winthrop, *Journal*, I, 228-229.

[44] Mention of Williams' letters to Vane and Winthrop appears in the latter's *Journal*, I, 227, 230, 234, *et seq.* Only those to Winthrop have been preserved. See *N.C.P.*, VI, 3-69.

[45] Winthrop, *Journal*, I, 234.

life, to the Sachem's house." For three days and nights he lodged with

> . . . the bloody Pequod ambassadors, whose hands and arms, methought, wreaked with the blood of my countrymen, murdered and massacred by them on Connecticut river, and from whom I could not but nightly look for their bloody knives at my own throat also.[46]

When Williams arrived, the Narragansetts had assembled in a general council to hear the Pequot emissaries. The Pequots made a strong argument. If their tribe was destroyed, they declared, the Narragansetts would not long be safe from attack and extermination. They outlined the strategy of guerrilla warfare. They could cut down the English in isolated attacks, destroy their cattle and crops, and defeat them without risk of open battle. Against persuasions such as this Williams had to marshal his greatest eloquence. Yet he succeeded. God wondrously preserved him, he declared, and helped him "to break to pieces the Pequods' negotiation and design."[47]

In his old age Williams recalled that when the hearts of his countrymen had failed him, God had "stirred up the barbarous heart of Canonicus to love me as his son to his last gasp." Through this friendship he won also the confidence of Miantonomu and all the lesser sachems.[48] His personal influence with the Narragansetts thus saved not only his own settlement but all of New England. "I had my share of service to the whole land in that Pequod business, inferior to very few that acted"; so wrote Williams to Mason years later when orthodox Puritan chroniclers with one exception, persistently passed over Williams' great services with never a word of them. The solitary exception was Winthrop, who gave credit in his *Journal,* wrote Williams a warm personal appreciation, and urged the magistrates to revoke the banishment. The magistrates refused.[49]

[46] Williams to Mason, *N.C.P.,* VI, 338.

[47] *Ibid.* See also Bradford, *History,* pp. 423-424; and De Forest, *Indians of Connecticut,* pp. 101-103.

[48] *Letters,* N.C.P., VI, 407.

[49] *Ibid.,* pp. 338, 339. Underhill, Vincent, Mason, and Increase Mather omit all mention of Williams in their accounts of the war. Gardener makes a casual reference (3 *Coll. M.H.S.,* III, 154). Bradford's account of the failure of the Pequot overtures to the Narragansetts contains no reference to Williams' intervention.

The magistrates nevertheless continued to rely on Williams' good offices. Upon receiving his report of thwarting the Pequot alliance, they sent for Miantonomu, who went to Boston with a royal retinue, dined with the magistrates, and averred that the Narragansetts "had always loved the English, and desired firm peace." A treaty was drafted; "but because we could not well make them understand the articles perfectly," wrote Winthrop, "we agreed to send a copy of them to Mr. Williams, who could best interpret them to them."[50] Nearly twenty years later, as president of his own colony, Williams was to remind the Bay magistrates of this treaty and tell them that he kept his copy of it yet "as a monument and a testimony of peace and faithfulness between you both."[51]

Diplomacy had won the Narragansetts, but the Pequots were still on the warpath. On October 24, 1636, Williams sent word to Winthrop that Connecticut Indians "have slain some of our countrymen. . . . I hope it is not true."[52] With the horrors of a border war now threatening in good earnest, Massachusetts sought to extricate herself from the trouble she had provoked by calling for help from the other colonies. Plymouth, protesting the war and bringing up old wrongs done her by Massachusetts, finally agreed to send fifty men.[53] Saybrook and the three Connecticut towns, faced with imminent attack, had no choice. The first general court of Connecticut assembled and managed to place ninety armed men in the field under Captain Mason. Connecticut received a dubious reinforcement from Uncas, a dusky and scheming ally who deserted the Pequots with a canny prescience of what was to come.

By May, 1637, when the English were ready to give battle, Williams informed Winthrop[54] that the Narragansetts knew of the preparations and were keeping faith. Canonicus was "very sour" because of a recent plague which he blamed on the English, but Williams had "sweetened his spirit." He had had "far better dealing" with Miantonomu who "kept his barbarous court lately at my house"; the stately savage had taken a fancy to visiting him at Providence and threatened to incommode his host again "eight days hence." The most important part of Williams' letter dealt with mili-

50 *Journal*, I, 237.
51 *Letters*, N.C.P., VI, 269.
52 *Ibid.*, p. 13.
53 Bradford, *History*, pp. 418-424.
54 *Letters*, N.C.P., VI, 16-20.

tary strategy. The Narragansetts, schooled in savage warfare, advised the English to feign a retreat, "as if you were departed," and then to return by stealth and fall on the Pequots "within three or four days, when they are returned again to their houses." The Narragansetts advised this ruse particularly against the Pequot stronghold, which was almost impregnable since it was located in a swamp some distance back of the outer fort. In his letter Williams drew a diagram giving "a rude view" of the Pequot defenses.

At the end of his letter Williams pleaded for humane warfare; the sachems told him "it would be pleasing to all natives, that women and children be spared." Canonicus, he added, would like a present of a box of sugar.

Williams' suggested stratagem for attack was substantially the plan which Captain Mason eventually adopted. After a show of force at Saybrook, where Captain Underhill's Massachusetts party joined Mason, the expedition retreated to the boats and sailed away eastward instead of risking a direct attack when the Pequots expected it. Arriving in Narragansett bay, the men disembarked and on May 24 started overland, leaving their boats to double back more slowly along the coast. After an all-day march the English forces closed stealthily in on the palisaded fort of the unsuspecting Pequots. The sun had gone down and, under cover of darkness, the men stretched out for a few hours of sleep, their presence wholly undetected. Several hours before dawn, they mustered in two bodies, one marching to the front entrance and the other cutting off retreat of the Pequots to their fortress in the swamp. Warned too late by barking dogs, the startled Pequots rallied and made a stiff resistance, but Mason set the torch to the wigwams and a strong wind carried the flames. The English forces retreated outside the fort and slaughtered the maddened fugitives as they tried to escape from the inferno within. Half a thousand Indians, women and children together with the braves, slowly roasted to their death. Some of the English soldiers went faint with the heat. God was above them, declared Mason, and

> Laughed his Enemies and the Enemies of his People to Scorn, making them as a fiery Oven: Thus were the Stout Hearted spoiled, having slept their last Sleep . . . Thus did the Lord judge among the Heathen, filling the Place with dead Bodies![55]

[55] *Pequot War*, 2 Coll. M.H.S., VIII, 140-141.

Subsequently the main forces from Massachusetts and Plymouth made a tardy appearance in the campaign, united with Mason's command, and succeeded in annihilating nearly the whole of the remaining enemy forces. The proud Pequots were no more. The English and their Indian allies hunted down the remnants and made them captive, some to be placed in servitude among the English and a few to be sent to the Bermudas as slaves. Accounts such as Mason's and Underhill's rang with Old Testament fervor the halleluiahs of triumph. "Sometimes," wrote Underhill, "the Scripture declareth women and children must perish. . . . We had sufficient light from the word of God for our proceedings."[56] Mason saw no need for apology: "Blessed be the Lord God of Israel . . . for the Lord was pleased to smite our Enemyes in the hinder Parts, and to give us their Land for an Inheritance."[57] With grim realism, Mason counted it fortunate that the Pequot fort on the night of the attack had been more crowded than usual.[58]

The heritage of the Pequot war was fear and hatred on the part of the natives and the establishment of slavery as a New England institution. Against indiscriminate slaughter of the Indians and enslavement of captives, Williams was almost alone in making a protest. "I fear some innocent blood cries at Connecticut," he wrote Winthrop.[59] If Pequots had been murderers, he was yet not convinced that the whole tribe deserved such vengeance. He added a wry postscript, "I observe our countrymen have almost quite forgotten our great pretences to King and State, and all the world, concerning their souls," and regretted the general talk that "all must be rooted out." As the work of hunting down and enslaving the fugitives went on, he made a final plea for a more humane solution: "since the Most High delights in mercy, and great revenge hath been already taken," might not the Pequots be made subjects of Connecticut and Massachusetts?—"which they will more easily do in case they may be suffered to incorporate with the natives in either places."[60] With this proposal Williams also suggested as sufficient punishment the ingenious penalty placed by "Edgar the Peaceable"

[56] *History of the Pequot War*, 3 Coll. M.H.S., VI, 25.
[57] Mason's account, reprinted by Increase Mather, *Relation of the Troubles in New England* (Boston, 1677), p. 41.
[58] *Pequot War*, 2 Coll. M.H.S., VIII, 141.
[59] Williams to Winthrop, July, 1637, *N.C.P.*, VI, 46-49.
[60] Same to same, February 28, 1638, *N.C.P.*, VI, 87 f.

upon the Welsh, "a tribute of wolves heads . . . which (with submission) I conceive an incomparable way to save much cattle alive
in the land."

Williams' proposal of incorporation of the remnants of the
Pequots with other tribes did credit to both his heart and his head.
It was a practical suggestion and calculated to please their Indian
allies by giving recognition to an old Indian custom. Connecticut
alone paid any great heed to the suggestion.

8

DEMOCRACY ON THE ANVIL

THE FIRST APOSTLE OF THE RIGHTS of man, declared a European pundit, "was not Lafayette, but Roger Williams."[1] Statements of this kind have been based on the tracts Williams began to publish in 1644 and in which he stood forth as an avowed apostle of individual rights. Whether he was actually the first to advocate the rights of man is doubtful, and certainly more relevant in evaluating his position as a seventeenth century prophet of democracy is the question of what his theories meant in practice. The words "sovereignty of the people" were bandied about freely in Williams' time but they meant far less than when they flamed from the pen of Thomas Paine. How the reputed father of American democracy applied his theories in his own town and colony is the crucial matter. When Williams wrote of the will of the "people" and consent of the governed, what people did he have in mind and to what extent did he conceive of popular participation in governing the community? Did he consider suffrage the privilege of the few or an individual right open to all? Did the liberty he extolled mean the right to agitate, organize, and oppose; in a word, the right of a minority to become the majority?

During the dark days of the Pequot war, Roger Williams was embarking upon a humble experiment of larger significance than that first bloody conflict between the Puritans and Indians. He proposed to the settlers three objectives cherished to this day as the essence of free government; he proposed nothing less than a lowering of class barriers to economic opportunity, a guarantee of civil liberties including freedom of worship, and the preservation of liberty and opportunity through popular organs for majority rule. The early government forged at Providence was cast in the mold of these three great ideas and hammered and shaped into a serviceable instrument for democratic rule.

Suppression of dissent and denial of civil liberties had no place in early Providence. "At their first coming thither," says Winthrop,

1 Georg Jellinek, *The Declaration of the Rights of Man and of Citizens* (trans. by Max Farrand, New York, 1901), p. 77.

"Mr. Williams and the rest did make an order, that no man should be molested for his conscience." Thus the Salem Separatists no sooner escaped from Massachusetts jurisdiction than they explicitly avowed the sect ideal, "that grand cause of Truth and Freedom of Conscience," as Williams called it. In conformity with Williams' conviction that magisterial power could intervene "only in civill things," the settlers made a covenant establishing liberty of conscience as a natural right. Presumably the covenant was written down on the lost records of the first year of the plantation. Its wording is unknown but its substance is clear. The new settlement was dedicated to freedom and diversity, not compulsion and orthodoxy. From the time of its founding Providence was never to know an established church.[2]

Williams' other major objects, to provide economic opportunity and a popular government, likewise led him to blaze a new trail. Providence he envisaged as "a shelter for persons destressed for Conscience" and a place of opportunity for "such as were destitute."[3] To give reality to his equalitarian social policy involved delicate tasks in the sphere of politics: first the creation of a government which would heed the popular will, and secondly the establishment of a land system which would promote the welfare of the first comers and yet not discriminate against the poor and needy who chanced to come later. Thus from the first the question of economic opportunity and political control went hand in hand, and Williams found himself facing the most fundamental problem of modern democracy. Looking back in 1654 upon the formula he devised to meet that problem, he declared proudly that he always had stood for "liberty and equality, both in land and government."[4]

Two or three months after the founding of the plantation Williams penned a description of his tiny commonwealth.[5] The householders or "masters of families" held regular fortnightly meetings where they settled questions of land and "planting." On the principle of "mutual consent" they "finished all matters with speed and peace." One, called "the officer," summoned them to town meetings, but otherwise they had no executive machinery. The diminutive

2 Winthrop, *Journal*, I, 340; *Prov. Recs.*, I, 1, 4; Chapin, *Doc. Hist. R. I.*, I, 32-33, 71-72. The phrase, "only in civill things," occurs in a compact of 1639.
3 *Prov. Recs.*, III, 307; Chapin, *Doc. Hist. R. I.*, I, 25.
4 *Letters*, N.C.P., VI, 263.
5 *Ibid.*, pp. 3-7.

primary assembly of the married men, who constituted the voters, retained full control of plantation affairs.

No other problem proved a more crucial test of Williams' capacity for leadership than the question of land. Virginia and Plymouth had already encountered serious difficulties from precisely this source. Williams and his associates adopted the current New England device of a town proprietorship, though varying from the norm in their firm insistence on equality between purchasers. In the early years the proprietorship and the town were one, constituting a joint land and political corporation. The political idea of freemanship was joined with the economic idea of proprietorship and, according to Williams' principle, the whole body of voters held the common or undivided land in trust for the town and possessed the power of making allotments. Thus with the right to vote went a proprietary right, which in Providence meant a grant of land equal to that of the other purchasers and an equity in the common or undivided lands on similar terms of absolute equality. Such a practice was rare indeed in New England towns, and Williams could well boast of his principle of liberty and equality in land and government.

In devising the New England land system, notes Egleston, "our ancestors were guided by no visionary theories of equality."[6] In Salem, Boston, New Haven, and other towns where administration of the land system slid into the hands of selectmen and committees of "allotters," there was never any thought of sharing on an equal basis, and the discriminatory character of grants allowed wide latitude in favor of the wealthy.[7] In Plymouth, when Williams was there, an inner oligarchy of proprietors rather than the whole body of freemen had the power of allotment, a monopoly broken in 1639 but restored in 1682. There were towns other than Providence where control of the land lay in the freemen, but in the realms of orthodoxy the freemanship was restricted; rarely did the bulk of the householders have a vote in town meeting and the decision on land policy.[8]

[6] Melville Egleston, *The Land System of the New England Colonies* (Baltimore, 1886), p. 54.

[7] See Chapter 6, p. 78. Also H. B. Adams, *Village Communities of Cape Anne and Salem* (Baltimore, 1883), p. 67; C. H. Levermore, *Republic of New Haven* (Baltimore, 1886), pp. 79-85; H. L. Osgood, *American Colonies in the Seventeenth Century* (New York, 1904-1907), I, 457-463; R. H. Akagi, *Town Proprietors of the New England Colonies* (Philadelphia, 1924), pp. 71, 73.

[8] Osgood, *American Colonies*, I, 464-465.

In dealing with Williams' part in establishing the Providence proprietorship, or "fellowship" as he called it, we enter a realm of perplexing controversy. Because of the destruction of many early records when Providence was burned in King Philip's war, historians have perforce filled in the gaps by referring to statements made by William Harris and Roger Williams toward the close of their lives. The two men at that time were engaged in a bitter public contest; and historians, misled by the hot words of the contestants, have pictured early Providence as chequered with controversies between Williams and the town. Thus in some accounts Williams is portrayed as far from a democrat in 1636, making himself sole proprietor and ruling the town as its feudal overlord.[9] According to another version he is regarded as prone to "vagaries" and is darkly suspected of a "communistic bent."[10] The engaging suggestion is made that until the issue was settled by a deed of 1638, the Providence settlers were reluctant communists, grumbling and arguing and sojourning in wigwams—a situation only relieved when the shrewd materialist, William Harris, emerges as the champion of free private enterprise, rallies the settlers against the utopian idealist, and plagues Williams into admitting the townsmen into a joint proprietorship. The realist triumphs over the impractical visionary and the sacred institution of private property is restored.[11]

Williams was certainly no communist, nor was he a feudal overlord. Suppositions that the settlers were arrayed against him in a contest for land overlook the fact that agreements as to the character of the new plantation had already been made before the land was purchased.

The first decisions affecting the Providence land system were made in Salem in 1635. Williams' immediate intention after his trial, as he explained in 1677 during his contest with Harris, was "to do the natives good" as a missionary among the Narragansetts. Because of this, he did not at first want "English company," nor "make covenant with any" to go with him, nor have any notion of founding

[9] Ernst, *Roger Williams*, pp. 167-172, 177; Osgood, *American Colonies*, I, 337 f.; Edward Channing, *History of the United States* (New York, 1905-1925), I, 383.

[10] W. B. Weeden, *Early Rhode Island* (New York, 1910), p. 26.

[11] I. B. Richman, *Rhode Island: Its Making and Its Meaning* (New York, 1902), I, 91; H. C. Dorr, "The Proprietors of Providence," *Coll. R.I.H.S.*, IX, 199; S. G. Arnold, *History of the State of Rhode Island and Providence Plantations* (New York, 1859), I, 101.

a plantation. Yet, as he long afterward reminded Harris, when the latter and other neighbors in Salem asked leave "to come along in my company," he consented and conceived his project of a plantation for the persecuted. Before Williams' flight from Salem his coterie —"above twenty persons," according to Winthrop—concerted plans for the settlement and Williams agreed to put Harris and the others "in the first grant equal to myself."[12] This agreement, or "covenant" as Williams called it,[13] marked the first stage in the evolution of the Providence proprietorship.

In accordance with this covenant the town in 1636 assumed title to Williams' purchase from the Indians and made allotment of land a matter of regular town procedure. It is true that the earliest surviving record[14] attesting the town title was drafted in 1638, but other evidence shows that Williams gave his purchase to the townsmen in the first days of the plantation. As William Harris testified in 1677, Williams "actually and immediately" put Harris and the rest "in equall possession" of the land "with himselfe."[15] This agreement of 1636 by which the town acquired the Providence tract, though probably oral, may have been entered in the lost records for the first year. The earliest records now surviving contain entries of land grants for 1637.[16] Since these records were neither kept by Williams nor entered in his name as sole proprietor, but were public records of grants by the town and entered as such by a town official, they substantiate the testimony of William Harris.

If we could recover the lost records of the town, they would reveal that six men composed the original fellowship. A record of June 10, 1638, refers back to six earlier proprietary grants to Throckmorton, Greene, Harris, Verin, Arnold, and Williams.[17] Since this appears among the records for the "second year of plantation," the entry for the first six grants must have been among the lost records of the first year. This evidence that Williams conveyed the land in 1636 and that five other masters of families were associated with him on equal terms is confirmed by Harris who testified in 1675 that he was "one of the first six persons" who became purchas-

---

12 Williams' Plea, 1677; printed in Carpenter, *Roger Williams*, p. 224.
13 Williams to Winthrop, 1636, *N.C.P.*, VI, 6.
14 The "initial deed"; see p. 113.
15 *Harris Papers*, p. 203.
16 *Prov. Recs.*, I, 3-5.
17 *Ibid.*, pp. 4-5.

ers.[18] Still more explicit, Verin in 1650 recalled the agreement by which "we six which Cam first should have the first Convenienc," including home lots and meadow. He referred also to the admission of later purchasers in 1638, "about 7," to make up the first thirteen.[19] A later record shows that the first six, like the seven whose grants were recorded on June 10, 1638, obtained full proprietary rights and were "all Intrested alike."[20]

From the foregoing it is apparent that Williams' tiny commonwealth not only varied from the New England pattern but bore little or no resemblance to English institutions. Providence was in fact one of the few early settlements where frontier conditions had a formative influence. Had its founders been men of means holding social views like the Massachusetts gentry and masters of the region by virtue of a patent, frontier conditions would have had little consequence; but Williams and his associates, few of them connected with families of the gentry, none of them possessing a quantum of capital, and all of them smarting from the buffets of arbitrary rulers, found on the frontier a singular opportunity. Here was room for all and no one to insist that privilege, wealth, or sanctification was essential for good order and equitable government. The Providence settlers accordingly established a land policy in the interest of small freeholders, a suffrage by which masters of families possessed the right to vote, and a primary assembly of the enfranchised as the immediate governing body for all affairs of the community. This combination of political and economic equalitarianism followed logically from the transplantation of English liberal ideas in American soil, from the presence of open land, from the prevailing equality of the settlers in material possessions, and from the fact that Providence was an autonomous plantation with no authorized regime bolstered by English law.

"We have no Patent," wrote Williams in 1636, "nor doth the face of Magistracy suit with our present condition." At this point, three months after the founding of the settlement, he was revolving in his mind the current European doctrine of the social contract and had drafted two civil compacts.[21] Under the first compact the mas-

---

[18] *Harris Papers*, p. 150.
[19] *Prov. Recs.*, XV, 37; Chapin, *Doc. Hist. R. I.*, I, 28-29.
[20] *Prov. Recs.*, XVII, 20.
[21] Williams to Winthrop, *N.C.P.*, VI, 4-5.

ters of families by their "free and joint consent" and for the "common peace and welfare" were to pledge themselves to abide by all orders and agreements "made by the greater number of the present householders." This plantation covenant would provide a more formal basis of authority and by signing it the married men would incorporate themselves as a patriarchal democracy. It is probable that this compact was adopted, though the loss of early records leaves the matter in doubt. The second compact was designed for young single men and newcomers "desirous to inhabit in this Town." Since by signing it these men were to "promise to subject" themselves to agreements made by a majority of the patriarchs, this instrument, like the Mayflower Compact, would have the force of a pledge of obedience.

Williams wrote to Winthrop of his two compacts, asking advice of the elder statesman of the Bay. He was perplexed because "some young men, single persons (of whom we had much need) . . . are discontented with their estate, and seek the freedom of the vote also, and equality." [22] He realized that a small, poor, unauthorized plantation could not flourish if the original settlers established themselves in a privileged position. Recognizing that a large influx of newcomers might challenge local authority, he turned to the idea of covenant as the best guarantee of cooperation in the absence of a charter. To prevent discontent he favored a broad policy by which those admitted as "inhabitants" should be advanced within a reasonable time to full local rights. As he informed Winthrop,[23] he already had obtained an agreement, "by consent," whereby acceptable new settlers were to pay "thirty shillings a piece as they come," thus qualifying at once for a proprietary right. Williams' ideal was that of a steadily expanding fellowship and both of his compacts expressly intimated that later comers were to be admitted "into the same fellowship and privilege" with the first six.

The suffrage as of 1636 reveals both the radicalism and the limitations of the Providence experiment. Already the town was inclining toward the stake-in-society principle which the town finally adopted in 1658 when all freeholders were made eligible to vote. The Providence leaders were drawn from the middle class and their

22 *Ibid.*, p. 4.
23 *Ibid.*, p. 6. Records of later grants show that this agreement applied to married men.

attitude toward the young men who were unenfranchised shows that they had no notion of complete equality. But Williams was not one to forget the destitute. Thomas Angell, not yet of age, who worked for the Williams family, and the "poor young fellow," Francis Weekes, presumably a hired hand of one of the others, both received a small grant of land in 1637. William Carpenter, though probably already married, apparently lived with the Arnold family and worked for his father-in-law. In 1637 he received land, established himself as a "householder," and the following year was admitted to the fellowship. John Smith, unenfranchised though married, may have worked for one of the purchasers, for it is not known that he had property of his own at this early date.[24] These grants of 1637 apparently eased discontent for the moment, for it was not found necessary to adopt the young single men's compact until 1639.

The thrill of horror which ran over the settlements during the Pequot war checked migration to Providence for more than a year. In 1637 the only newcomers were two young men, Edward Cope and William Reynolds, both of whom were promptly given small grants of land. The aftermath of the war left many burdens on the Williams family, involving entertainment of English soldiery and bands of Narragansetts, and the cost of sending messengers, for which the only recompense was shipment of supplies from Winthrop.[25] During July, 1637, Mary Williams was occupied with the care of a wounded soldier, a Boston man who some years later became a Providence citizen.[26] Her husband, ambassador extraordinary in all Indian affairs, was busy penetrating the tangle of native intrigue left in the wake of war, keeping Miantonomu and Canonicus faithful to their pledges, pacifying the Narragansetts who smarted from affronts at the hands of their imperious white allies, and keeping Winthrop informed of the double dealing of Uncas.

To procure a better livelihood for his family, Williams established a trading post in the Narragansett country, profiting by his friendship with the two great sachems. Even in such busy months of trade, travel, and diplomacy, he did not lose sight of his old desire to "do the natives good," and to Winthrop he lamented that the colonists

[24] He may have been unenfranchised because of bad conduct. See *N.C.P.*, VI, 90; Chapin, *Doc. Hist. R. I.*, I, 76.

[25] *N.C.P.*, VI, 32, 89, and *passim*.

[26] *Ibid.*, p. 39.

had forgotten their "great pretences" of Indian labors. Subsequently
he reported that he had found "what I could never hear before, that
they have plenty of Gods"—he had brought home the names of
thirty-eight! Williams had "great hopes," for he had found "many
a poor Indian soul enquiring after God."[27]

In the midst of "barbarous distractions" Williams was also concerned for a more generous piety in realms of the lordly whites. In
July, 1637, at the request of two ministers, Peter Bulkley and Hugh
Peter, he forwarded a thirty-eight page manuscript in which he
asserted that only the ancient Jews had warrant from God for an
established church. Massachusetts had proceeded too far already
on the model of Israel; "the further you pass in your way," he wrote
Winthrop, the further you have "to come back, and the end of one
vexation will be but the beginning of another, till conscience be permitted (though erroneous) to be free amongst you."[28]

Massachusetts leaders learned nothing from such warnings, and
when a Providence man on a visit to Salem in July, 1637, dared to
speak his mind, the weight of authority fell harshly. John Greene,
accosted by Edmond Batter, a Salem deputy, gave a Yankee answer
to the question whether he was returning to live there: "how could
he unless he might enjoy the freedom of his soul and conscience?"
Deputy Batter's smooth denial of the insinuation led Greene to
respond hotly that the Bay magistrates had usurped power over conscience and persecuted Roger Williams. Endecott, now restored to
office as a magistrate, happened along the street at this point
and the upshot was a heavy fine on Greene of £20 from which he
escaped only by a humiliating retraction. Williams interposed in
behalf of Greene, declaring there had been no breach of the civil
peace. "Mr. Endecott," he asserted to Winthrop, "had need have a
true compass for he makes great way."[29]

In 1637 the Providence settlers offered land to others of their
group who remained in Salem. Endecott, Batter, and Hugh Peter in
Salem and the general court of the Bay added inducements of
another kind. At a church meeting the Visible Saints of Salem
catechised Margaret, the wife of Francis Weston, for taking excep-

[27] *Ibid.,* pp. 48, 88.
[28] *Ibid.,* pp. 50-51.
[29] *Ibid.,* pp. 52-54; *Mass. Bay Recs.,* I, 200, 203.

tion to Batter as a juryman on a case which concerned her.[30] Francis Weston, Thomas Olney, and other Separatists, likewise summoned before the inner circle of the church, were charged with holding it a grievance that they had "no liberty of objecting in the Church against what is taught." Owning up to this grievance, Weston, true to the teachings of his exiled pastor, declared he felt bound "to object and so seek clearing of truths." Olney, demanded a text for separation, answered "2 Cor. 6, be not unequally yoked."[31]

Following the synod of 1637 and the suppression of Anne Hutchinson and the Antinomian heresy, the Bay oligarchy was in no mood for moderation. The general court, meeting on March 12, 1638, dealt with Ezekiel Holliman "for seducing many" and refusing to attend Salem church and issued warrants to four others of Williams' following in Salem, Richard Waterman, Stukley Westcott, Olney, and Weston, and to leaders of the Antinomians to appear at the May session if they and their families had not "removed." The same court received a letter from Providence in which John Greene reiterated the statements he had recently retracted; whereupon the court ordered exclusion from the Bay colony of all Providence persons who were of the "same corrupt judgment."[32] This order amounted to banishment of all Rhode Island from Massachusetts soil.

Such severity merely promoted the growth of new settlements in the Narragansett basin. Before winter was over Williams was corresponding with the Antinomians about lands near Providence as a "shelter for their wives and children."[33] With Williams as negotiator the Antinomians, headed by William Coddington and John Clarke, obtained on March 24, 1638, a deed from the sachems for Aquidneck, the great island in Narragansett bay later called Rhode Island. On its northern tip at Portsmouth was presently settled a larger and wealthier group than Providence could boast for many years.

Others from Massachusetts "who were of the rigid separation, and savored anabaptism," noted Winthrop, "removed to Provi-

30 Daniel A. White, *New England Congregationalism* (Salem, 1861), p. 28. See also "Salem Quarterly Court Records," *The Essex Antiquarian*, III (1899), 83.
31 White, *Congregationalism*, pp. 31-32, 36.
32 *Mass. Bay Recs.*, I, 221, 223, 224.
33 *Letters*, N.C.P., VI, 89.

dence."[34] The new refugees from Salem included Mrs. Sweet, who soon married another Salem exile, Holliman, a widower, Mrs. Daniell, who became Greene's second wife, Robert Cole, Waterman, Westcott, Olney, and Weston. Before Margaret Weston's departure the stewards of the Lord subjected her to public ridicule by condemning her to two hours in the bilboes at Boston on "lecture" day, and two more at Salem.[35] Thomas James, former minister at Charlestown, and Richard Scott, brother-in-law of Anne Hutchinson, also took refuge in Providence, and from the household of Governor Winthrop came Joshua Winsor who, developing scruples of conscience, transferred to service in the Williams family with the connivance of Winthrop!

The eight new Salem families, inclusive of the children, brought the total migration from Williams' old congregation to about sixty persons, and the total of newcomers by the end of 1638 increased the town population to some eighty-five. Four of the refugees had been Massachusetts freemen, and one, Weston, had been a deputy at the general court. Despite the increase of population, Providence, unlike the Antinomian plantation, remained a straggling frontier village peopled by men drawn from the class of small farmers or artisans with little capital to bring in livestock and make improvements. As compensation for primitive living conditions, one of the new settlers, Robert Cole, whom the Massachusetts sleuths of God had decorated with a large red D for frequenting the bottle and "intiseing" another's wife,[36] found a welcome relief from the rigors of the Bay in the disinclination of Providence to establish governmental regulation of private lives.

The high regard of Williams and his associates for individual freedom occasionally brought perplexities. On May 21, 1638, the town suspended Joshua Verin's "liberty of voting" until he should agree not to break the "covenant" for freedom of conscience.[37] On the following day Williams notified Winthrop of this first tempest in the Providence teapot. Though Jane Verin, a "gracious and modest woman," had been attending the Separatist meetings at Williams' house, her husband for the past twelve months had carried

[34] *Journal,* I, 322.
[35] *Mass. Bay Recs.,* I, 233.
[36] *Ibid.,* pp. 107, 112.
[37] *Prov. Recs.,* I, 4.

liberty of conscience to the ultimate, eschewing all churches and services—for which "we molested him not." Failing to persuade Jane to the same ungodliness, Joshua had "trodden" her underfoot and beat her with such "furious blows" that she went in danger of life. For this "bruitish carriage" the town disfranchised him.[38]

Some four months later Williams wrote Winthrop that Verin and William Arnold were circulating "odious accusations in writing," slandering Providence, and asked him not to believe their "malicious falsehoods."[39] It does little credit to Winthrop's historical judgment that he subsequently accepted Arnold's version of the episode; his journal suppressed the fact of Verin's brutality toward his wife, pictured Williams as enticing Jane to attend so many services that she had time for little else, and capped the story with remarks made in town meeting by "one Arnold, a witty man," who said religious liberty did not abrogate God's ordinance for "the subjection of wives to their husbands" and that what Verin did "he did out of conscience."[40]

Verin took his wife back to Salem where the superior rights of the male were better understood. Because of Jane's Separatist views, the Bay court on December 4 referred her to the Salem elders; three weeks later she was still in trouble for refusing to attend church despite repeated conferences with the magnetic Hugh Peter.[41] William Arnold remained in Providence to plague the town for many years. Unaware of Winthrop's misplaced confidence in the man, Williams late in 1638 wrote of Arnold as an "unruly person" who had aggrieved most of the townsmen and openly favored royal intervention to establish "better government" by a general governor. Williams knew what to expect of a royal governor while Laud was head of the Lords Commissioners for Plantations. He had previously told Winthrop that Portsmouth settlers proposed Sir Henry Vane as general governor and that he had "endeavored to discover the snare in that";[42] and now, in remarking on Arnold's schemes, he warned Winthrop of the common interest of all New England: "The white [of the target] which such a speech or person levels at can be no

---

[38] N.C.P., VI, 95-96.
[39] Ibid., pp. 124-125.
[40] Winthrop, Journal, I, 340-341.
[41] Mass. Bay Recs., I, 247; "Salem Quarterly Court Records," The Essex Antiquarian, III (1899), 85.
[42] N.C.P., VI, 92.

other then the raising of the fundamental liberties of the country, which ought to be dearer to us then our right eyes."[43]

The arrival of so many new settlers at Providence and the founding of the nearby Portsmouth plantation produced a series of changes in Williams' little commonwealth. On March 24, 1638, when Williams drafted the deed for Aquidneck and induced Canonicus and Miantonomu to sign it, he had the foresight to get their signatures on another document which defined the boundaries of the Providence purchase of 1636 and granted him a new tract, the Pawtuxet lands lying on the west shore of the bay just south of Providence.[44] During the next eleven weeks the town fellowship expanded to thirteen, including the recent arrivals, each of the seven new members paying thirty shillings and receiving home lots, meadow, and upland to make a total of 100 acres equivalent to the shares of the first six.[45] On or before October 8 Williams drafted and signed the "initial deed" and turned it over to the settlers together with the Indian deed or "town evidence." In its primary effect, the initial deed gave the town a formal record of Williams' conveyance of the new Pawtuxet purchase. Serving to remove any ambiguity arising from the fact that the town evidence recorded the sachems' grants as made to Williams alone, the initial deed also confirmed the town's title to the original purchase of 1636.[46]

Williams was careful to insert in his initial deed a declaration that the thirteen who were already enfranchised and those whom the "Major part" of them admitted into the "fellowship of Vote" should have "Equall Right" in disposals of the town land. Williams did not contemplate a body of proprietors separate from the body of voters and possessing the special privilege of dividing the land. In spite of his liberal purpose, a majority of his associates made an agreement on Pawtuxet which violated the spirit of the initial deed. The Pawtuxet agreement, dated October 8, 1638, "impropriated" the new purchase to the first thirteen, "to be equally divided."[47] Since it did not specify the admission of later comers, the agreement obviously implied that Pawtuxet belonged to a closed body of proprietors.

43 *Ibid.*, p. 23.
44 *Prov. Recs.*, IV, 70-71.
45 *Ibid.*, I, 4-5; Chapin, *Doc. Hist. R. I.*, I, 75-76.
46 *Prov. Recs.*, III, 90-91; XV, 86.
47 *Ibid.*, XV, 31.

As a result of this transaction Providence was rent by one of the controversies so characteristic of the New England town land system. There was an inherent weakness in the system which made it an easy matter for first comers to intrench themselves in possession of the undivided land. Since only freemen had a voice in dividing land, they could not only grant the largest and best lots to themselves but a majority could at any time vote to sequester all the remaining common land as their joint possession. In nearly all New England settlements this latter device was shrewdly exploited; the freemen denied new voters any voice on future allotments and transformed the body of existing "purchasers" into a company of "proprietors" exclusive in membership and eventually divorced from the town government. Through this weakness in the land system, private interest thwarted the original public purpose; the public domains of New England towns passed slowly into the control of self-perpetuating real estate corporations which, subject to little or no democratic check, wrung a speculative profit from the rise in land values.

In the Providence of 1638 there was no body of unenfranchised sufficiently powerful to spike the Pawtuxet deal, but as newcomers arrived the opposition mounted. To bolster authority, Williams in 1639 drafted a compact modeled on the one which he had previously submitted to Winthrop. The five young men who had come earlier and eight new inhabitants, at least three of whom were married men, were induced to sign this, thereby binding themselves to submit to the rule of the thirteen incorporated "maisters of families."[48] The newcomers apparently paid ten shillings and received small grants of land.[49]

Despite this compact, the desire of the unenfranchised for equality soon produced conflict. To the patriarchs the nub of the question was not equality but Pawtuxet. Hastily they divided some of the Pawtuxet lands, and William Arnold, Carpenter, Cole, and William Harris moved their families there, forming the nucleus of a new settlement. Inasmuch as most of this fertile tract was still undivided, the men who had sequestered it were reluctant to enfranchise later comers so long as they contested their monopoly on Pawtuxet.

Williams, thinking from the first in terms of a "homestead" policy, always maintained he intended Pawtuxet to provide for the

48 *Prov. Recs.,* I, 1; Chapin, *Doc. Hist. R. I.,* I, 97.
49 See the Combination, "Agre. 12"; *Prov. Recs.,* XV, 4.

destitute.[50] When the patriarchs voted through the Pawtuxet agreement, he found himself in a minority of one. In December, 1638, his associates presented him with a cow as payment for the tract, which he accepted, but until settlement of the dispute he refused the share in the division of Pawtuxet.[51] Soon afterwards, when drafting the compact for the unenfranchised, he took care to employ language which implied continuation of his policy of steady enlargement of the town fellowship.

In the twenty-one months following the Pawtuxet agreement the town population rose to a total of nearly 120 persons. By the summer of 1640 the unenfranchised included about twenty men, of whom Chad Brown, Scott, and three or four others were men with families. The young single men and the half dozen who were married now outnumbered the voters and, as William Harris complained, "by the sugjestions of Mr. Williams," they "rose up" in a mutinous manner against the rule of the patriarchy and "claymed patuxet."[52] Williams, by his own account, aided by his friend Chad Brown, "a wise and Godly soul . . . brought the murmuring after comers, and the first monopolizing 12 to a oneness by arbitration."[53]

The arbitrators, William Harris and Robert Cole representing the Pawtuxet men and John Warner and Chad Brown representing the new comers, were chosen by the "inhabetance" and authorized not merely to settle the Pawtuxet dispute but to devise a new instrument of government. On July 27, 1640, they presented the town with an elaborate plantation covenant known thereafter as "The Combination."[54] The first article of this document ceded the disputed territory to the Pawtuxet men—"to the great Regret of most," according to Williams—[55] and defined the boundary between Pawtuxet and Providence, leaving the original Providence purchase, three-fourths of the combined area, to the town.[56] The second article lodged the power of granting land in the "hole inhabetance." The twelfth provided that those previously unenfranchised, who had already paid ten shillings for small grants, were to "make up" that

[50] Plea of 1677; printed in Carpenter, *Roger Williams*, p. 225.
[51] *Ibid.*, p. 226; Chapin, *Doc. Hist. R. I.*, I, 79; *Pub. R.I.H.S.*, VIII, 157.
[52] *Harris Papers*, pp. 199, 252.
[53] Plea of 1677; printed in Carpenter, *Roger Williams*, p. 226.
[54] *Prov. Recs.*, XV, 2-5.
[55] *Pub. R.I.H.S.*, VIII, 157.
[56] *Harris Papers*, pp. 66, 199.

amount to thirty shillings, thereby becoming "Equall with the first purchasers."

Scattered through the twelve articles of the Combination were provisions to reinforce the authority of the town meetings by means of new officials and procedures. The clerk was to summon regular town meetings every "quarter." In the interim a board of five "desposers," elected every three months, was to oversee allotments, issue written deeds, and administer town affairs. "We aprehend," stated the third article, "no way so sutable to our condition as Government by way of Arbetration." This mode of settling disputes was a favorite of Williams' who had learned its value when serving as an arbitrator in Massachusetts.[57] To make the system effective the Combination provided that arbitration should be compulsory and authorized the disposers to enforce the award. The second article recorded agreement on another of Williams' cherished principles: "As formerly hath benn the libertyes of the Towne: so Still to hold forth Libertye of Conscience."

With good reason the Providence compact of 1640 won praise nearly three centuries later from an historian interested in the "direct democracy" advocated by the elder La Follette and Theodore Roosevelt.[58] The Combination represented in fact a literal application of the democratic theory of social contract. As its preamble indicated, it was a constitution drawn up by a committee elected by the inhabitants to effect a combination for "unitye and peace." Unlike most plantation covenants, it was not framed and adopted on the authority of magistrates but was initiated and ratified by the whole body of townsmen. Nineteen new voters and all but two of the first purchasers,[59] signified assent by signing their names.

Harris, Brown, and the others who drafted the Combination frequently consulted Williams and the fruit of their labors represented a triumph for Williams' program. The new covenant abolished the earlier patriarchal government and established a broader base for Providence democracy. The young single men and substantially all townsmen became freemen at once with full rights in the land; and for the next two decades the ranks of the town fellowship expanded rapidly, ultimately including 101 members. Pawtuxet was yielded to

[57] *Mass. Bay Recs.*, I, 151.
[58] Charles S. Lobingier *The People's Law* (N. Y., 1909), p. 79.
[59] Weston and Greene; see *Harris Papers*, p. 199.

the first comers but the impulse toward an inner proprietorship was checked. Pawtuxet itself was then only a small tract, "a small addition to Providence," and not until several decades later when Harris repudiated Williams' leadership did it become a vital factor in an attempt to establish a landed aristocracy. As Williams reminded Harris long afterward, the freemen "confessed themselves" merely trustees for the town and later comers "paid the 30 s, not to the purchasers (so called) as proprietors, but as feoffees for a Town Stock."[60] Williams' "grand desire" of propagating a "public Interest" had been vindicated and Providence democracy had reached its high point.

[60] Williams' Plea, printed in Carpenter, *Roger Williams*, p. 225.

9

THE RHODE ISLAND WAY

IN THE EYES OF ORTHODOX PURITANS the people of Rhode Island
were outcasts, banished men, radicals, and dangerous fanatics.
Providence and soon Aquidneck had embraced the alleged new light,
liberty of conscience, and in consequence Rhode Island began to be
looked on as a madhouse. The Rhode Island way, the free church
system, was something not to be comprehended by the rigid authoritarian Puritan mind. It was too sharp a break from Puritan devotion to ecclesiastical unity and government-controlled uniformity.
Freedom of conscience was soul-license. The secular state was a god-
less state in which the will of man was set above the will of God.
The reign of Belial was broken forth anew, under the very noses of
the horrified saints—and just beyond their jurisdiction.

The multiplication of new lights and schisms in Rhode Island
became a perennial scandal to orthodox neighbors. Roger Williams
not only introduced the impiety of a secular state but committed the
weak and pitiable error of wavering in his faith. Tossed like a lost
soul, as his former orthodox associates saw it, he had cast adrift and
now veered giddily from Brownism to Anabaptism and Seekerism,
from excess to extravaganza. To add to confusion, the Antinomians
on the Island broke forth into worse blasphemies, errors, and
heresies, sinking ever more desperately into the bitter depths of
Familism.[1] Then came Samuel Gorton with his mad rout and swept
through the Rhode Island settlements like a plague, spreading his
wild fanaticisms to the utter rending of civil society and the distraction of Christian order.

All this, to one who comprehended, might signify the freshness
and confidence of men released from the fetters of the past and the
vigor and variety of intellect of ordinary men engaged in the task
of creating a new society. But scandalized saints like Thomas Weld
saw here only the ignorance and depravity of men who rejected the
sacred discipline. As the years passed their animosity deepened and

[1] See Winthrop and Weld, *A Short Story*.

118

their statements about Rhode Island were increasingly marked by distortion and detraction. "There they live to this day," wrote Weld of the Antinomians, "hatching and multiplying new opinions, and cannot agree, but are miserably divided into sundry Sects and Factions."[2] In the same spirit Edward Johnson ten years later wrote down in his *Wonder-Working Providence* that those banished from the society of the saints had gone to Providence and Aquidneck, "where having Elbow roome enough, none . . . to interrupt their false and deceivable Doctrines, they hamper'd themselves fouly with their owne line, and soone shewed the depthlesse ditches that blinde guides lead into."[3]

By this campaign of detraction New England leaders attempted to retard Rhode Island's growth and discredit her freedom as a profligate license. Restless and dissatisfied persons in the orthodox commonwealths were likely to hesitate long before venturing to take up residence in a community such as the Rhode Island settlements were represented to be. Carl Becker has remarked that the ideas of Williams "were too relevant not to arouse controversy but too remote from the spirit of the age to win many adherents."[4] Rhode Island ideas, however, were not so remote from the spirit of the age but that they might have won many more converts had not Puritan authorities employed vigorous propaganda as a means to prevent it. Free speech and free inquiry were not allowed in Massachusetts and the people never got the real facts about liberty of conscience and the Rhode Island way. Ministers and magistrates succeeded for the most part in keeping the populace from straying off, but denunciation of Rhode Island frequently had the inverted effect of producing conviction. Measures of repression and the inevitable infection of the prospect of liberty resulted accordingly in a small but steady migration to Narragansett bay.

It was a favorite pretense of defenders of orthodoxy that Rhode Island had no churches. When Francis Hutchinson of Portsmouth asked to be dismissed from the Bay covenant, John Cotton replied that such a dismissal would be "from a church to no church."[5] It

---

[2] *A Short Story*, p. 5. This slander was seized upon at once in the mother country and Robert Baillie promptly quoted this very passage; *Dissuasive*, p. 72.

[3] *Wonder-Working Providence* (Poole ed., Andover, 1867), p. 132.

[4] Carl Becker, *Beginnings of the American People*, Houghton Mifflin Co. (Boston, 1915), p. 101.

[5] 2 *Coll. M.H.S.*, X, 184-185.

was perhaps a half-truth that there was at first no formal church in Providence. The Separatists from Salem held services, however, and Providence soon could boast of a more considerable battery of ecclesiastical talent than any settlement of similar size. Three trained ministers, William Blaxton, Thomas James, and Roger Williams, preached to those who cared to harken, one representing the Anglican tradition, one the Congregational discipline, and one the Separatist doctrine.

Catherine Scott and Ezekiel Holliman soon introduced a fourth way to salvation, that of the Baptists. At Providence, noted Winthrop in March, 1639, "things grew still worse"—Roger Williams was "taken" by the persuasive Catherine, sister of Anne Hutchinson. Since the new sect denied the validity of infant baptism, Williams was rebaptized by Holliman; "then Mr. Williams rebaptized him and some ten more."[6] Among the members of this first Baptist church in America were Chad Brown, John Throckmorton, Thomas Olney, and William Harris.

Infant baptism is today largely a dead issue among the many that lie on the theological scrap heap, but it was becoming a live issue in those years in New England; enough so to lead shortly to the cashiering of one president of Harvard, Dunster, and to intrigue his successor, Chauncey, to the point of belief in "dipping," the later Baptist practice of total immersion. Neither the Bible nor early church tradition provided support for infant baptism, and to Williams with his own insatiable literalness, the rigid insistence of the Baptists upon scriptural authority may well have appealed as one of their merits.

The larger explanation of Williams' spiritual migration lay in the appealing alternative offered by the Baptists to one who was increasingly dissatisfied with outward ordinances and authoritarian pretensions. Williams' views had long been converging in the same direction as the Baptists. Like them, he denied the validity of theocratic precedents of the Old Testament as a basis for modern disciplines and employed the New Testament to support religious liberty.[7] Since 1610 London Baptists had consistently denied the power of the state over belief and worship and some had suffered in prison for circulating pleas for liberty of conscience. Here was a communion allowing

[6] *Journal,* I, 352-353.
[7] See letter of 1637, *N.C.P.,* VI, 51.

election of officers by the entire congregation and acknowledging the complete autonomy of its separate churches. A body of "come-out-ers," the Baptists agreed as heartily as Williams on ecclesiastical democracy and the right of free private judgment.

Despite the similarity of his own views and Baptist teachings, Williams shortly found that even in his new spiritual haven his critical turn of mind would allow him no rest. By June or July, 1639, according to Winthrop's chronology, he left the Baptists and made his last and greatest plunge into the darker depths of heterodoxy. He became a Seeker.[8]

The peregrinations of the tender conscience of Roger Williams had long astounded and scandalized orthodox English and American acquaintances. His new heresies of 1639 were the final proof of eccentric delusions and unsound judgment. John Cotton called him "a haberdasher of small questions" and William Coddington, at a time when he had long proven himself no friend of Williams, labelled him "a meer Weather-Cock, Constant only in his Unconstancy." Cotton Mather pleased himself and his readers with the fancy that Williams had a windmill in his head. Hubbard in the same spirit seized on Williams' rejection of his new baptism as a convenient vehicle for complacent satire. One of the Providence Baptists, he related, "of a like capricious brain," raised an objection which none of them could answer: if they renounced their former baptism because it was unlawful, "then what right had Holeman to baptize Mr. Williams; which so gravelled them all, both the baptizers and the baptized, that they turned Seekers, and so continued ever after."[9] Williams, despite Hubbard's implication to the contrary, did not secede from his new church because lay baptism was improper.[10] His baptism by Holliman was not a theological absurdity. In the primitive church which orthodox Puritans as well as Baptists took as a model such a procedure was lawful where ordained clergy were not available.

Williams lay down his pastorate in the Baptist church because of what was ever after his sticking point: no church, he believed, could present any clear proof of a true apostolic succession. He had

[8] *Journal*, I, 307; Chapin, *Doc. Hist. R. I.*, I, 95-96.

[9] *History*, 2 Coll. M.H.S., VI, 338.

[10] For a sympathetic explanation from the Baptist point of view, see J. D. Knowles, *Memoir of Roger Williams* (Boston, 1834), 166-167, 170-173.

reached a point where he could not conscientiously remain in any church. The Baptist faith was valid by the same logic through which the Anglican church under Cranmer derived its apostolic succession from the Catholic church, but this reasoning no longer satisfied the inquisitive Williams. He questioned his second baptism, as Winthrop noted, because he was unable "to derive the authority of it from the apostles" except through the Anglican clergy, "who he judged to be ill authority." With his tongue in his cheek the Massachusetts governor added that his erstwhile young friend was now expecting "to become an apostle."[11] Winthrop and orthodox scoffers overlooked the point that Williams' objections were valid against their own church as against the Baptists.

Puritan logic brought Williams to the dilemma of those who insisted on an uncorrupted apostolic succession and upon church ceremonies in their original purity, but who were forced to derive the one through the channel of the medieval church and the other from the welter of contradictory precedents of the Bible and early church writings. Facing this dilemma with all the honesty and logic of a trained and critical intellect, he succeeded only in multiplying his scruples; and he now groped his way through to the ultimate scruple which was the key to all the others. His difficulties, he realized at last, revolved upon this one point: all churches, all ordinances, all true apostolic succession, had been lost in the apostasy of the Roman church, by the accretions through the ages of man-made rites and articles of belief—"inventions of men." With Williams' criticism of the medieval church for divergence from primitive Christianity other Protestants, whether Anglican, Lutheran, or Puritan, would have been in general accord. But in making his further contention, that it was impossible at that late date to recover the authentic sacred original now so long obscured or obliterated, Williams passed beyond. He proceeded through Protestantism by means of its own premises and its own rationalism, to its logical end.

Henceforth there would be no church in which Williams could believe, because no church might demonstrate to one of his mind that its authority indisputably was derived from God and not from man. Only an infallible church, founded upon incontestable revelation, or resolving moot points in the future by continual visible manifesta-

11 *Journal*, I, 307.

tions of the divine will, could have met his needs. Guided by his original Puritan orientation, Williams had lost faith in the Puritan church but still held with full Puritan zeal to his belief in God. He required infallibility, as did the orthodox; but he was unable to perceive such divinity in any of the brands of infallibility then passing for God's own. Had he been born a little later and more subjected to the intellectual currents which influenced the Deists, he might not have expected so much of God.

By becoming a Seeker Williams did not change his principles any more than he had by becoming a Baptist. Seekerism was but the ultimate logic to which his principles carried him. It was the solution of his intellectual dilemma. By this solution, "discarding all theologies," Roger Williams "came as near as his age would permit, in the case of a soul at once supremely honest and truly devout, to being an Agnostic."[12] Henceforth there were no doubts, no waverings; he had found his faith—the certainty of uncertainty; disbelief in the unproved.

Religious ferment in Aquidneck steadily increased the contempt of the orthodox for the people they had banished. Mistress Hutchinson and the Antinomians daily "fell into new errors," and one of them, Nicholas Easton, "a man very bold, though ignorant," gathered a following of his own and created a schism.[13] In 1639 Samuel Gorton, whom Cotton and Hubbard called the most "prodigious minter of exorbitant novelties," introduced additional blasphemies, "the very dregs of Familism."[14] Anne Hutchinson denied that sanctification—as defined by ministers in the Bay—was the first evidence of salvation; Easton preached that the elect had an "indwelling" spirit; Gorton held that all might be saved. The popularity of such teachings showed how eagerly the average man, relieved of compulsion, turned from orthodox formalism to those who spoke from "mere motion of the spirit."

By 1641 when the Baptist leaven began to spread from Providence, many at Aquidneck were reputed to have "denied all magistracy" and the legend grew that Rhode Island had neither churches nor government.[15] There was more befuddlement here than sense,

12 I. B. Richman, *Rhode Island, Its Making and Its Meaning,* G. P. Putnam's Sons (New York, 1902), I, 111.

13 Winthrop, *Journal,* I, 338; II, 48-49.

14 Hubbard, *History,* 2 Coll. M.H.S., VI, 402.

15 Winthrop, *Journal,* II, 46; Robert Baillie, *Anabaptism* (London, 1647), p. 59.

for there were devotion and worship in Rhode Island; it was simply
that the Puritan mind could not grasp a system which denied magisterial power over religion, secularized the state, and put the churches
on their own.

Although Portsmouth had not originally embraced democracy or
religious liberty, the example of Providence was a challenge, the
absence of chartered government an invitation, and the medley of
religions a dynamic propulsion. The immediate impetus was supplied
by the despised outcasts, Gorton and Anne Hutchinson, who swiftly
drew from their individualistic doctrines the interwoven logic of
religious liberty and government by the people. When Gorton
arrived in Portsmouth, William Coddington, wealthy stock farmer
and former Massachusetts oligarch, ruled the plantation under a
compact which was strictly theocratic. Finding the Hutchinson
group already opposing this conservative regime, Gorton promptly
joined his forces to theirs, complaining that Coddington's men had
not gained power by "choice of the people, but set up themselves."[16]

The result was the election of William Hutchinson as chief officer in April, 1639, and the departure of Coddington and his angry
followers to the southern end of the island where they founded Newport. The Portsmouth reformers meanwhile established a more
popular government, "a Civill body Politike," abolishing theocracy.
Libertarianism was soon attracting John Clarke, Nicholas Easton,
and others who had gone to Newport and although the old guard
party scored a triumph in 1640 when the two Aquidneck settlements
united under the domination of Coddington, the popular movement
was not to be checked. In March, 1641, Aquidneck proclaimed itself
"a Democracie or Popular Government," lodging legislative power
solely in the hands of the assembly of freemen. None was to be
accounted a "Delinquent" for "Doctrine." The multiplication of
sects and increasing individualism had as in Providence produced
religious liberty, a broadened suffrage, and control of policy by the
body of freemen.[17]

As the tide of individualism grew stronger in Rhode Island,
orthodox neighbors lost all hope of reclaiming the outcasts. Overtures from Aquidneck for intercolonial amity were rejected by the
Bay oligarchs on the ground that the Rhode Island men were "not

[16] N.E.H.G.R., IV (1850), 205.
[17] See Chapin, Doc. Hist. R. I., II, 58, 108, 112, and passim.

fit to be capitulated withal by us."[18] In 1639 Salem church passed the "great censure" on those of its former members who had been re-baptized at Providence. This "bull of excommunication," as Williams called it, was issued against Roger and Mary Williams, Holliman's wife, Widow Reeves, and Throckmorton, Olney, Westcott and their wives.[19]

Cotton broke off correspondence with Williams and later, in the days of their debate on toleration, cast a slur on Williams' character and mode of living. God had not prospered Williams, Cotton asserted, for he refused to serve the Lord as he should and had taken to "merchandise" at his Narragansett post, a calling "unto which he was never brought up."[20] Williams, however, generally escaped the worst forms of abuse and Cotton Mather eventually admitted that many "judicious persons" judged him to have "the root of the matter" in him.[21] Williams had the gentlemanly distinction of university learning and the New England squirearchy could not say he was a mere ignoramus and disciple of the devil. Toward Anne Hutchinson and Samuel Gorton they felt no such restraint and descended to language of coarse vilification. Hubbard, writing in the second generation, undoubtedly expressed the view current in the generation of the founders: "Every year they broached new errors, the issues of their depraved minds, more misshapen than those monsters, which were credibly reported to be born of the bodies of some of them."[22]

Venomous and insinuating publicity made notorious the miscarriages of the unfortunate Mary Dyer and Anne Hutchinson. In the interests of orthodox piety gentlemen and ministers circulated the story that Mary Dyer bore a horned monster with claws on its feet and "sharp talons." John Cotton improved the occasion at a public lecture by giving his congregation an unsavory description of the "monstrous birth" reported of Anne.[23] As late as 1685 one of the Mathers suggested perpetuating the hideous libel by preserving it in print, a suggestion which bore fruit in a lurid passage in Cotton

[18] Winthrop, *Journal*, II, 24; *Mass. Bay Recs.*, I, 305.
[19] Hutchinson, *History*, I, 371; *Bloody Tenent More Bloody*, N.C.P., IV, 55.
[20] *Reply to Mr. Williams*, N.C.P., II, 86.
[21] *Magnalia* (Hartford, 1820), II, 433.
[22] *History*, 2 Coll. M.H.S., VI, 341-342.
[23] Winthrop, *Journal*, I, 313-316, 326-328; Winthrop and Weld, *A Short Story*, Preface, and pp. 43-45; Johnson, *Wonder-Working Providence*, p. 133.

Mather's famous *Magnalia*.[24] Rhode Island people had a more humane opinion of the two women. Robert Baillie reported that Roger Williams "spake much good" of Anne Hutchinson.[25] The Gortonists bluntly told Massachusetts authorities that their detestation of Anne sprang from their failure to suppress her "light"; the real object of the Bay was to bound and measure the infinite word of God "according to your own shallow, human and carnal capacities."[26]

Blunt retorts by the Gortonists increased the animus against Rhode Island at a time when vindictive leadership was driving the Bay colony steadily nearer to action more menacing than mere verbal abuse. Prior to the Antinomian expulsion, Governor Winthrop was reprimanded for moderation and acquiesced in the judgment. Following the institution of the synod in 1637, the way of the New England churches was clarified and the harsher lineaments of reaction began to show more sharply. Cotton drafted and sought adoption of "Moses His Judicialls," a code of laws which carried the dogma of absolutism and compulsion to its logical conclusion. It proposed that those who rejected correction by the church should be banished and that outright heretics should be "punished with death."[27] Cotton's code was not adopted but these two harsh provisions presently appeared among Massachusetts statutes.

As reaction gripped the Bay, heterodox Rhode Island seemed increasingly the embodiment of Belial let loose. Many of its people were accounted "loose and degenerate in their practices,"[28] and on authoritarian premises the accusation was true. Under the sect ideal compulsions to piety were conceived as inward and subjective; it was no function of a secular state to manufacture saints and knock down sinners through the agency of laws. Galled by such impiety, Winthrop described the Narragansett bay settlements as "under no government" and increasingly "offensive."[29] They had no religious tests for the right to vote or hold office, no laws to compel church attendance nor to restrain Sabbath-breaking, no ministers' lots or

---

[24] 4 *Coll. M.H.S.*, VIII, 58-59; *Magnalia*, II, 448-449.
[25] *Dissuasive*, p. 150.
[26] Randall Holden to Massachusetts, 1643, 3 *Coll. M.H.S.*, I, 14.
[27] *An Abstract of the Laws*, Force's Tracts, III, No. 9, p. 12.
[28] Winthrop and Weld, *A Short Story*, Preface.
[29] *Journal*, II, 102.

tithes to support churches. More unfortunate, from the modern
view, they made only a few haphazard attempts to provide support
for schools. Rhode Islanders, charged a Massachusetts squire, were
"very ignorant and easily perverted."[30]

To the minds of orthodox gentry, the absence of rigorous social
discipline in Rhode Island, the laxity which made the common man's
private life largely his own business, produced a scandalous condition of morals and manners. Forward women and brazen jezebels
like Anne Hutchinson "exercised publicly," set themselves up as
women preachers, and profaned the Holy Word.[31] A wife like Jane
Verin was encouraged in the strange delusion that she had a "right"
to her own religious views when they differed from those of her
lord and master. Winthrop noted—without recording the exten-
uating circumstances—that the wife of "one Beggerly" had remarried in Providence, "and no divorce."[32] Those who had run the
gamut of stocks, pillory, and whipping post in the realms of orthodoxy found on Narragansett bay much the same freedom as marked
the frontier of later America.

The Rhode Island way had passed beyond the ken of the Puritan
mind and its real significance was almost completely lost on those
who had most to say about it. Condemned as a sewer for the poor
and ignorant, the deluded and fanatical, Rhode Island was, in fact,
a melting pot where liberating forces were being released in health-
ful vigor. Embodying the social freedom of the secular state, the
Narragansett bay settlements were an embryo of the America that
was to come. They were not to be understood or appraised correctly
by those bred to English notions of class and privilege and wedded
to the compulsory asceticism of the New England discipline.

After 1641 the chasm between the Rhode Island settlements and
neighboring colonies steadily widened. The fear that their indentured
servants would run away to Rhode Island, the darker fear that the
leaven of Rhode Island liberality would bewitch their own submerged populace, and the obstinate fact that the melting pot of cast-
offs and come-outers grew and flourished, betraying the fallacy of
orthodox predictions, caused the policy of New England magistrates
rapidly to stiffen. In 1642 Governor Bellingham of the Bay urged

[30] Johnson, *Wonder-Working Providence*, p. 132.
[31] Hubbard, *History*, 2 Coll. M.H.S., VI, 338, 341.
[32] *Journal*, I, 341. *Cf. ibid.*, II, 421.

Plymouth authorities to adopt common measures against Rhode Island. Their emissaries "have latly come amongst us," he wrote, "and have made publick defiance against majestracie, ministrie . . . secretly also sowing the seeds of Familisme, and Anabaptistrie, to the infection of some, and danger of others."[33] Plymouth rejected the Massachusetts overtures, but within two years the orthodox colonies were to initiate a policy of intervention in Rhode Island and subjugation of its people.

[33] Bradford, *History*, p. 461.

10

INSECURITIES AND ALARUMS

ALTHOUGH ONE MAY SUSPECT THE REITERATION by the saints that Rhode Island individualism amounted to anarchy, there was fire under the smoke. The Narragansett bay settlements had their stormy petrels. In the years from 1640 to 1643 Samuel Gorton contributed more than his share, certainly all that the leather lungs, compelling personality and rugged self-assertion might effect, toward sustaining the propagandists in their lurid pictures of Rhode Island anarchy. Here was a man who attacked the oligarchy of New England squires and ministers as "artificiall and self seeking" and boldly arraigned it for employing power and civil policy "to get riches and honour" and "lord it over men's consciences."[1] Of all the outcasts in the Rhode Island brood, none matched Gorton in the power to inspire fear, loathing and wrath among the godly, and there was no one whom orthodox magistrates denounced more hotly as anarchist, blasphemer and rogue.

But to the historian this is not the real Gorton. Gorton's moral character was of the highest, and if he differed from orthodox Puritans in religion, he was not less devout than they. He objected to the ways of government wherever he went and answered the invective of adversaries with stentorian billingsgate, but he was neither a blasphemer nor an anarchist. He was a champion of liberty in its larger sense and English to the core in his insistence on legal process and the rights of an Englishman.

Gorton began the meteoric part of his strange career in Plymouth and swept successively through Portsmouth and Newport, Providence, Pawtuxet, and on to his final home in Shawomet. His difficulty with Plymouth authorities arose in part from their disregard for the legal forms and practices of English law.[2] Gorton was right in his contention, but it is also true that when strong hands were laid upon

---

[1] *Simplicities Defence,* Coll. R.I.H.S., II, 31.

[2] Winslow, *Hypocrisie Unmasked* (Chapin ed.), pp. vii, 55, 67. For Gorton's complaints against disregard of English law, see *Simplicities Defence,* Coll. R.I.H.S., II, 46-47, 80.

him, he displayed qualities which the popular mind associates with the radical agitator and gave vent to his spleen and voice to his principles in an outburst of vituperation and scandalous defiance. A similar incident occurred soon after his banishment and removal to Aquidneck. The Gortonists and the Hutchinson party, when they temporarily upset Coddington's regime, laid stress on obedience to English law.[3] In 1640 when Coddington reëstablished ascendancy over Portsmouth, Gorton once more found himself under an arbitrary government which violated the proprieties of English law. Again he ran amuck of the authorities and once more when strong hands were laid upon him employed language which was something less that subtle. He called the justices of the court "just Asses" and "corrupt Judges," demanded trial by English law, and compared his treatment with that at Plymouth where the magistrates "condemned him in the Chimney corner, ere they heard him speak." At the command to take him to prison he shouted out to take Coddington to prison. Coddington cried out instantly, "All you that owne the King, take away Gorton and carry him to prison." Gorton shouted in turn, "All you that owne the King, take away Coddington, and carry him to prison."[4]

As at Plymouth, Gorton received a lashing and was urged to move on. Early in 1641 he bobbed up in Providence, accompanied by Randall Holden and a train of followers, and soon by his mystical preachings made converts of Weston, Waterman, Greene, and several other Providence citizens. By the end of winter Williams was writing plaintively to Winthrop: "Master Gorton having foully abused both high and low at Aquidnick, is now bewitching and bemadding poor Providence." On grounds of civility Williams had reproved Gorton for his sharp censure of orthodox Puritan ministers. He also confessed privately to Winthrop that he could not sympathize with Gorton's denial of "all visible and external Ordinances."[5] A Seeker whose rational mind could be satisfied with nothing less than objective proof of the divine will could repose no confidence in the mystical ideas of Samuel Gorton. Williams "was for outward ordinances to be set up again by new apostles," explained the last of the Gortonists in 1771 to the president of Yale, whereas Gorton

---

3 Chapin, *Doc. Hist. R. I.*, II, 56-59.
4 Winslow, *Hypocrisie Unmasked* (Chapin ed.), pp. 54-55.
5 *Letters*, N.C.P., VI, 141.

"beat down all outward ordinances of Baptism and the Lord's Supper."[6]

Though Williams could not approve of the inner light of the Gortonists, it never occurred to him that whipping or banishment was the way to save the plantation. However, when Gorton asked grant by the town of the privilege of inhabitancy, without which he could not become a permanent resident, Williams, Arnold, and the majority opposed it. Under the terms of the Combination admission as an inhabitant would have opened the way to enfranchisement and rights in the land. Williams favored granting Gorton admission and "town privileges" if he pledged respect for authority and reformed the "uncivil" practices which got him in trouble at Portsmouth.[7] William Arnold disagreed with Williams and was determined to keep Gorton out regardless of any pledge of good conduct.

Following the rejection of their request for admission as townsmen, the Gortonists renewed the request and remained in Providence. In a public letter of May 25 William Arnold protested this as contempt of authority, assailed Gorton as a "turbulent person" who used "words unsufferable," and declared the intruders were "not fit persons" to be received under such a weak government.[8] Roger Williams, remembering Arnold's share in the maneuver to monopolize Pawtuxet and his confederation with Verin and slanders on the Providence government, may have detected insincerity in this plea for law and order. Arnold in his letter did in fact lay naked the real fear that haunted him: if the Gortonists remained, they might win a majority and "get the victory" over the rest of the townsmen, "specially of those that laid the first foundation of the place." Arnold had been, and was, a troublemaker himself; but after all he had been one of the patriarchs and had a vested interest in Pawtuxet to protect against newcomers.

In fairness to Gorton one should distinguish between the violence of his language and the moderation of his principles. Having smarted from the large, loose discretionary authority of arbitrary colonial governments, he believed in subjection to English law as a protection of civil rights. Nevertheless his application for citizenship indicated his willingness to submit to government under the Combination.

[6] *Coll. R.I.H.S.*, II, 19-20.
[7] *Letters*, N.C.P., VI, 142.
[8] Winslow, *Hypocrisie Unmasked* (Chapin ed.), pp. 59-62.

Gorton in fact thought so well of the Providence system of arbitration that he later adopted it at Shawomet and boasted of its virtues.[9]

The humanity of Williams and his associates in giving refuge to the Gortonists soon produced a situation which exhibited a weakness of government by social compact. "Mr. Williams and divers others," according to Edward Winslow, originally took the Gortonists in and treated them with "humane curtesie" because of the "sharpe" winter season. Once housed in the town, the six Gortonists from Aquidneck won over an equal number of Providence men. Although still a minority, their party was large enough so that it was "beyond the power" of the town either to rule them or "drive them out" except by threat of force. In consequence, related Winslow, Gorton "soone undermined their Government" and eventually, "to the great distraction of Mr. Williams, and the better party," contended "against their Laws, and the execution of Justice, to the effusion of blood."[10]

The effusion of blood occurred in a riot which broke out when the Gortonists resisted enforcement of a judgment for £15 against one of their members, Francis Weston. The case had been heard by eight arbitrators, as provided by the Combination, and on November 15 a body of the townsmen attempted to enforce the judgment. As they "went orderly, openly, and in a warrantable way" to attach some of Weston's cattle, Gorton and his followers met them in the street. The result was a "tumultuous Hubbub" during which "some few drops of blood were shed on either side." When order was restored the committee of enforcement made their way to Weston's cornfield to impound the cattle, but Weston came on the run flourishing a flail and crying for help. The rest of the Gortonists "came riotously running," calling the committee cattle stealers, and in the resulting melee drove off the cattle.[11] Both parties would have "fought it out, had not Mr. Williams used means for pacification."[12]

The upshot of this situation was the division of the Providence settlers into three factions: the Gortonists, the Williams party favoring peaceful conciliation, and a faction led by the Arnold clan and William Harris favoring intervention by Massachusetts. Two days after the riot some of the latter group addressed a plea asking the Bay

[9] *Simplicities Defence*, Coll. R.I.H.S., II, 96.
[10] Winslow, *Hypocrisie Unmasked* (Chapin ed.), Epistle dedicatory, and pp. 1, 54.
[11] *Ibid.*, p. 57.
[12] *Ibid.*, p. 1; Winthrop, *Journal*, II, 71.

colony to help "ease" Providence of the "burden" of the Gortonists. The authors of this letter, misrepresenting the principles of Gorton, charged him and his followers with desiring "no manner of honest order, or government." Not satisfied with calling them anarchists, Harris and his associates, like later red-baiters, also accused the Gortonists of a strong bent toward communism and free love. Unless restrained, they would contrive "cunningly to detaine things" and finally would seize the property of others; then "to maintain licentious lust, like savage brute beasts, they will put no manner of difference between houses, goods, lands, wives, lives, blood, nor any thing will bee precious in their eyes."[13]

This letter was written by Benedict Arnold[14] and signed by Harris, William Carpenter, and others of the Arnold faction. Roger Williams, Chad Brown, and the party of peaceful conciliation had no part in it. Williams, although opposed to Gorton, saw neither safety nor honor in reliance upon Massachusetts; and events were soon to indicate that his attitude was wise. Less than a third of the enfranchised citizens are known to have supported the plea to Massachusetts. The larger party seems to have supported Williams in the determination to find a solution without resort to an unsafe alliance with Massachusetts. The Bay authorities declined aid to the Providence red-baiters, but their reply was not reassuring to the Williams party. The magistrates were ready to intervene if the Providence settlers would simply submit themselves to their jurisdiction.[15] This suggestion was not long lost on William Arnold.

The Gorton episode furnished lively material for Rhode Island's detractors and served as perfect proof of the evil consequences of democracy and religious freedom. Edward Winslow made a masterly presentation of this argument, the 1649 edition of his tract bearing the significant title, "The Danger of Tolerating Levellers in a Civill State." The conduct of the Gortonists was, in truth, a serious test of Providence democracy, but such disorders were not chronic and except for new disturbances some fifteen years later, Providence maintained as good order as New England towns on other frontiers.[16]

Roger Williams and the party of peaceful conciliation soon

[13] Winslow, *Hypocrisie Unmasked* (Chapin ed.), p. 56.
[14] 3 *Coll. M.H.S.*, I, 4.
[15] Winthrop, *Journal*, II, 71.
[16] See study by Chapin, *Doc. Hist. R. I.*, I, 125, and *passim*.

scored a triumph, and for the first time Samuel Gorton departed from a New England plantation without the marks of the lash searing his back. Providence returned to its normal course, and the Combination and its system of arbitration continued to serve local needs. But there were a number of Providence citizens, Roger Williams among them, who had learned something from Samuel Gorton —that the time had come when a charter was imperative.

As winter came on the Gortonists moved to the land of John Greene on the west side of Pawtuxet where they built houses for their families. Even here they were to find no security. Before the spring of 1642 William Arnold, most ruthless of the Pawtuxet proprietors, concocted a neat stratagem to rid himself of his unwelcome neighbors and ingeniously acquire a claim to the possessions of others. His first step, in conjunction with his son-in-law, William Carpenter, and Robert Cole, was to obtain from Socononoco, the local chieftain, a spurious deed granting title to nearly half of the original Providence purchase and to all of Pawtuxet.[17] Subsequently Arnold mutilated Williams' Indian deed which the town had entrusted to him, cutting out the section relating to Pawtuxet, thereby destroying the evidence of the original title.[18] Arnold's second step was to take his cue from the Massachusetts magistrates and submit Pawtuxet to the jurisdiction of the Bay. On September 8, 1642, the Pawtuxet secessionists, Arnold, his son Benedict, Carpenter, and Cole were welcomed under the "government and protection" of Massachusetts and given commissions "to keepe the peace in their lands."[19] As a justice of the peace for the great northern colony Arnold could now eject the Gortonists and contest the jurisdiction of Providence over the whole of Pawtuxet.

The Massachusetts governor made a notation which would have interested his old friend Roger Williams. The ulterior object of the Bay's protectorate over Pawtuxet, confided Winthrop to his *Journal*, was "to draw in the rest of those parts, either under ourselves or Plimouth"; moreover the place was likely to be of use as an outpost against the Narragansetts and as an "outlet" for Massachusetts on Narragansett bay.[20]

17 Chapin, *Doc. Hist. R. I.*, I, 147.
18 *Ibid.*, I, 61-69.
19 Winthrop, *Journal*, II, 102; *Mass. Bay Recs.*, II, 26, 27.
20 *Journal*, II, 102.

For the imperial purposes of the saints William Arnold and his associates were unworthy but useful tools. Gorton considered Arnold "ill-bred, apostatized" and commented sardonically on his violation of the Massachusetts code by habitual Sabbath-breaking. Cole, likewise harboring contempt for the ordinances of his former persecutors and new protectors, was known to have declared that the heathen religion of the Indians was the same as that of Massachusetts! Gorton later reminded the Bay magistrates of what they conveniently forgot: they had cast out Robert Cole for scandalous offenses and compelled him "to wear a D on his back for a whole year" to stigmatize him for the sin of drunkenness. The Gortonists saw at once that such "subjects" were acceptable to the Bay magistrates only as a pretense for "stretching their line" southward to put an end to Rhode Island as "a refuge for such as were oppressed."[21]

As Williams and the moderates had feared, a menace more serious than the riot of the Gortonists had resulted from the appeal for Massachusetts aid. Meanwhile, eleven days after the secession of the Arnold men, the Aquidneck assembly, recognizing the immediate need of union with the Providence settlers, proposed consultation about a charter.[22] In the following spring Roger Williams was bound for England to procure a charter for all the settlements of Narragansett bay.

Denied the liberty of taking ship at Boston, Williams was "forced to repair unto the Dutch" and arrived at New Amsterdam just in time to witness the outbreak of a bloody conflict.[23] In February, 1643, the Dutch emulated the Massachusetts policy toward the Pequots and fell on the Mohawks to force them into submission. In retaliation the Mohawks carried the war into the white settlements and burned many houses. Williams found that the Dutch were bent on a war to the finish and when he offered to mediate, discovered that the notion of peace "was foolish and odious" to the aroused Dutchmen. The authorities of New Amsterdam were to regret their rashness. Before his ship weighed anchor, related Williams, "their bowries were in flames" and Dutch settlers and Long Island English were slain. "Mine eyes saw their flames at their towns, and the flights and hurries of men, women and children, the present removal of all

---

[21] *Simplicities Defence,* Coll. R.I.H.S., II, 48-52, 79.
[22] *R. I. Col. Recs.,* I, 125.
[23] *Letters,* N.C.P., VI, 272.

that could for Holland. . . ." After vast expense and four years of "mutual slaughters of Dutch, English and Indians," New Amsterdam was saved from ruin only by a patched-up peace with the Indians.[24]

While Williams waited a ship, the Mohawks were joined by the Indians of Long Island who slaughtered many of the English who had previously fled there from the intolerance of New England. Anne Hutchinson and her family, newly arrived from Aquidneck, perished at Hell Gate. Hard pressed, the Dutch were now glad to avail themselves of Williams' skill in Indian affairs, and he proceeded to mediate with the Long Island Indians and reëstablished peace between them and the Dutch. Williams himself never mentioned this achievement, but word of it came to Boston and Winthrop recorded it in his account of the war.[25]

On the voyage to the homeland he had not seen for thirteen years, Williams occupied his time in completing a work which was to be one of his most enduring contributions, a study of the native dialects and tribal lore and customs of New England Indians. Upon arrival in London, he faced a situation which portended little hope for the success of his mission. Laud and Charles had sown the dragon's teeth and armed men were now locked in mortal combat. Already Lord Strafford had been executed and the hated Laud confined in the Tower. Charles, fleeing from London, had raised his standard and at Edgehill turned on his pursuers in the first bloody encounter of the great civil war. Just as Williams arrived in London, the parliamentary leader, valiant John Hampden, fell mortally wounded on the field of battle. Amid such a mighty conflict, English authorities were likely to brush aside a small Rhode Island project as of slight importance.

Yet the menace to Rhode Island was becoming daily more acute and only a charter from the mother country could preserve its people from new persecutions. Even before Williams sailed for England, the dire threat implied in a warrant from Massachusetts scared off the Gortonists from their homes in Pawtuxet. On January 12, 1643, the twelve Gortonists purchased from the great sachem, Miantonomu, a large tract on the west shore of the bay ten or twelve miles south of Providence. One of the signers of the deed was Pomham,

[24] *Letters*, N.C.P., VI, 272-273
[25] *Journal*, II, 116-117.

chieftain of the small local tribe of Shawomets. As the Gortonists abandoned their Pawtuxet property to clear the forest at Shawomet and build houses anew, they sent a reply to the "irregular" warrant from Massachusetts. The Gortonists knew English law well enough to remind the Bay authorities that they had no "power to enlarge the bounds, by King Charles limited unto you."[26]

The illegality of claiming jurisdiction some twenty miles beyond their boundaries was no obstacle to men who in the name of God set their own power above the law of England. Shawomet was south even of the Pawtuxet line, but the Gortonists soon discovered that Governor Winthrop and his council had found a new excuse "to make an inroad" upon them. "Old malicious Arnold" and the other "low stringed instruments" of the Bay proceeded to "insinuate" themselves with Socononoco and Pomham. At Boston in June, 1643, with Benedict Arnold acting as interpreter, the Pawtuxet and Shawomet chieftains were persuaded to renounce allegiance to the Narragansett sachems and place their tribes and lands under Massachusetts jurisdiction.[27] Winthrop and his associates now had pretext for intervention both against Providence men and the despised Gortonists. In October, 1643, Massachusetts troops invaded Shawomet, rejected offers of arbitration, besieged the Gortonists for several days and took them captives and their cattle as booty. Banished from their own homes, the wives and children of the Shawomet settlers were left to shift for themselves over the winter while their husbands were clapped in irons and incarcerated in scattered Massachusetts towns.

Thus before Roger Williams in England had so much as gained a hearing, the fears which sent him overseas had rapidly materialized. To the minds of the Bay leaders, England's distress was Massachusetts' opportunity. In May, soon after Williams sailed, the orthodox colonies formed the New England Confederacy, presenting a solid phalanx against the generous liberalism to which Rhode Island was dedicated. Rhode Island, to these Puritans of the Confederation, was a land of lost souls, whither fled all the perverse, unmannerly, ignorant, and irreligious, the schismatics and unbelievers, drunkards and insolvents, agitators and radicals; a land of the bewitched and the damned: where Anne Hutchinson and her sister-in-law gave birth

---

[26] *Simplicities Defence*, Coll. R.I.H.S., II, 60, 62, 83 n.
[27] *Ibid.*, p. 92; 3 *Coll. M.H.S.*, I, 5-7.

to strange monsters; where the souls of all men were certain to be imperiled, and where God's grace was like to fall on no man. The duty of the godly was manifest, the power of Laud broken, Charles I in hopeless conflict with parliament, and the way was now clear for the imperial advance of the ubiquitous saints.

Upon Roger Williams' skill as a negotiator hung the fate of the few straggling plantations which had dared to believe in the common man and to disbelieve in castes or creeds which sundered men from their fellows.

11

DICKERING FOR A CHARTER

THE PURITAN REVOLUTION PRESENTED WILLIAMS with what was at once an opportunity and a gamble. His Essex friends and their powerful connections might gain him a favorable hearing before the revolutionary leaders; but of what avail an irregular patent from parliament if the king should win? Thus the fate of his mission hung upon the success of English squires and merchants in their struggle for power.

Williams consulted at once with his old patron, Sir William Masham, and Sir Thomas Barrington, but though their influence would count with their kinsmen, Oliver St. John and Cromwell, parliamentary leaders were too distracted in the summer of 1643 to deal with colonies. In the eastern counties Cromwell was building a model regiment soon famous as the Ironsides. Sir Henry Vane, already prominent in the councils of the revolutionaries, had scarce time to greet Roger Williams before leaving London on great affairs of state.

The gods of battle were smiling on the king's arms, and as the summer waned London burghers watched the clouds of war rolling up steadily more ominously about the metropolis. At the end of June the Fairfaxes were routed and northern England lay at the king's mercy. In July the parliamentary forces under Sir William Waller were cut to pieces in the west, and Prince Rupert took Bristol, the second seaport of the realm. Many voices cried for peace, even in the House of Commons, and on August 10 the desperate revolutionaries, unable to enlist in their cause large masses of the people, pushed through an ordinance for compulsory recruitment. With three quarters of England under royalist sway, alarm gripped the capital lest the triumphant columns of the king's forces converge on the metropolis simultaneously from the north, west, and south. Hastily parliamentary adherents, Williams perhaps one of them, rallied the faint-hearted; a crusade was preached throughout the city, the prentices were mustered and the shops closed as London turned out to wish Godspeed to her famous train-bands. Six sturdy regiments marched out to reinforce the beleaguered troops under the hesitant Essex and fight their way across England to raise the siege of Gloucester and prevent the convergence of the royalist armies. Meanwhile on August 8, Sir Henry Vane, conferring in Edinburgh with Scottish leaders, sued for military aid from the northern kingdom.

Since a charter was out of the question for the moment, Williams completed his study of the Indian language. Very likely it was John Milton,[1] now devoting his great literary talents to the production of inspired pamphlets for the parliamentary cause, or another of the inner circle of radical Puritans with whom Vane associated, who directed him to a printer. Gregory Dexter, a radical Baptist, was Milton's printer and he became Williams'. On September 7, 1643, bearing the imprint of Dexter's press, Roger Williams' *Key into the Language of America* appeared in London bookstalls. To Lady Judith, wife of Sir Thomas Barrington, the author promptly presented an inscribed copy.[2]

His *Key,* declared Williams, was intended to "unlocke" the Indian language and "some Rarities concerning the natives themselves."[3] A pioneer work, it proved a storehouse of information to all who came after. Systematically arranged with appropriate vocabularies accompanying each of its thirty-two chapters, it ranged with an anthropologist's curiosity over the Indians' diet, family life, housing, and tribal mores, including chapters on "their Nakednesse and clothing," "their Government," religion, trading, "Debts and Trusting," sports, hunting, and war. In a chapter on coin, Williams told how shell money became an inflated currency and childlike natives bedevilled him to explain the white man's mysterious economic laws by which "for English commodities they pay so much more" than they received for their own. When beaver fell on the English market, the Indians cried "the English cheat and deceive them."[4]

Native hospitality, strong family affection, and communal concern for the unfortunate won Williams' praise. "There are no beggars amongst them, nor fatherless children unprovided for."[5] The Puritan in Williams led him to feel that overly affectionate Indian fathers

---

[1] H. M. Chapin, "Gregory Dexter," *Coll. R.I.H.S.,* XII, 105-121; G. R. Potter, "Roger Williams and John Milton," *ibid.,* XIII, 113-129.

[2] *Coll. R.I.H.S.,* XIII, 104.

[3] *Key into the Language of America,* Coll. R.I.H.S., I, 17.

[4] *Ibid.,* p. 129.

[5] *Ibid.,* p. 45.

spared the rod and spoiled the child. But he admired the natives' skill with a dugout in rough water, their woodcraft, endurance, and communal spirit. When a new field was to be cultivated, they had "a very loving sociable speedy way to dispatch it": all the neighbors, men and women, forty or a hundred or more, "come in to helpe freely."[6]

A thoroughgoing liberal, Williams found in his copper-skinned friends neither the noble savage nor the contemptible offspring of an inferior race. "Nature knowes no difference," he declared, between Europeans and Indians, "God having of one blood made all mankind. Acts 17." To point this sound biological conclusion, he added several lines of verse:

> Boast not proud English, of thy birth and blood
> Thy Brother Indian is by birth as Good.[7]

Thus through broadly understanding eyes England was introduced to the natives of New England—and Puritans in the homeland began to ask why, if the savage was so human and approachable, had few other than Williams labored amongst them.

Upon his arrival in London Williams had visited his family. Soon after his new book appeared, he and his brother Sydrach commenced a lawsuit against the third brother, Robert, and several of his associates. When Mrs. Williams died in 1634, she left legacies to her sons, Sydrach £100 and Roger £200, to be paid over a period of years. After the mother's death Robert Williams, executor of the estate, traveled abroad as a merchant and "being beyond the Seas failed in Creditt and became unexpectedly much impoverished." With one brother in America and the other in the Levant, he discovered a ready means to relieve him of his misfortunes and "confederated" with the overseers of the will to appropriate the income from the estate of Alice Williams. Failing to get satisfaction from the conspirators, Sydrach and Roger Williams initiated a suit in chancery. The case, however, was soon continued and did not come up for final judgment until the summer of 1644.[8]

Sydrach and Roger exchanged anecdotes of strange peoples and

---

[6] *Ibid.*, p. 92.

[7] *Ibid.*, p. 61.

[8] S. S. Rider, "The Ancestry of Roger Williams," *Book Notes*, XXIX (Providence, 1912), no. 11, pp. 83-86; no. 12, pp. 89-93.

high excitements which they had encountered. The elder brother, prospering as a merchant taylor, had traveled widely, marketing serges and other fine products of English guilds in Italy and Turkey. To match Roger's stories of Massachusetts Puritans and copper-colored savages, he could relate the tales of old tars who had sailed to Greenland and tell of his purchase of "sea horse teeth," of the arctic walrus, which he had shipped to Constantinople. One rare prize which he had acquired awakened in his brother the envy of a bibliophile; long afterward Roger recalled how Sydrach showed him "the Old Testament of the Jews, most curious writing," which had cost £60.[9] Sydrach had suffered great losses during the war between France and Spain and had run afoul of persecutors when he went to Italy to straighten out his affairs. Matching Roger's account of his inquisition at the hands of Massachusetts Puritans, Sydrach could tell of similar treatment at the hands of the Papists—his seizure and imprisonment "by the Inquisition at Milan."[10]

Several weeks after Williams commenced the suit in chancery, Sir Henry Vane returned from Edinburgh with a treaty of alliance to bring the armed might of Presbyterian Scotland upon the back of Charles. Years before when Williams was banished, Vane, newly arrived in Massachusetts, had favored strict discipline, but when his Antinomian friends were expelled he looked with different eyes upon the policy of persecution. He had not forgotten the year of his governorship in Massachusetts when Williams had served him wholeheartedly in the stirring days of the Pequot war, nor had he forgotten his own subsequent humiliation at the hands of the Bay oligarchy. The two men, as Robert Baillie noted, soon developed a "great friendship," and in after years Williams alluded affectionately to "that truly noble Sir Henry Vane" as chiefly instrumental in furthering his suit for a charter.[11]

The time was not ripe in the fall of 1643 to press for a charter and both Vane and Williams became absorbed in a great internal conflict which eventually split the ranks of the revolutionists. Down from Edinburgh came the Solemn League and Covenant, a good Scotch bargain which neither Vane nor Williams could relish but

[9] *George Fox Digged*, N.C.P., V, 146.

[10] *N.E.H.G.R.*, XLIII (1889), 427; LXXV (1921), 234-235; LXXXVIII (1934), 387.

[11] Baillie, *Dissuasive*, p. 63; *Williams' testimony, 1658*, N.C.P., VI, 306.

which English Puritans must accept as the price of the Scottish alliance. As the Anglican hierarchy was harried from the land, its place would be taken by "a new clericalism, Laud with a Scotch accent."[12] The Scottish army might withdraw if the war were successful, but the Scottish kirk must remain.

On August 26 the Solemn League and Covenant was presented to parliament for ratification. Parliamentary liberals swallowed the bitter medicine, trusting to Vane's sly reservation that the new reformation should be founded directly on the "Word of God" rather than explicitly on the practice of the Scots. On September 25, under the relentless prodding of the brethren from Scotland, the House of Commons and the assembly of Puritan clerics at Westminster swore to the covenant. With the great body of authoritarian English Puritans now rallying to their support, the intolerant majority in the Westminster assembly hailed a modified Presbyterianism as a bulwark against the rapidly growing left-wing sects and laid plans for a rigid national church either on the New England model or in the image of the Scottish kirk. The Independents, led by Vane, Oliver St. John, Cromwell, Haselrig, in whose circle Williams now moved, perceived the dire threat to latitude for dissenters and maneuvered skilfully in parliament and the Westminster assembly to block the Presbyterians. Meanwhile the alarm sounded and the radical sects rallied to the cause of Independency and religious toleration.

These events were enough to stir Roger Williams to defense of his own radical vision of full religious liberty, but as if to add to the provocation there appeared in London bookstores in the fall of 1643 a personal challenge from overseas New England. In *A Letter of Mr. John Cotton to Mr. Williams,* the great spokesman for the New England model took Williams severely to task, extenuated his banishment and defended coercive orthodoxy. It was not surgery "but Butchery," said Cotton, "to heale every sore in a member with no other medicine but abscission from the body."[13] Issued at such a moment, Cotton's pamphlet furnished the supporters of the Westminster assembly with strong arguments against Separatists and toleration of dissent.

The gauntlet had been thrown, and Williams immediately set to

---

12 John Buchan, *Oliver Cromwell,* Houghton Mifflin Co. (Boston, 1934), p. 151.
13 *N.C.P.,* I, 309.

work on a series of bristling tracts which were to win him fame among the ranks of the revolutionists. Much of his writing was done under great difficulty, for as cold weather gripped London, Williams found another outlet for his abundant energies. With the king's forces occupying the north and west, the supply of coal from New-castle was cut off and the people of London shivered in cold houses. A broad-sheet of the time, advertising a scheme of an enterprising quack, recommended an artificial substitute for coal as a means to prevent thievery by those that "never stole before" but who now appropriated "posts, seats, benches from doors, rails, nay, the very stocks that punish them."[14] Williams, who witnessed "the mutinies of the poor for firing," devoted himself to a more disinterested means of relieving the distress. During the hard winter his time was "eaten up" by serving parliament and the municipality, ranging about the countryside superintending "the supply of the poor of the City with wood"; and he was forced to gather his "loose thoughts and papers" and snatch odd moments for writing "in change of rooms and corners" and sometimes in the fields in the midst of travel.[15]

As the winter months came on, Williams at last had opportunity to petition for a charter. The Scottish alliance immeasurably strengthened the parliamentary cause, and although the issue was still uncertain, parliament encroached further on royal prerogative by assuming authority which had gone by default in the turmoil of war. Holding the key to the colonies through control of the fleet, parliament in November, 1643, established new imperial machinery and named the Earl of Warwick the governor-in-chief and lord high admiral of English plantations. Among the members of the commission were Vane and several Independents friendly to Williams : War-wick himself, Lord Saye and Sele, Sir Arthur Haselrig, Cornelius Holland and Cromwell.[16]

Williams scarcely had time to congratulate himself before his hopes were dashed by a sudden onslaught from an unexpected quar-ter. Seizing the main chance, Massachusetts planned a bold coup to legalize its recent seizure of the Gortonists, consolidate its position in Pawtuxet and Shawomet, and extend its jurisdiction over all

14 Masson, *Milton,* III, 36-37.
15 *N.C.P.,* IV, 103-104.
16 *Cal. State Papers, Col., 1574-1660,* p. 324.

Rhode Island. Since 1641 Thomas Weld had been in London as agent for the colony and now, striking quickly with all the prestige and influence of the governor and company of Massachusetts bay, he petitioned for a patent to the lands of Narragansett bay. Massachusetts authorities might well be confident of an easy victory, for their colony was orthodox and highly advertised, while the Rhode Island settlers were relatively unknown and reputed to be sunk into chaotic sectarianism.

Fate gave the small, radical Rhode Island settlements an advantage. On December 8, 1643, the moderate chieftain of the revolution, John Pym, died and the two great Independents, Vane, a republican with democratic leanings, and St. John, a man with little respect for monarchy, became the most powerful leaders in parliament. Vane, as Williams declared, became the "sheet anchor" of Rhode Island's hopes; among the twelve commoners on Warwick's commission he alone had been in America and his influence would probably outweigh all others'.

Unwittingly Williams provided one of the strongest arguments in his own behalf. As the commissioners and other members of parliament read his recently published *Key into the Indian Language,* his prestige grew rapidly and his fame spread as a missionary among the Indians. Puritans in the mother country had long been disappointed at the failure of New England to convert the natives. A year before, 1642, Thomas Lechford, speaking with authority as a former Massachusetts resident, charged that there had been "and is much neglect of endeavours, to teach, civilize, and convert the Indian Nation." No one had been sent out by the churches to learn the natives' language or to give them Christian teaching: "First, because they say they have not to do with them being without, unlesse they come to heare and learn English."[17]

Roger Williams' substantial account of tribal life and customs and study of the native tongue brought assurance that at least one of those who had gone to New England with high professions had harkened to the Macedonian cry. Before long, John Eliot was to undertake endeavors as notable as Williams', but as late as 1645 Robert Baillie remarked sourly that "of all that ever crossed the American seas," the Puritans of New England had most neglected

[17] *Plain Dealing,* 3 Coll. M.H.S., III, 80, 109.

the work of conversion. "I have read of none of them that seem to have minded this matter: onely Williams in the time of his banishment from among them, did assay what could be done with those desolate souls, and by a little experience quickly did finde a wonderful great facility to gain thousands of them. . . ."[18] This high reputation gave Williams a distinct advantage in his plea before the commission.

Thomas Weld, who had done nothing for the natives, proved himself for all that no mean adversary. Some time between November 24 and March 14, by means never wholly explained, he persuaded nine of the commission to sign his proposed patent. This document, the so-called Narragansett patent, was a masterpiece of special pleading. Massachusetts, it affirmed, was already overpopulated and its original boundaries would soon "bee too streight and narrow." Weld and his supporters, alleging this with their tongues in their cheeks, also took care to insert a wily allusion to the unredeemed paganism of Narragansett tribes and the heterodoxy of their neighbors, the Rhode Island English. Annexation of Rhode Island by Massachusetts would permit orthodox gospel to be "conveyed and preached to the natives that now sitte there in darknes" and would bring the English there under "God's true Religion" by extension of the Massachusetts ecclesiastical system.[19]

The Narragansett patent presents a critical problem. For formal approval Weld needed the endorsement of only one more member of the commission. The signatures on the patent appear in irregular order and suggest that Weld, employing the devious arts of a lobbyist, sought out individual members of the commission at varying times and managed to induce nine of them to sign. Rhode Island representatives asserted to the government of Charles II that the Weld patent was obtained by "under-hand" methods and was invalid, "being never passed the council-table nor registered."[20] Weld eventually forwarded the document to Massachusetts where it became the basis of a claim to Rhode Island, but since it was never formally

---

[18] *Dissuasive*, p. 60. Baillie calls attention to Lechford's criticism; *ibid.*, p. 69. See also the appreciation of Williams in Thoroughgood's *Jews in America* (London, 1651).

[19] The text of the Narragansett patent has been printed in *N.E.H.G.R.*, XI (1857), 41-43.

[20] *R. I. Col. Recs.*, II, 162.

enrolled, lacked seals, and bore a forged date, December 10, 1643, the Massachusetts claim was fraudulent.[21]

As a shrewd piece of propaganda to bolster his cause, Weld sent a sizzling manuscript of Winthrop's to the press. Appearing by February 10, 1644, under the title, *A Short Story of the Rise, reign, and ruine of the Antinomians,* this book made a biting attack upon the "Antinomians, Familists and Libertines" who had infected Massachusetts Bay and related how they were "confuted" by the ministers and magistrates. Containing the story of the monstrous birth of Mary Dyer, it was the least creditable of Winthrop's writings, and Weld perhaps did a kindness in keeping the authorship anonymous. The preface, written by Weld, gave an account of "the lamentable death" of Anne Hutchinson and her family at the hands of the Indians and drew the lesson of the wrath of God against fomenters of heresy. The abominations pictured in the *Short Story* caught popular attention and the work was republished several times, becoming a storehouse of arguments for those who pleaded for compulsory uniformity.

On February 5, just before this damning picture of Rhode Island came from the press, Williams, engaging in publicity on the opposite side, published *Mr. Cotton's Letter Examined and Answered.* A month earlier the five Independent divines in the Westminster assembly had precipitated the most heated and portentous religious controversy England had yet known[22] and on January 3 published the *Apologetical Narration,* posing the crucial question of what degree of compulsion would be required by the new national church. The issue was publicly joined and all minority parties, fearing Presbyterian intolerance, rallied to the Independents. Williams' reply to Cotton became at once a part of the great contest over toleration. But where the five dissenting divines asked only for latitude for tender consciences within the framework of the new national church, Williams justified separation and sectarianism, affirming an absolute right to free private judgment.

On February 9 Williams sounded forth another blast on his "despised ram's horn," his second challenge in a resolute campaign

---

21 See Thomas Aspinwall, "The Narragansett Patent," *Proc. M.H.S., 1862-1863,* pp. 41-77.

22 W. K. Jordan, *The Development of Religious Toleration in England,* vol. III (Cambridge, 1938), pp. 44-53.

for England's liberation. His *Queries of Highest Consideration,*[23] which he cast into the halls of debate at this critical juncture, established him as one of the most effective pamphleteers in the rising host. Modest in size and anonymous as to authorship, it dodged no issues and spoke directly to those whom it wished to convince. It was addressed, in three separate dedications, to the five Independents, to the Presbyterian divines from Scotland, and—for good measure —to parliament itself. Going far beyond the *Apologetical Narration* and striking at the roots of both Presbyterianism and New England Congregationalism, Williams contended vigorously for entire separation of church and state, declaring without equivocation that it would never be possible to fit one church to every conscience because the only conceivable result would be "a world of hypocrites" and a "wracking and tormenting" of souls.

Williams' *Queries,* although addressed to the public conflict between the rival Puritan and sectarian ideologies, bore, as did Weld's edition of the *Short Story,* a subtle relevance to the contest for a charter. How Warwick and his commission regarded the religious question would affect profoundly their decision as between Thomas Weld and Roger Williams. Seven months later on his return to New England Williams presented to the Bay magistrates a letter which cited approvingly Williams' Indian labors and expressed regret at the differences between Williams and the Bay and hope for greater tolerance.[24] Among its signers were Lord Wharton, Miles Corbet, and Cornelius Holland, who also approved and signed Williams' charter. Holland, who had once been in the service of Sir Henry . Vane, Sr., supported Williams as actively as the son of his old employer and remained in after years a warm friend of Rhode Island. One of the peers on the commission, Lord Saye and Sele, was also a member of the circle where Williams' reputation was high and, like Lord Wharton, refused to approve Weld's patent and signed Williams'. Both Wharton and Saye had opposed the Solemn League and Covenant in the House of Lords and as lay members of the Westminster assembly were now in alliance with Vane, St. John, and the growing body of Independents, contending for toleration.

The influence of Vane, Wharton, and Saye was probably decisive in winning over Sir Arthur Haselrig and the Earl of Warwick who

[23] Reprinted in *N.C.P.,* II.
[24] Winthrop, *Journal,* II, 236-238.

had previously signed the Weld patent. Lord Saye had been closely connected with Haselrig in the Saybrook colony and with Warwick in the Providence company. Warwick, as an old associate of Sir William Masham and Sir Thomas Barrington, was likely to hear good opinions of Williams, and he had also other reasons for favoring Rhode Island. Because of his efforts to divert colonists to the West Indies, he had had a tilt with Massachusetts, and his sympathy for the Bay colony had waned as reports of her intolerance came back to England. To the signatures of Warwick, Saye, Wharton, Haselrig, Holland, Corbet, and Vane were added those of Lord Pembroke, never a man of deep convictions, and three lesser figures.

On March 14, 1644, Williams had his charter at last; a charter very different from that of Massachusetts bay, one in which the way was left open for democracy and in which civil power over ecclesiastical affairs was significantly absent. The Narragansett bay settlements were granted full power to rule themselves by whatever form of "Civil" government "as by voluntary consent of all, or the greater Part of them, they shall find most suitable."[25] In after years the general assembly of Rhode Island declared that freedom of conscience had been requested in Williams' "sute" for the charter and had been the "true intent" of those who granted it.[26]

Williams remained some months yet in England and his homeland was to hear more blasts of revolutionary gospel from the ram's horn. By March, 1644, English presses were groaning as the war of the pamphleteers raged over an ever broadening field. The Presbyterian phalanx in the Westminster assembly looked with dread on the cry for toleration and on February 29 Adam Steuart, a Scottish member, attacked bitterly even the mild latitude of the *Apologetical Narration*.[27] Late in March a hard-headed English merchant, Henry Robinson, published anonymously a pragmatic condemnation of intolerance as harmful to business enterprise.[28] On May 3 John Goodwin replied to Steuart in defense of the five Independent divines in the assembly.[29] A month later authoritarian Puritans of the Congregational persuasion rejoiced as their great champion, John Cotton, entered the lists. Cotton's celebrated tract, *The Keyes of the King-*

---

[25] *R. I. Col. Recs.*, I, 145.
[26] *Ibid.*, I, 378 f.
[27] *Some Observations upon the Apologeticall Narration* (London, 1644).
[28] *Liberty of Conscience* (London, 1644).
[29] *M. S. to A. S.* (London, 1644).

dom of Heaven, became the indispensable handbook for those who wanted a national church on the New England model. Finally on July 15 appeared *The Bloudy Tenent of Persecution for Cause of Conscience,* published anonymously but soon known as Williams'.

This famous tract, a passionate assault on persecution and flaming defense of a noble vision of religious liberty and free government, exploded the vast body of apologetics by which persecutors put the gloss of piety upon acts of brutality, stupidity, and avarice. Quoting Bacon, Williams stigmatized those who upheld "pressure" of conscience as "guided therein by some private interests of their owne."[30] His definition of persecution cut the ground from under the equivocators.[31] In passages rising to fiery eloquence, he warned reasonable men against the folly contemplated by English Puritans and Scottish Presbyterians; of what avail to throw off one species of intolerance and place the neck of the people in the yoke of another? Here was not merely another plea for toleration of lesser differences. *The Bloudy Tenent* made a devastating frontal attack on the hoary principle of a national church, summoned all humane men to stand firm for separation of church and state, and struck with impassioned conviction for religious liberty as a matter of *right.*

To justify such revolutionary proposals, Williams resorted to an equally radical political philosophy. Government was man-made; it rested on consent of the governed and existed for the common peace and welfare of the people—"so farre as concernes their Bodies and Goods."[32] Since government was by nature humane and civil, "it must consequently be of a humane and Civill operation."[33] Secular authorities were bound to promote civic virtue, but it was an abomination if they confused good citizenship with religious sanctification.[34] Magistrates or rulers were not stewards of the Lord but civil servants of the people;[35] their duty toward religion was to protect the right of the citizen to freedom of worship, not to determine whether the citizen's religion was true or false.[36]

[30] *The Bloudy Tenent,* N.C.P., III, 9.
[31] See the excellent appraisal on this and other points by W. K. Jordan, *Religious Toleration,* III, 489 and *passim.*
[32] *The Bloudy Tenent,* N.C.P., III, 249, 364.
[33] *Ibid.,* 372.
[34] *Ibid.,* 170-172, 246-247.
[35] *Ibid.,* 161-162, 343, 354-355, 398.
[36] *Ibid.,* 129, 372-373.

These demands for a secular state Williams grounded solidly on his deep faith in the common man and the power of reason in a free people; and on page after page he drove home the revolutionary democratic doctrine that governments derived their powers solely from consent of the governed:

> From this Grant I infer . . . that the Soveraigne, originall, and foundation of civill power lies in the people. . . . And if so, that a People may erect and establish what forme of Government seemes to them most meete for their civill condition: It is evident that such Governments as are by them erected and established, have no more power, nor for no longer time, then the civill power or people consenting and agreeing shall betrust them with. This is cleere not only in Reason, but in the experience of all commonweales, where the people are not deprived of their naturall freedome by the power of Tyrants.[37]

These memorable phrases were soon seized upon by political radicals among the people and in the army, but the Puritan squirearchy shrank in horror from such leveling doctrine. Parliament found the book pernicious and ordered it burned. Two editions subsequently escaped the vigilance of the censor and found a widening audience. In the ensuing years *The Bloudy Tenent* was to be attacked and applauded, but not forgotten. Together with William Walwyn, John Lilburne and others of the radical school, Roger Williams was to have a large share in pressing England forward in her great march toward democracy.

Williams added to his reputation as a radical by preaching to the left-wing elements among London Independents, and soon the English Presbyterian, Richard Baxter, berated him as "father of the Seekers." The Seekers of London were among the most individualistic of the many sects spawned by the Civil War. Their principles had appeared in England earlier, but as a recognized group the Seekers were new and Williams was soon regarded as their outstanding sponsor. In the summer of 1644 Robert Baillie remarked that his "good acquaintance Mr. Roger Williams" had drawn a great number to a "singular Independencie," denying there were any true churches and urging "every man to serve God by himselfe alone, without any church at all." Williams' agitations "made a great and

---

[37] *Ibid.*, 249-250; see also pp. 214, 297, 355, 366-367, 418.

bitter schisme" and many of the Independents left the English church.[38]

Baillie attacked Williams' ideas with forthright bitterness, but he knew Williams personally and seems to have conceived both liking and respect for him. The great Scottish divine, pressing forcefully in the Westminster assembly for Presbyterianism in England, hated New England Congregationalism as strongly as Williams. He talked often with the Rhode Island agent and gathered information about New England which he later employed shrewdly in attacking the theories both of Cotton and of Williams. On May 17, 1644, having heard that some of the Boston magistrates favored the death penalty for the Gortonists, Baillie declared that "only they in New England are more strict and rigid than we, or any Church, to suppresse, by the power of the magistrates, all who are not of their way, to banishment ordinarilie, and lately, even presently to death. . . ."[39]

Williams deferred return to Rhode Island pending settlement of his suit in chancery. On June 21, 1644, the court decreed that "Roger Williams should have noe benefitt" of the proceedings and adjudged him in contempt because he refused to answer according to the court's order.[40] The court had ordered Williams to take oath. Long afterwards Williams informed the Quakers that he agreed with their objection to oaths and could tell them how "in the Chancery in England" he had chosen to bear "the loss of great Sums" rather than play hypocrite with his conscience.[41]

After failure of the chancery suit Williams wound up his affairs and took ship for New England, anxious to see his family and his infant son, Joseph, whom Mary Williams had borne during his absence. With him went Robert Williams, the brother he had just sued, and Gregory Dexter who had printed his book on the Indians. A tract printed by Dexter had brought down the wrath of the parliamentary censors and in consequence the last work to issue from his press was *An Almanack for Providence Plantations in New England for 1644.*[42] Roger Williams had made one more convert to his broad notions of liberty, and Providence was to be the refuge of a master printer from Stationer's Hall.

[38] *Letters and Journals* (Edinburgh, 1841-1842), II, 191-192, 205.
[39] *Ibid.*, 183.
[40] S. S. Rider, *Book Notes,* XXIX (1912), p. 90.
[41] *George Fox Digged,* N.C.P., V, 412-413.
[42] *Coll. R.I.H.S.,* XII, 120.

12

NABOTH'S VINEYARD

On September 17, 1644, Roger Williams disembarked at Boston. By landing on Massachusetts soil Williams defied the sentence of banishment, but he nevertheless coolly requested a safe conduct to Rhode Island, presenting a letter in his behalf signed by prominent lords and commoners, including Northumberland, Wharton, Oliver St. John, Sir William Masham, and Thomas Barrington.[1] The letter spoke of Williams' "good affections," his sufferings at the hands of the prelates, and "his great industry and travail in his printed Indian labours in your parts, the like whereof we have not seen extant from any part of America," and expressed sorrow at the disagreement which had cut Williams off from the Bay colony. The signers bespoke their "great desires" of utmost endeavors for a reconciliation.

This mild reproof came from men whom they respected, but the Bay authorities received it coolly. Williams' old friend Endecott, now governor, and his associates, Dudley, Bellingham, and others, "saw no reason to condemn themselves for any former proceedings against Mr. Williams," nor any reason to concede "free liberty of ingress and egress."[2] Nevertheless, for this once, they allowed him to pass through their territory.

The unpleasant chill of Williams' reception in Boston was dissipated in the warmth of his welcome on reaching Rhode Island. At Seekonk a flotilla of fourteen canoes with friends from Providence gave him a rousing homecoming, and the whole flotilla escorted him across the river to Providence with Williams "hemmed in in the middle" in the place of honor.[3] A few weeks later the general assembly of the colony met for the first time and Williams was elected as "chief officer," a position equivalent to that of governor. Records of early proceedings have perished but apparently the assembly first met in November, 1644, and held subsequent

[1] Winthrop, *Journal*, II, 236-237.
[2] Hubbard, *History*, 2 Coll. M.H.S., VI, 349.
[3] George Fox, *A New-England Fire-Brand Quenched*, II, 247.

meetings in May and August, 1645, and May, 1646. Through the period down to 1647 when the colonial government was established on a more lasting basis, Williams continued to hold the chief office.[4] Coddington's aristocratic faction held aloof, but democratic leaders in the Aquidneck settlements cooperated with the men of Providence and Shawomet. The Gortonists renamed their town Warwick in testimony of their gratitude for the charter, and Samuel Gorton, though still anathematized by Coddington, was welcomed by the party of union and served under Williams as one of the commissioners.[5]

The new colony had to struggle to maintain its existence. It was soon evident that the cool reception given Williams at Boston was based on more than the oligarchy's fear that free ingress into Massachusetts might result in the spread of Rhode Island heresies. Hopeful of the triumph of orthodox Puritanism in England, the United Colonies were driving ahead impetuously on a course of imperial expansion, contesting the claims of Gorges and Mason northward in New Hampshire and Maine and of Rhode Islanders and the Dutch on the south and southwest. In July, 1643, when Williams was in England, a war between Uncas of the Mohegans and Sequasson, tributary of the Narragansetts, provided opportunity for Haynes, Winthrop, and Bradford to push their design to obtain suzerainty over all Rhode Island.

The great sachem Miantonomu had long chafed at the desertion of tributaries who, under the encouragement and protection of Connecticut, Massachusetts, and Plymouth, renounced their obligations to the Narragansetts. Realizing that only energetic assertion of its power could maintain the integrity of his tribe, Miantonomu at last determined to put an end to the intrigues of Uncas, ally of Connecticut. In accordance with his treaty commitments, he inquired whether the United Colonies would object if he dealt with Uncas by force of arms. Haynes and Winthrop replied that if the Mohegans had given injury and refused justice he was free to fight it out. This solemn assurance by the great white fathers was to prove the sheerest hypocrisy, and when Miantonomu took the warpath Hooker hailed the opportunity to humble the Narragansetts.[6]

[4] "Early Sessions of the General Assembly," *Coll. R.I.H.S.,* XIV, 7; Chapin, *Doc. Hist. R. I.,* I, 219, 221-231, 238.

[5] Chapin, *ibid.,* 221-223, 225, 256-257, 260.

[6] Mather, *Magnalia,* I, 312.

By intrigues of the very sort which Miantonomu sought to avenge, the wily Uncas won the battle. The great Narragansett sachem, betrayed by some of his own tributaries, was defeated and captured. The sequel is well known. The commissioners of the United Colonies, meeting at Boston, took under advisement the question of whether Miantonomu deserved execution. It was a consummation devoutly to be wished, but there was the troublesome question of law: they had "no civil ground to put him to death." There was, however, another way of attaining the same result. Five of the most "judicious elders," called in for advice, rose to the occasion and found a higher sanction for immediate execution. The commissioners thereupon handed Miantonomu over to the tender care of Uncas with full knowledge of the inevitable. The Mohegans, accompanied by some of the Connecticut settlers, took Miantonomu from his prison in Hartford. A brother of Uncas came up suddenly upon Miantonomu from behind and buried a hatchet in his head. Thus was set an early and interesting precedent for judicial murder in New England history.

The hostility of the Puritan colonies toward the Narragansetts was a matter of policy and not of principle. Security against a powerful tribe was the ostensible object. But the Narragansetts were a relatively peaceful confederacy, willing to negotiate, and deeply impressed with the power of the English. By contrast, the policy of the militant Puritans was an interesting foreshadowing of the later devices of imperialism by which world powers were to penetrate into backward regions by playing off one group of natives against another and assuming protection over that particular group which favored their enterprise. Plymouth "protected" Massasoit and his Wampanoags, former tributaries of the Narragansetts, and whittled away the power of the Rhode Island Indians on the east. After Miantonomu's death Plymouth laid claim to suzerainty over Pomham and the Shawomets. Without sanction of a charter, Connecticut laid claim to lands of the conquered Pequots and reached out toward the western hunting grounds of the Narragansetts. Simultaneously the long arm of Massachusetts was stretching forth to encourage the defection of the natives at Pawtuxet and Shawomet and to utilize William Arnold and the Pawtuxet secessionists as an advance guard for the imperial saints.

In October, 1643, within a few weeks of Miantonomu's death,

Massachusetts seized and imprisoned the Shawomet settlers. The magistrates soon found they had caught a Tartar. Even in chains a Gortonist had the use of his voice and the authorities discovered that Gorton would be less dangerous to orthodoxy when at liberty in Rhode Island than while a captive in Massachusetts. Released after a winter in irons, the Gortonists returned to Rhode Island, reporting that the sermons they were forced to hear in Massachusetts were meat fit to be digested only by an ostrich.[7] Their release had been accompanied by a stern warning that on pain of death they were to keep out of Pawtuxet and Shawomet, both of which were subject to Massachusetts,[8] and in consequence the Gortonists dared not return to their own lands at Shawomet and took refuge at Aquidneck. In October, 1644, when Roger Williams arrived with a charter which left no legal pretext for Massachusetts claims, the magistrates again warned the Gortonists to keep out of Shawomet.[9] Meanwhile, the refugees took a shrewd step to protect the Narragansetts and Rhode Island against further encroachments. On May 24, 1644, at Gorton's suggestion, Canonicus subjected his tribe directly to the king of England. The legal case against unlawful dominion by the great Bay colony was now complete.

During these same months the infant colony was beset by another dire threat to its existence. Arrogantly indifferent to the fierce passion of resentment which burned in the hearts of the Narragansetts in consequence of the betrayal of Miantonomu, the federated colonies were goading them to the brink of savage war. In May, 1644, Massachusetts sent ten men "well armed" to reinforce Pomham and Socononoco and build "a strong house of pallizado," later called Pomham's Fort, as an outpost in the northern Narragansett country.[10] In June, when summoned by the commissioners of the United Colonies, Canonicus, now holding himself subject only to England, refused to appear. In September the Narragansetts sent notice that Uncas must return the ransom paid for Miantonomu or submit to judicial settlement for his murder, otherwise they would take the warpath against the Mohegans. The commissioners promptly held a hearing on the complaints of the Narragansetts,

---

[7] *Simplicities Defence*, Coll. R.I.H.S., II, 127.
[8] *Ibid.*, 152; *Mass. Bay Recs.*, II, 57.
[9] *Simplicities Defence*, Coll. R.I.H.S., II, 166.
[10] *Mass. Bay Recs.*, II, 55.

but the pretense of justice by men who had handed Miantonomu over to Uncas was an obvious mockery. Uncas was supported on every count.[11]

In the spring of 1645 the Narragansetts took matters into their own hands and 1000 warriors led by Pessicus, brother of Miantonomu, descended upon the Mohegans and defeated them with a heavy slaughter. In this and subsequent battles only the intervention of Connecticut and New Haven troops saved Uncas.[12] This partiality was the last straw, and in May, 1645, when Benedict Arnold of Pawtuxet and other Massachusetts agents ordered the Narragansetts to appear before the commissioners, Pessicus and Ninigret coolly refused. If the Narragansetts were now not only thirsting for the blood of Uncas but suspicious of his white champions, the commissioners had only themselves to blame. On June 25 Williams reported to Governor Winthrop of the Bay colony that despite his dissuasions the Narragansetts, fallen into "a spirit of desperation," were resolved to revenge the murder of their sachem and recover the ransom or else to perish with him. The only way to prevent English blood from being "further spilt" was by "mediation or prudent neutrality."[13]

In July, 1645, the commissioners decided to declare war and force the Narragansetts into subjugation to the United Colonies. Forty men from Connecticut and thirty from New Haven colony soon assembled under Captain Mason with instructions to attack the Niantics, while 190 Massachusetts men under Major Gibbons prepared to join a Plymouth detachment and march through Rhode Island to the stronghold of the Narragansetts. Anticipating this and condemning hotly in his heart the rashness of his countrymen, Roger Williams as chief officer of his colony took the only course left to secure Rhode Island from the horrors of a border war. He negotiated a neutrality with the Narragansetts.[14] In August the Plymouth forces under Miles Standish reached Rhode Island and Captain Standish discovered that some of the Providence settlers "received the Indians into their houses familiarly" although aware that the natives were preparing to resist the United Colonies. This

11 Winthrop, *Journal,* II, 243.
12 DeForest, *History of the Indians,* pp. 213-216.
13 *Letters,* N.C.P., VI, 145.
14 *Plymouth Col. Recs.,* IX, 33.

so enraged the fiery little captain that he ordered Rhode Islanders "to lay aside their neutrality, and either declare themselves on the one side or other."[15] The friendship of the Gortonists and the Narragansetts similarly infuriated the Massachusetts commander and he gave order that any in Rhode Island who showed favor to the natives should be taken captive.[16] To members of the Puritan confederation the question of lawful jurisdiction was secondary and the Rhode Island charter of no consequence.

Trusting to their impressive show of force, the United Colonies made one last overture for peaceful settlement, ordering two messengers to proceed with Benedict Arnold to the Narragansetts. The messengers were unable to find Benedict Arnold "and heard he durst not adventure himself againe amongst the Narrohiggansets Indians without a sufficient guard."[17] Because of the Narragansetts' accusation that Arnold had played them false during the previous negotiations, his usefulness as an interpreter had ended. But the messengers of the United Colonies found a substitute who had the full confidence of the Indians. Learning that Williams had been "sent for by the Narrohigganset Sachems" and was going down to them, they "acquainted him with their message, shewed him their Instruccons, and made use of him as Interpretor."[18] The man whom Massachusetts had banished thereupon saved the confederacy from its own folly and once more proved himself the ablest peacemaker living in New England. Through his mediation arrangements were made for a peace conference and a treaty was signed at Boston on August 27. Winthrop and the other commissioners of the United Colonies, far from thanking Williams for his intervention, rebuked the Massachusetts agents for employing him as interpreter and censured them for acceding to Williams' request that they write to Captain Mason to postpone hostilities.[19] According to Gorton, John Cotton, still smarting from Williams' pamphlet war on his principles, publicly belabored the agents for their employment of such a renegade as a Massachusetts negotiator.[20]

The terms of the treaty bore hard upon the Narragansetts and

15 Winslow, *Hypocrisie Unmasked* (Chapin ed.), p. 85.
16 *Plymouth Col. Recs.*, IX, 51.
17 *Ibid.*, 42.
18 *Ibid.*
19 *Ibid.*, 43.
20 *Simplicities Defence*, Coll. R.I.H.S., II, 171.

the records show that they scarcely obtained a fair hearing. The representations of Uncas were accepted without adequate investigation, while the Narragansett chieftains who had trusted to the white man's justice discovered during the negotiations at Boston that they were prisoners of war. It was a treaty imposed by force, exacting of the Narragansetts an indemnity of two thousand fathoms of wampum and surrender of four sons of the sachems as hostages. Complaining bitterly, the Rhode Island Indians signed the treaty. The colonial forces were disbanded, and a day of general thanksgiving was proclaimed; the Narragansetts had been humbled.

For three years the resentful Narragansetts chafed at payment of the indemnity until in 1648 war clouds rolled up again and it looked as though the Narragansetts would fight rather than submit to the injustice of the treaty. The United Colonies sent Captains Atherton and Prichard to negotiate; and once again the agents of the confederation found the services of Williams indispensable. Williams placated the fears of Pessicus and arranged a conference at which the Narragansetts agreed not to "meddle" with Uncas and to pay the remainder of the indemnity; but they declared that once the payments were finished "they would require satisfaction for all the wrongs Uncas had done them, and if the English would not see them satisfied, they would consider what to do."[21]

Williams stated flatly that the Narragansetts had never really "intended hurt against the English."[22] After the crisis of 1645 William Pynchon admitted that even the Mohegans testified to the honesty and good faith of the Narragansett sachem.[23] In the absence of justice to Uncas from the whites, the Narragansetts desired only freedom to settle the score for themselves. This the commissioners would never grant unless the Narragansetts submitted their lands and tribe to the jurisdiction of the confederated colonies. In 1647 the younger Winthrop was asked by a Narragansett sachem how he might enjoy the love of the English. Winthrop told him he must "attend their order in all things," for that was "the only way to attaine his desire of peace."[24] Roger Williams believed that the

[21] Backus, *The Baptists*, I, 195; Winthrop, *Journal*, II, 407.
[22] *Letters*, N.C.P., VI, 157.
[23] 4 *Coll. M.H.S.*, VI, 374.
[24] 5 *Coll. M.H.S.*, VIII, 38.

United Colonies joined "most unjustly" with Uncas and explained their policy as rooted in aggrandizement, based on envy of the Narragansetts' lands and "Riches" and their friendliness to himself "and other Heretiks."[25]

The suspicion that subjugation of the Narragansetts was merely part of an imperial policy of conquering Rhode Island and subjugating its English plantations was substantiated at the very moment when Pessicus was signing the treaty of 1645. As assurance to the sachems that no harm would come to them if they attended the peace conference at Boston, Williams voluntarily placed himself as a hostage among the Narragansetts[26] and while there received an extraordinary communication from Massachusetts. The Bay magistrates, having "receaved lately out of England" a charter which included Providence and Aquidneck, "thought fitt" to give Williams notice to surrender "any Jurisdiccon therein, otherwise to appeare at our next Generall Courte . . . to shew by what right yow claime any such jurisdiccon."[27] The rulers of Massachusetts, though perfectly aware that Weld's Narragansett patent was a bogus document, hoped by force and guile to override Williams' charter as they were soon to do with the patent of Gorges and Mason. As chief officer of his infant colony, Williams sent Governor Winthrop a reply which he believed "righteous and weighty," but, ominously, "to that answer of mine I never received the least reply."[28]

Winthrop, governor of the Bay and presiding officer of the commissioners of the United Colonies, was a prime mover in the concerted drive of the saints against the Narragansetts and the Rhode Island heretics. Williams' pamphleteering against Cotton and triumph over Weld in the battle for a patent cast a cloud over his old friendship with Winthrop. Correspondence between the two dwindled, and Winthrop ceased to record in his *Journal* Williams' manifold services as peacemaker among the Indians. On June 25, 1645, Williams wrote to Winthrop of his "fear that all sparks of former love are now extinct":

[25] Williams to Whipple, *R. I. H. Tracts*, XIV, 26. The prospect of rich booty was not absent from magisterial calculations; Emanuel Downing wrote to Winthrop that captured Narragansetts could be exchanged for Moorish slaves—a neat solution for high wages and the servant problem; 4 *Coll. M.H.S.*, VI, 65.

[26] Gorton, *Simplicities Defence*, Coll. R.I.H.S., II, 171.

[27] *Mass. Bay Recs.*, III, 49.

[28] *Letters*, N.C.P., VI, 341.

> Sir, (excepting the matters of my soul and conscience . . .)
> you have not a truer friend and servant to your worthy person
> and yours, nor to the peace and welfare of the whole country,
> then the most despised and most unworthy
>
> Roger Williams.[29]

This was one of the last letters known to have passed from Williams
to the elder Winthrop.

On October 1, 1645, Massachusetts, following up its assertion of
jurisdiction over Rhode Island, authorized thirty-two families to
settle at Shawomet and preempt 10,000 acres of the land confiscated
from the Gortonists.[30] This would establish the Massachusetts claim
on a solid *de facto* basis. Plymouth dignitaries, however, also had
taken the Shawomet natives under their protection and, hoping "to
drive a trade with the Indians," warned the Massachusetts interlopers to keep out.[31]

The United Colonies found a solution for this dispute but not by
due process of law. The Massachusetts contention of sovereignty by
virtue of submission of the Pawtuxets and Shawomets had no more
validity in English law than Weld's patent, nor was Plymouth's
claim any more substantial. Moreover, as Roger Williams always
maintained, interference with Indian nations to encourage secession
of minor chieftains like Pomham broke "the law and tenor of the
natives" by which inferior sachems and tribes could only "plant and
remove at the pleasure of the highest and supreme Sachems."[32] The
royal commissioners later reminded the magistrates of New England
that the king had given them no "commission to alter the Indians'
laws and customs."[33] Much as John Marshall ruled in the days of
Andrew Jackson, Indian tribes were domestic dependent nations
protected by the central government.[34] Nevertheless, the United
Colonies sat on the case and awarded Shawomet to Massachusetts.
The only vital document from a legal point of view—the Rhode
Island charter—was not even considered in the evidence. By a
strange coincidence John Cotton was at this time composing his
Reply to Mr. Williams in which he justified the famous banishment

---

[29] *Ibid.*, 144-145.
[30] *Mass. Bay Recs.*, II, 128; Winthrop, *Journal*, II, 308.
[31] *Ibid.*
[32] *Letters*, N.C.P., VI, 300.
[33] *Ibid.*, 326.
[34] See the celebrated Georgia Indian cases.

on the ground that Williams' attack on the Massachusetts charter "subverted" the government!

Massachusetts' pretensions under the Weld patent encouraged Coddington's faction at Newport to undermine the new government under Williams' charter, and like William Arnold before him, Coddington made overtures looking toward secession. The growing spirit of manifest destiny among the saints, however, had a contrary effect upon Rhode Island democrats and drove Samuel Gorton into action. By the latter end of 1645 Gorton and Holden were on the high seas, bearing with them a petition to parliament and Gorton's manuscript, *Simplicities Defence,* which they soon published, savagely exposing the persecutions and aggrandizements of the New England oligarchy. Gorton knew his rights by law and exhibited copies of Massachusetts warrants served in Rhode Island "after the Charter was established amongst us."[35] In September, 1646, Holden returned, brazenly landing at Boston with official documents which proved the alleged Weld patent a fraud and called a halt to the imperial sweep of magisterial policy. An order from Warwick's commission commanded Massachusetts to allow the Gortonists "freely and quietly to live and plant upon Shawomett" and reminded the squires of the Bay that their jurisdiction was limited not by the will of their God but by the law of England.[36] Incensed, the Massachusetts oligarchs considered clapping Holden into jail and went so far as to debate seriously whether they need any longer acknowledge the authority of Warwick or parliament itself.[37] In the end they allowed the hated Holden free passage and dispatched Edward Winslow to obtain Warwick's sanction to their claims in Rhode Island. Meanwhile at long last the Gortonists returned to possession of their hard won plantation.

During this long struggle to organize the colony and protect its independence, Providence town affairs were proceeding in an orderly course. Sometime between 1641 and 1645, possibly after Williams' return with the charter, the five disposers who had acted as selectmen gave place to two town deputies.[38] The town was relatively free from troublemakers and the local device of settling disputes by arbi-

---

[35] *Simplicities Defence,* Coll. R.I.H.S., II, 166.
[36] Winthrop, *Journal,* II, 342-344.
[37] *Ibid.,* 334, 340-341, 344-346.
[38] Chapin, *Doc. Hist. R. I.,* I, 235.

tration was adequate for the ordinary needs of a frontier Puritan community. Perhaps the most colorful brawl was one precipitated by William Harris who for years had lived in the woods at his remote habitation in Pachasit, "like another Nebuchadnezzar," as his neighbors remarked, "not fit for the Societie of Men."[39] Generally shrewd and calculating in business matters, Harris had a hot head, leather lungs, and corrosive talents in the realms of contention. According to Williams, he sometimes aped English gentry in a display of mettle, issuing "Challenges to fight (yea with pistolls and Rapier)."[40]

One day in 1644, Harris, though a town official, got into a wrangle with Adam Goodwin and "fell on the sayd Adam and beate him in the open street." At the conclusion of the fracas, Harris was set down in the town records as a common brawler and when confronted by the forces of law and order, expressed unmitigated approval of his own conduct. The town felt otherwise, and disfranchised him "for fighting and shedding blood in the street" and "for maintaining it and allowing it." Freedom to violate the civil peace and run amuck at will was not accounted by his neighbors as among the liberties of the citizenry. The strong-willed Harris was not one to take too seriously a mere town ordinance and after a while his irritated neighbors complained that Harris came to town meetings and voted regardless.[41]

More important in Providence history was a new attempt to restrict allotments of land to men of substance. Although in the years since 1640, eleven newcomers including Robert Williams and Gregory Dexter signed the Combination and became townsmen with full rights,[42] about an equal number of landless working men, servants, or poor men obtained neither a purchase right nor vote. Proponents of vested rights in Providence pushed through "an Order to receave no more" as purchasers, but Roger Williams and those who shared his belief in a refuge for the destitute soon defeated this project and made a new compact which granted poor men twenty-five acres apiece and a "quarter right" in the use of the common land.[43] This agreement remained in force for many years and later

39 *Prov. Recs.*, XV, 122.
40 *Ibid.*
41 *Ibid.*, 121-122; *Harris Papers*, p. 70.
42 Chapin, *Doc. Hist. R. I.*, I, 119-120.
43 *Pub. R.I.H.S.*, VIII, 157-158; *Prov. Recs.*, II, 29-31.

comers continued to sign it until the total number grew to thirty-five.[44] The social significance of the twenty-five acre compact has been overlooked. Practically all the signers were poor men, many of them young and unmarried, and nearly half, who made their signatures by mark, were presumably illiterate.[45] These men lacked the wherewithal to pay thirty shillings for a full purchase right of one hundred acres and buy stock and supplies to improve a large farm, but twenty-five acres—more than enough for good farming by an ordinary family—gave them the desideratum which lured so many from England, the opportunity to rise from the ranks of the landless.

Relative to time and place, the essentially democratic character of the twenty-five acre agreement is clear if one compares it to practice elsewhere in New England. Whereas Providence was following a cheap land policy in accordance with what was to become a characteristic American frontier formula, towns in the orthodox colonies, despite the abundance of land, introduced to some degree the contrary principle of an economy of scarcity. In his *Abstract of the Laws,* John Cotton, voicing the aristocratic pretensions of the Puritan squirearchy, called for unequal division of land so "Eminent respect (in this case may be given to men of eminent quality and descent) in assigning unto them more large and honorable accommodations, in regard to their great disbursements to publike charges."[46] Salem, Plymouth, Hartford, Guilford, New Haven, and most early towns, even frontier settlements like Springfield and Hadley, frankly based rights to the land on "quality," wealth, and size of family.[47] Political and religious acceptability was also a factor affecting allotments, and the land system was often an instrument for the earthly

[44] The eight whose names are crossed out did not become permanent residents. Exclusive of these, the first nine names in the left column seem to have been early signers; the next seven, Clawson to John Fenner, obtained grants between 1650 and 1652; grants to the last five, Northrup to Way, were not earlier than 1655. The first four in the right column signed in 1646 or soon after. *Prov. Recs., passim.*

[45] Tillinghast, Jones, D. Brown, E. Olney, B. Smith and probably others were young single men. Sayles, Sucklin, Clawson, and others had been servants. The twenty-five acre men paid the smallest taxes on the lists for 1650 and 1652, showing their original poverty.

[46] *Force's Tracts* (Washington, D. C., 1836-1846), III, no. 9, p. 8.

[47] P. W. Bidwell and J. I. Falconer, *History of Agriculture in the Northern United States* (Washington, D. C., 1925), pp. 52-54; Akagi, *The Town Proprietors,* pp. 155-159 and *passim.*

reward of saints.[48] Massachusetts provided that only freemen, "church members," could vote in town meeting on admission of inhabitants or the granting of land.[49] The enactments which prevented residence in any town except by consent of the magistrates or freemen, together with town restrictions on selling land to outsiders, although not wholly successful, served to limit the opportunity of the discontented and unorthodox for acquisition of land.[50]

By 1646 "purchasers" in Watertown, Dorchester, Boston and other towns were already making themselves "proprietors," restricting membership, and establishing themselves among the wealthy and privileged through their opportunity to speculate on the growth of the town.[51] Poor men, although not completely shut out by the little oligarchies of the towns, frequently received no more than an acre or so as a town lot, with no "right" as "purchasers" to share in future allotments of the town lands. The "aristocratic aversion" against generous grants to the lowly arose in part from a desire to prevent hired hands and craftsmen from bargaining for a high return for their labor or from joining the ranks of independent farmers if they did not get it. Because of the sheer abundance of land, the more enterprising of the common folk frequently bettered their condition, but the indubitable evidence of countless town records shames Edward Johnson's zealous boast of "the poorest sort" receiving handsome farms and humble laborers winning lordly incomes.[52] After a careful study of the Cape Anne settlements, Herbert Baxter Adams compared a cottage right in Salem to the shanty right of the Irish along later western railroads and concluded that poor white trash had less opportunity in early Massachusetts than Virginia.[53]

The Providence compact of 1646 was remarkable as a free concession by the men of property to a minority group of landless men who had no political power and whose only reliance was the spirit of liberality which Williams and his followers had frequently pro-

[48] Nathaniel Ward to the younger Winthrop, 4 *Coll. M.H.S.*, VII, 24; "Boston Records, 1634-1660," 2nd *Rpt. of Record Com.* (3rd ed., Boston, 1902), pp. 5, 6.

[49] *Mass. Bay Recs.*, I, 161.

[50] *Ibid.*, I, 167, 168, 196, 228; *Conn. Col. Recs.*, I, 8, 185, 210, 351; F. J. Turner, *The Frontier in American History* (N. Y., 1920), pp. 54-55; C. M. Andrews, *The River Towns of Connecticut* (Baltimore, 1889), p. 83.

[51] Akagi, *The Town Proprietors*, pp. 53, 71-73, 138-141, 175 and *passim*.

[52] *Wonder-Working Providence*, pp. 175, 176.

[53] *Village Communities of Cape Anne and Salem* (Baltimore, 1883), pp. 64-67. See also Turner, *Frontier in American History*, pp. 60, 62; L. W. Labaree, *Milford* (Conn. Tercentenary Pubs., New Haven, 1933), pp. 4, 10, 13, 28.

fessed. Fortunately a majority of the "purchasers" recognized the logic of frontier conditions: Providence was a struggling wilderness settlement, government under the charter still weak, land abundant, and satisfaction of the humbler inhabitants would strengthen the colony and broaden the base of the town democracy. Williams himself detested the system of exclusive proprietorships which he saw emerging in many New England towns. Six years after adoption of the twenty-five acre agreement, he sharply criticized the class concept and religious exclusiveness which dominated the proprietorship in Taunton, a town nearby in Plymouth patent:

> . . . the said (reputed) Minister Mr Streete, publikely and earnestly perswaded his Church-members to give Land to none but such, as might be fit for Church-members: yea not to receive such English into the Towne, or if in the Towne, yet not to Land, that if they lived in the Towne or place, yet they might be knowne to be but as Gibeonites, hewers of wood, and drawers of water for the service of them that were of the Church.[54]

Taunton's aristocratic land policy, Williams pointed out, was likely to cause dissension and "Departures of divers, and Barres to the comming of others, to the spoile and hindrance of a most likely and growing Plantation."[55]

More extreme Providence equalitarians like Williams and Gregory Dexter may have felt that the twenty-five acre compact did not go far enough. Since it bound its signers "not to clayme any Righte" to share in future divisions of the town land, "Nor any privillidge of Vote" until "received as free Men" by the town, it betokened middle-class liberalism rather than thoroughgoing equalitarianism. In 1654 Williams said that he had been charged with folly for upholding "freedom and liberty . . .; I say liberty and equality, both in land and government."[56] Despite this statement, it is doubtful that he held any absolute ideas of equality, and if he did he certainly did not win full acceptance of them. Though Williams spoke of the rights of man and consent of the governed, the practice in his colony restricted "consent" to men who held property. On the other hand, one cannot miss the fact that in Providence there were

[54] *Bloody Tenent More Bloody*, N.C.P., IV, 471-472.
[55] *Ibid.*, 472.
[56] *Letters*, N.C.P., VI, 263.

no barriers in the way of a religious test or pronounced discrimination along class lines. Orthodoxy was irrelevant and it was easy to acquire property.

The phraseology of the twenty-five acre agreement indicated that the signers could look forward to future admission as voters with full rights in the town lands. They had not long to wait. By 1655 nearly half of the twenty-five acre men were accorded full status as voters and purchasers, three more were admitted in 1656, and by an order of 1658 a twenty-five acre man or any one with even a small parcel of land was entitled to vote as a freeman of the colony.[57] By that date certain fortunate early families were acquiring relative wealth and social prestige; but democracy was not yet on the retreat.

[57] *R. I. Col. Recs.,* I, 299; *Prov. Recs.,* II, 85, 96, 112.

13

A MORE PERFECT UNION

THE COLONIAL GOVERNMENT INAUGURATED BY Williams in November, 1644, was hardly a glowing success. After a decade of town sovereignty, William Coddington and his following in the wealthier and more populous plantations of Aquidneck were disinclined to risk diminution of their power and refused to support a union in which Providence and Warwick would enjoy equality with Newport. Concurrently the United Colonies' contemptuous disregard of Williams' charter encouraged the Newport magnate to emulate the Pawtuxet secessionists, and on August 5, 1645, Coddington made an overture to his former associates, the Massachusetts oligarchs. Despising the Gortonists, whom he confessed were now considered "so much strength to the place," shrinking from democracy and finding his party a minority, Coddington informed Winthrop that he believed in the Massachusetts system "both in Church and Commonwealth" and proposed "alyence with yorselves or Plimouth, one or both."[1]

To consolidate the colony and ward off secession and territorial encroachment by Plymouth and the Bay, Williams and the patriotic elements rallied the people to strengthen the central government and place democracy on a firm foundation. Working from the grass roots they organized a movement in town meetings for a root and branch reorganization of the government. Prior to the general assembly of May, 1647, the towns thrashed out many questions by committees of correspondence and prepared instructions for their representatives in the forthcoming assembly. In the Providence town meeting Williams acted as moderator and drafted the Providence plan for the new government. This plan stipulated a code of laws; reservation of small cases for trial in the town, but a court of "generall Tryalls" for the colony; home rule in matters of strictly town concern with "noe inter mixture" of town and colony offices; a system of appeal from the local to the colony court; and, finally, a charter of civil incorporation for each town.[2] Subse-

[1] Chapin, *Doc. Hist. R. I.*, II, 176-179.   [2] *Prov. Recs.*, XV, 9-10.

training of the militia, and poor relief—and prescribed also the privileges of towns such as the initiative and referendum.[9] The federalism of Rhode Island was subordinated to popular sovereignty and parliamentary supremacy. To appease Aquidneck citizens who desired local home rule, special privileges were accorded Portsmouth and Newport, but in 1649 when the assembly granted Providence a town charter, it reserved power "from time to time" to make alterations "most conducing to the generall good."[10]

Judicial provisions completed the framework of 1647. Jurisdiction over local affairs was left to monthly courts of the towns, but for disputes between town and town and other cases of greater moment, a colony court of trials was created. In subsequent years the assembly placed increasing reliance upon the courts in dealing with disorderly factions, tax-resisters, recalcitrant towns, or town officials neglectful of duties,[11] but while the courts were thus a useful arm of the central government, the assembly remained the master. There was no separation of powers or insulation of the judiciary against popular clamor through security of tenure. The president and assistants, popularly elected, served as judges in the court of trials. Above them as a court of last resort sat the assembly which, when its legislative work was finished, constituted itself a high court of justice, as in the early days of parliament, and dispensed law and equity. Thus, adapting to democratic purposes the emerging English theory of parliamentary supremacy, Williams and his associates made both local government and the judicial power directly subject to the will of the people expressed in elections.

The unionists of Rhode Island, individualistic yeomen farmers though they were, feared not so much strong government as arbitrary power in the hands of a few. Williams, with a confidence in popular rule equal to that of Thomas Paine and eighteenth century purveyors of the "enlightenment," consistently maintained that in civil things a government had a right to do what the majority desired; and that this sovereignty of the people extended to all things essential for their "commonweale or safety" in "bodies or goods." Civil constitutions were men's ordinances and as such subject to change whenever a majority became convinced of the sufficiency of need.[12]

9 *Ibid.*, I, 148-154, 184, 188.
10 *Ibid.*, I, 216. See also resolution of 1656, *ibid.*, 333.
11 *Ibid.*, I, 422, 424, 481.
12 *The Bloudy Tenent*, N.C.P., III, 108 f., 249, 354, 364, 398.

The organic laws of Rhode Island were accordingly not final or fundamental, and the legislators specifically provided that the freemen should review the measures of 1647 at the next general assembly and amend anything not "suitable to the Constitution of the place."[13] There was here none of the aristocratic republicanism of American federalists of 1787 or shrewd maneuvering to beguile the populace. Williams and his associates clung literally to the doctrine of a social compact continuously reaffirmed by each generation; and they set no comfortable precedents for later champions of separation of powers, fixed written constitutions, or judicial review.[14] "The forme of Government," proclaimed the assembly, "is DEMOCRATI-CALL; that is to say, a Government held by the free and voluntarie consent of all, or the greater parte of the free Inhabitants."[15] By virtue of the extraordinary effort to give this democratic faith a reality in practice, the Rhode Island freeman gained a "wider field in which to exercise his suffrage" than contemporary voters in any other colony,[16] and Williams could justly hail the "inestimable" liberties enjoyed by his fellow citizens: security in lives, persons, and estates, "not a peny to be taken by any rate from us, without every mans free debate by his Deputies," and freedom "of choosing and being chosen to all offices, and of making or repealing all Lawes and Constitutions among us."[17]

After settlement of the form of government, it remained to chart the wide domain of individual freedom and shape legislative policy to promote the social welfare. Confronting defiant obstructionists at Aquidneck who supported Coddington and the equally defiant secessionists at Pawtuxet, Rhode Island unionists were face to face with a

---

[13] *R. I. Col. Recs.,* I, 148.

[14] Subordination of judicial power persisted so long that by 1900 a local historian felt called upon to apologize: "To one accustomed to the acknowledged position of the judiciary, it seems scarcely credible that for some years after 1856 this power could be questioned. The union of the judicial with the legislative power in Rhode Island; the existence of a department that could make, interpret and enforce its own acts, had for so long been a recognized fact in this State that it was difficult for the people to realize, even sixty years after the adoption of the federal constitution, that the judiciary—so long the creature of the legislature—was in many ways its master." Edward Field, ed., *State of Rhode Island and Providence Plantations at the End of the Century: A History,* The Mason Publishing Co. (Boston and Syracuse, 1902), III, 89.

[15] *R. I. Col. Recs.,* I, 156.

[16] A. E. McKinley, *The Suffrage Franchise in the English Colonies* (Philadelphia, 1905), p. 443.

[17] *Letter to the Town of Warwick, 1666,* Pub. R.I.H.S., VIII (1900), 149.

profound problem of free government. Victims of persecution who had proclaimed religious liberty, men who had fled to the wilderness from the arbitrary regimes of kings and gentry, could not lightly ignore the rights of minorities or sanction compulsion in the name of the majority. Counsels of experience and the long speculations of Williams on the nature of liberty warned that government by consent depended upon civil tolerance of political differences; conflicts in a democracy must be resolved by discussion, compromise, arbitration, and orderly processes for restraining governors from disregard of law, majorities from arbitrary coercion of the opposition, and minorities or individuals from illegitimate obstruction of the popular will.

To guarantee the traditional rights of Englishmen and promote decency and justice between man and man, Williams on May 19, 1647, submitted the Providence request for a "Modell" or code based on the "Lawes of England."[18] Almost the first act of the assembly was a formal vote of approval.[19] In the next few days committees toiled over English statutes and common law, modifying precedents to suit local needs. As the assembly adjourned it declared itself "unwilling" that "popularity" should prove, "as some conjecture it will," an "Anarchie, and so a common Tyranny" and proclaimed the completed code as a "hopeful assurance" to every man of "peaceable and quiett enjoyment of his lawfull right and Libertie."[20] Every town was to have a copy of the laws,[21] there to be accessible to the lowliest inhabitant so he might read and know his rights and obligations.

The idea of codifying the laws was not unique, and progressive spirits both in England and New England had long sought to bolster liberty through "known" laws. The deputies of the Bay colony had rejected the theocratic "Judicialls" of Cotton, except for the capital laws, but Nathaniel Ward's Body of Liberties, adopted in 1641, failed to satisfy their demand for legal limitations on magisterial omnipotence. The first of the Liberties, which provided that no one should be banished except by "some expresse law," took away with one hand what was given with the other: magistrates were to judge

[18] *Prov. Recs.*, XV, 10.
[19] *R. I. Col. Recs.*, I, 147.
[20] *Ibid.*, I, 156, 158.
[21] *Ibid.*, I, 148, 155.

"by the word of God" if the existing law failed to cover a particular case.[22] Stewards of the Lord recognized no fixed legal limitations, and in 1645 Hingham inhabitants protested that magistrates were "so waspish they might not be Petitioned."[23] In 1646 courageous Massachusetts men led by Robert Child, remonstrating against the lack of an adequate bill of immunities and deploring persecution and the "overgreedy spirit of arbitrary power," petitioned for a broader suffrage and a code of laws to give such assurance of lives, liberties, and estates "as all Freeborne enjoy in our native Country."[24] Ruthless suppression and confiscation of estates through inordinate fines were the rewards of the remonstrants; but the Bay oligarchy met the demand for legal reform by expanding Ward's codification into the General Laws and Liberties of 1647, published the following year. Connecticut forestalled trouble by adopting a code in 1650, an almost verbatim copy of that of Massachusetts. Since 1636 Plymouth had operated under certain legal restrictions, but New Haven, frankly theocratic, framed austere Mosaic laws on the anomalous pattern of Cotton's Judicialls.

Inspired in part by Massachusetts experience, Rhode Island in its third year under a charter adopted a code of a liberality which more than a decade of struggle in the Bay had failed to wrest from Winthrop and his peers. Williams had had the foresight to obtain in the charter a liberty which he proudly pointed out "other charters have not," to conform to English law with a "favourable mitigacion viz: not absolutely but respecting our Wilderness estate and Condicion."[25] Taking advantage of this leeway, Rhode Island legislators drafted a code which gave point to James Harrington's prediction of a "levelling of the laws" as a natural consequence of equalitarian conditions. In contrast to English and colonial laws which allowed discretion in accordance with Nathaniel Ward's dictum that political and "personal" respects would not "admit one and the same remedy for all,"[26] the Rhode Island code assumed equality before the law and recognized no mitigation of penalties in favor of gentlemen offenders. The levelling spirit of freeholders which from the first settlements

---

[22] 3 *Coll. M.H.S.*, VIII, 216.
[23] *New-England's Jonas*, Force's Tracts, IV, no. 3, p. 6.
[24] *Ibid.*, pp. 9-11.
[25] *Pub. R.I.H.S.*, VIII, 149; *R. I. Col. Recs.*, I, 145.
[26] *The Simple Cobbler*, Force's Tracts, III, no. 8, p. 13.

had rejected feudal tenure and opposed accumulation of land by the few, likewise pervaded the law of inheritance. Ignoring the English system of primogeniture and the Hebraic "double portion" which was allowed the eldest son in orthodox Puritan colonies, Rhode Island legislators vested town councils with the unique function of making "equal" and just distribution of possessions to the heirs of persons dying intestate.[27] The levelling impulse had naturally the limitations of early agrarian democracy. Labor regulations in the Rhode Island code, although by no means incorporating the comfortable class assurances of English law nor emulating early Massachusetts legislation which sought to prevent laborers from demanding high wages, followed Elizabethan statutes in the proviso that when a contract was made, neither a free laborer nor an indentured servant had a right to strike for better terms or accept an offer from another master unless lawfully released.[28]

A frontier humanism infusing the new body of laws gave token of the inner springs of the levelling spirit. Rhode Island people, unencumbered by the old discipline of church and state and believing with Williams, Gorton, and the Baptists in the gospel of common brotherhood and the power of reason among the mass of men, were moving toward a new social psychology. Logic based on an abundance of land and a scarcity of settlers strengthened a doctrine of man that made human worth the basic determinant. Population was sparse and man precious, and the refugees of the colony were imbued with Williams' vision of an asylum from brutality and a haven where the destitute could find friendliness and opportunity. This spirit of hospitality dictated the omission of the usual "Stranger" law such as that of the Massachusetts code which forbade towns or individuals to allow habitation to newcomers or convey land to them except by consent of a member of the oligarchy.[29] The same humanist spirit led Williams and his fellow lawmakers to abolish imprisonment for debt. In an age which everywhere treated an insolvent like a criminal, they provided that if a debtor agreed to a "course" of payments, "he shall not be sent to prison, there to lye languishing to no man's

---

[27] R. I. Col. Recs., I, 188-190. For cases of equalitarian division, including girls with boys, see Prov. Recs., II, 58; VI, 282-284; XV, 157.

[28] R. I. Col. Recs., I, 176-177, 182-184.

[29] Book of General Lawes and Libertyes (Farrand ed., Cambridge, 1929), p. 49. Rhode Island's policy of welcome accounts for the liberality of its subsequent stranger laws; R. I. Col. Recs., I, 230, 307.

advantage."[30] Frontier humanism ran counter to long penal servitude or the dire resort to capital punishment. For riots the code
provided imprisonment for two weeks or a month: "Such long times
of imprisonments mentioned in the Statute, 2 Hen. v. 8, suits not the
constitution of our place."[31] Largely abolishing the many score
death penalties of the English penal code, Rhode Island lawmakers
listed only nine crimes as capital.[32] Even in this slender list the
death penalty was not always mandatory and in the case of burglary
sweeping exceptions were made, including the mentally deficient,
children, and "poore persons that steale for Hunger," who were to
receive mild punishment. Barbarous colonial legislation providing
brutal punishment or death for a servant who struck a master or a
child who struck a parent found scarcely a faint echo in the Rhode
Island stipulation that such offenders be sent for a short time "to
the House of Correction."[33] Inspired by a belief in the regeneracy
of man and freedom of the will, Rhode Island leaders recoiled from
corporal punishment, bodily mutilation, and the cruelty of a law of
vengeance and framed a humane legal code, seeking to reduce crime
by clemency coupled with correction and encouragement of reform
of the individual culprit. Only once did they specify punishment by
whipping; and only for a thief guilty twice of grand larceny did they
stipulate the branding iron—a penalty abolished nine years later
when Williams was president.[34] Other than this they abandoned the
innumerable harsh physical punishments, tortures, brandings, and
mutilations which dotted the penal codes of the time.

The new psychology exemplified in the humane and equalitarian
character of the code leavened laws touching manners and morals
and placed high esteem upon social freedom and personal liberty.
Bred to Puritan and English *mores,* the "come-outers" of Rhode
Island could not condone a free and easy morality, and Williams,
their chief philosopher and spokesman, acknowledged it a duty of
the state to promote "civility." Secular officials, he contended, should
be authorized to restrain "scandalous offenders" lest society lapse
into a "wilderness of life and manners," but such regulations should

---

[30] *R. I. Col. Recs.,* I, 181.

[31] *Ibid.,* I, 170.

[32] Treason, murder, highway robbery, arson, burglary, witchcraft, sodomy,
buggery, rape; *ibid.,* I, 160-161, 163-164, 166-168, 172-173.

[33] *Ibid.,* I, 162.

[34] *Ibid.,* I, 174, 350.

conform "to the Nature and Constitution" of the nation or people and not to a biblical or rigorous absolute standard.[35] In this spirit the code of 1647 duly followed English statutes in prohibiting sex crimes, fraud, slander, assault and battery and regulating tippling and gaming in public houses. With a striking modernity these enactments largely avoided the medieval and Puritan confusion of sin and crime and exhibited more confidence in the conscience of the citizen than in scarlet letters, stocks, whipping post, and hangman's noose. For "false witness" or perjury, punishable in Massachusetts and Connecticut by death, the Rhode Island penalty was the pillory. The laws against adultery and fornication were mild as compared with the Hebraic laws of neighboring colonies and included no alphabetic badges of shame.[36] Tippling was permissible for twice as long as in Massachusetts and drunkenness cost the offender half as much— without the Bay colony's sterner threat of ten stripes or imprisonment for repeaters.[37] The code makers recommended hot heads convicted as "Common Scoulds" to the sobering effect of the ducking stool, but with few exceptions[38] stocks, pillory, and ignominious punishments were noteworthy for their absence. No law against idleness nor sumptuary legislation sought to compel thrift or impose "seemly" fashions of dress and adornment on persons of low estate. On the whole Rhode Islanders respected a man's private life and their laws had little of the sweeping assortment of minute regulations of daily conduct and threats of public shame by which sleuths of God in orthodox colonies prodded saints and knocked down sinners.

The more radical Rhode Islanders who supported Williams combined with their democratic faith a broad social conception of state intervention for the general welfare; recognizing no acquisitive vested rights above the rights of society, they were nevertheless deeply convinced of the wisdom of erecting legal bulwarks for civil liberties. Specific enactments affecting political opposition, freedom of speech, assembly, and petition, were framed not for the purpose

[35] *Bloody Tenent More Bloody,* N.C.P., IV, 222, 485; *The Bloudy Tenent,* N.C.P., III, 108-109, 170-171.

[36] See A. M. Davis, "The law of adultery and ignominious punishments," *Proc. Am. Antiq. Soc.,* N. S., X (1895), 97-127.

[37] *R. I. Col. Recs.,* I, 185-186; cf. *The Book of General Lawes and Libertyes,* p. 30.

[38] *R. I. Col. Recs.,* I, 180, 182, 185, 186.

of restraining the liberty of the ordinary citizen but to assure him a maximum of freedom.[39] Rhode Island defined treason not as opposition to the colonial government but correctly, as a grievous offence against the king or "State Regall . . . See 25: Ed. 3, 2." and followed Tudor statutes for treason committed beyond the realm by ordering transfer of such cases to the mother country for final trial and sentence—a definition and procedure the reverse of that in Massachusetts where the oligarchy converted the law into a potent threat against political opponents. The Rhode Island law of libel and slander, declaring a good name "better than precious ointment" and slanderers "worser than dead flies," granted offended persons the right to bring action; but, affirming a principle celebrated a century later in the Zenger case, provided that if the charge could be proved true the case was not actionable. A bill of rights, almost the first thought of the law makers, was given preeminent position immediately following the preamble of the code.[40] Echoing and improving the language of a famous clause in Magna Carta, article one proclaimed that no man should be deprived of his lands or liberties or imprisoned or exiled save by lawful judgment of his peers "by some known Law, and according to the Letter of it." The second and third articles, forbidding officers or assemblies at their peril to "presume" to more authority than was vested in them by "those that had powre to call" them, affirmed the great principle of direct and immediate responsibility to the electorate. Implementing this general declaration of civil rights, a lengthy appendix to the code defined the "due course" of law, made all officials liable for infraction of it, and safeguarded the common rights to trial by jury, legal counsel, benefit of witnesses, and speedy trial.[41]

The last clause of the code summed up the Rhode Island conception of rights and duties: "These are the Lawes that concerne all men, and these are the Penalties for the transgression thereof," ratified and established by "common consent"; and "otherwise than thus what is herein forbidden, all men may walk as their consciences perswade them, every one in the name of his God."[42] In accordance with the philosophy of Williams, Rhode Island assumed religion

[39] See the laws of high treason, "misbehavior" or contempt of authority, unlawful assembly, slander and libel; R. I. Col. Recs., I, 160, 163, 169, 184.
[40] Ibid., I, 157-158.
[41] Ibid., I, 191-208.
[42] Ibid., I, 190.

beyond the scope of civil authority and dignified freedom of worship as a fundamental right coexistent with and limiting the natural order by which all forms of government must ultimately derive power from consent of the governed. A right of man, religious freedom was not to be regarded as a concession of authority. Long afterward a German scholar tracing the antecedents of the famous French Declaration of the Rights of Man concluded that religious liberty as a natural right first found recognition in law in the Rhode Island code of 1647.[43] The Rhode Island declaration was broader than religious liberty. The term employed was "conscience," a spacious word as Williams explained on countless occasions, meaning literally and necessarily freedom of thought, expression, and action in the fullest measure consonant with civil order. Thus all men were guaranteed their privileges and immunities under common law and statute and free to walk according to conscience up to the point of transgression upon the rights of society. Free churches depended upon religious liberty and free government upon civil liberty. But socially minded men like Williams were wary of an anarchistic individualism garbed in the language of natural law and making private rights paramount to those of society. In the last analysis Williams looked to the vigilance of the democracy as the ultimate safeguard of civil rights and with high confidence revered government by majority as an "inestimable" jewel: "No Life no Limbe taken from us: No Corporall punishment no Restraint, but by knowne Lawes and Agreements of our owne making."[44]

Despite a generally sharp contrast with the codes of the confederated colonies, the Rhode Island code in several respects was scarcely more modern. The capital laws of Massachusetts, Plymouth, and Connecticut, though harking back more than twenty centuries to the law of the primitive Jews, effected a reduction of death penalties almost as drastic as Rhode Island's. In one vital respect there is no question of the greater foresight of the orthodox colonies. While the Massachusetts code of 1647 inaugurated the celebrated New England system by which the colony compelled all towns to maintain schools, Rhode Island, clinging to the English tradition, left educational standards in the hands of localities. Instruction in the family, private tutoring, and dame schools prevented an abysmal increase of

43 Jellinek, *Declaration of the Rights of Man and of Citizens,* p. 69.
44 *Public Letter of 1666,* Pub. R.I.H.S., VIII (1900), 149.

illiteracy in Williams' commonwealth, but during his lifetime spo-
radic efforts to support town schools were generally ineffective.

In other respects the vast chasm between the scale of human values
of Rhode Island freemen and the gentry of the United Colonies was
writ visibly in the law. With the exception of provisions aimed at
blasphemers, schismatics, Jesuits, and worldlings, the Massachusetts
and Connecticut codes generally preferred Coke to Moses, but for a
generation after 1647 law in the orthodox colonies was like an edi-
fice of solid English brick cemented with crumbling Old Testament
mortar. The arbitrary impulse of oligarchs died hard and the doctrine of an angry God animated the court in the enforcement of
statutes English in substance. The interpretation of law lay in the
breasts of magistrates and afforded no tempered security for persons
or property. Radical books were burned, the Cambridge press cen-
sored, and agitators and non-conformists like the Southwicks of
Salem and the Rogerenes of New London found their estates diminished or confiscated by exorbitant fines and their bodies delivered to
merciless correction by jailings and scourgings. In the seventeenth
century Roger Williams, and in the eighteenth century Thomas
Hutchinson, the learned Tory governor of Massachusetts quoting
Williams, concluded that the founders of New England penalized
moral and spiritual deviations with a rigor more Mosaic than English and tended to confuse religious taboo or sin with crime, exacting
punishment out of proportion to the harm done society.[45] In his
great tract of 1652 Williams expressed scorn for Paul Prys who
aspired to be their brother's keeper and held them "censurable" for
casting suspicion without "proof and evidence."[46] Blasting the
Massachusetts provision of death for heresy, adultery, and witchcraft, he remarked that "spiritual whoredoms and witchcrafts might
stand with civil peace," the more so because "Body killing is but once
and forever, but a soule killed may recover."[47] He objected to "con-
founding Heaven and Earth" and drew an absolute distinction between the two sorts of laws and transgressions, civil and spiritual.[48]
About the time Connecticut adopted its code, he heard of harsh
measures there and wrote to the younger Winthrop that modern

[45] Hutchinson, *History*, I, 386-389, 393.
[46] *Bloody Tenent More Bloody*, N.C.P., IV, 136.
[47] *Ibid.*, 241, 434, 488.
[48] *Ibid.*, 360.

nations should not be bound by the laws and punishments of ancient Israel. Convinced by Winthrop's answer that orthodox magistrates still clung to the spirit of *Moses His Judicialls,* he replied that "too sharp" a penalty for licentiousness was "destructive" and that many who saw cause "to sigh at the filthiness in this land" might sigh "also at the unchristian ways of punishments."[49]

The draftsmen of the Rhode Island code betrayed a lack of technical proficiency in law but they made up for it by a liberal understanding and common-sense reliance on the statute book, Coke, Dalton, Stamford, and the *Doctor and Student,* a sixteenth century discussion of fundamental rights destined to be a favorite of Thomas Jefferson.[50] Early Rhode Island judges, self-trained, included men like John Clarke, Gorton, and Williams. Neither fettered by narrow devotion to precedent nor inflated by a conception like the elder Winthrop's that judges were "gods upon Earthe," they administered law with a warm humanity, and during Williams' lifetime only two men were executed, both for murder. Records of the early courts exhibit relatively little enthusiasm for the stocks and whipping post and more of the moral tolerance of the frontier than of the righteous wrath of stewards of the Lord.[51] Enemies of the colony, Williams observed, "told tales . . . that we are a profane people."[52] As this reputation spread, fugitive sinners from the realms of orthodoxy invaded Rhode Island, and after 1668 town fathers became somewhat sterner.

Rhode Island laws and courts offered more than an escape from the moral rigors of Puritanism. Religious and political refugees like Samuel Hubbard from Fairfield, Connecticut, who became an outstanding Baptist minister and warm friend of Roger Williams, Peter Folger, ancestor of Benjamin Franklin and a Baptist laborer among the Indians, and John Smith, the "remonstrant," continued to find in Providence plantations a freedom they had failed to find elsewhere. After 1647 witch hunting began to bear its gnarled fruit in Massachusetts and Connecticut. Prosecutions gradually mounted to a total of eighty or more cases prior to the final outburst at Salem and led to nine or eleven executions in Connecticut alone. The Gortonists immediately cried out "against them which putteth people to death

49 *Letters,* N.C.P., VI, 191, 193, 198.
50 See legal references, *R. I. Col. Recs.,* I, 163, 165, 168, 169, 172.
51 See *R. I. Court Records, 1647-1670,* 2 vols., Providence, 1920.
52 *Williams to Mason, 1670,* N.C.P., VI, 346.

for witches" and the colony opened arms to James Walkley, Goody Seager, and other escaped or suspected witches.[53] It cannot be presumed that witches avoided such a likely place as Rhode Island—but perhaps it required the trained eye of a Visible Saint to detect one. No witches were ever hailed into a Rhode Island court and the law against them was a dead letter from the start.[54]

There was no James Madison at the assembly of 1647 to take notes on debates, and one must draw one's own inference as to particular contributions of individual members. Roger Williams held a strategic position as chairman of the Providence delegation, and his university training, unequalled grasp of first principles and gift of speech easily ranked him the outstanding personality. Measures such as the allowance for those who "scruple the giving or taking of an oath"[55] echo principles he had long championed, and the preamble of the code of laws, the bill of rights, and the declaration of liberty of conscience are turned in language which strongly suggests his personal touch. But the new framework was the joint creation of many men who had followed the beckoning horizon and won to the sound core of their philosophy by strenuous experience. Prominent among the members from Aquidneck were the Clarkes, John and Jeremy, Nicholas Easton, William Dyer, and John Coggeshall, the new president; while from the mainland towns came forceful men like John Smith, who had taken his stand with Robert Child for reform of the Massachusetts government, Gregory Dexter, Robert Williams, John Greene, and Randall Holden.[56] Absent overseas, Samuel Gorton found voice through his followers whom he had schooled to insistence on the rights of Englishmen under English law. William Harris most likely had no part in the work of the assembly, since after his disfranchisement at Providence he hibernated at Pawtuxet and until 1656 held aloof from colonial affairs. Coddington, though elected assistant in the hope of conciliation, refused to recognize the charter and according to Plymouth testimony abstained from meetings of the assembly.[57]

[53] *R. I., Col. Recs.*, I, 235; *The Connecticut Magazine*, V (Oct., 1899), pp. 557, 559.
[54] See W. R. Staples, *The Code of Laws of 1647* (Providence, 1847), p. 27 n.; Arnold, *Rhode Island*, I, 525.
[55] *R. I. Col. Recs.*, I, 181.
[56] *Ibid.*, I, 42, 148.
[57] Chapin, *Doc. Hist. R. I.*, I, 225; II, 179.

After adjournment, President Coggeshall recorded agreement in the assembly "beyond expectation" and general "satisfaction" with its accomplishments.[58] A more perfect union had been created, and a freeholder's democracy bred from the soil and dedicated to liberty had won an impressive triumph. But secessionists in the colony, their allies of the New England Confederacy, and the bungling intervention of the mother country were to cause another decade of struggle before Rhode Island democrats could consolidate the gains of 1647.

[58] *Ibid.,* II, 183.

14

INDIAN TRADER AND FRONTIER PEACEMAKER

DURING THE FOUR YEARS FOLLOWING MAY, 1647, Williams withdrew when he could from the responsibilities of public office and sought to repair his private fortunes. The colony had not reimbursed his heavy expenditures for the charter, and since 1642 and 1643 when his sons, Daniel and Joseph, were born, he had six children to support. While the main source of livelihood was his farm at Providence, the small trade he had established with the Narragansetts in 1637 had grown, and by 1645 he was keeping an agent regularly employed at his Cocumcussot post.[1] From May, 1647, to September, 1651, Williams plunged wholeheartedly into the life of a fur trader, and except for occasional forays into public affairs, spent long periods at Cocumcussot, accompanied sometimes by Mary Williams or one of his elder daughters. Thriftily he engaged also in "improving some Goats" on an island in the harbor and urged the colony to liquidate its debt "about the charter" by stocking his island with "Cattell of that kind."[2] At intervals he found spiritual release by continuing his missionary work, visiting the little wigwam villages to preach simple homilies or to administer medicines to those who prayed for the white father's help in their sickness.

Williams' trading post soon netted an average of £100 a year. Richard Smith, whose family were his sole white neighbors at Cocumcussot, and Dutch interlopers competed for the rich Narragansett trade, but Williams, through fair dealing and the gratitude of the natives for his diplomatic services, kept pace with his rivals. Conscience, to be sure, interfered with profit. Without regret Williams remarked that he could have made "thousands" if he had stooped as the Arnolds and others did to the "murderous" traffic in guns and liquor. With his hearty support, Rhode Island soon passed a law against the sale of "strong waters" to Indians; though the assembly made a special exception of Williams who had leave to dole out small amounts for "natives in theare sickness."[3]

[1] 2 *Proc. M.H.S., 1892-1894*, VIII, 11.   [2] *Prov. Recs.*, XV, 39.
[3] *Letters*, N.C.P., VI, 180, 296; *R. I. Col. Recs.*, I, 219.

The white man's economic system was not the red man's, and Williams discovered that his friendship with Canonicus was not always a business asset. Williams sometimes declared that the sachems made him a "gift" of Providence, Pawtuxet, and the site of his trading post which Canonicus marked out "with his own hands"; but these were gifts only in the sense that there was no stipulated payment of "purchase" money. Settlers who knew less of the natives than Williams would have called Canonicus an "Indian giver," for he was steadfast in the simple tribal faith in community of possession which recognized no private right in land but only a privilege of occupancy in return for tribute. Williams respected the principle of the natives, but it cost him dear. While they lived, Miantonomu and Canonicus had the engaging habit of dropping in at his Providence house or his trading post and helping themselves to trinkets or commodities that caught their princely fancy. Canonicus "never traded with me," remarked Williams, "but had freely what he desired, goods, money," and in 1647 when he lay dying, "sent for me and desired to be buried in my cloth of free gift and so he was."[4]

Williams' trading post lay on the sandy western shore of Narragansett bay many miles south of the nearest white settlement. Beyond, along the lower reaches of the great bay toward the open sea stretched the rolling tidewater plain studded with villages of the Narragansetts—the picturesque south country which in two generations would become a fertile principality for wealthy white planters, slave-owners, and horse fanciers. Round about Cocumcussot the primeval forest, extending down from the rough, shaggy hill country of the interior, pressed in on Williams' little outpost, broken only by Indian traces like the Pequot Path. Though an English parson city-born and college trained, Williams took naturally to the life of a fur trader and revelled in the solitude and untamed charm of wilderness and shoreline. His book on the language and customs of the natives betrayed an enthusiast's relish for things woodsy and wild, and his curious and observant eye noted birds unknown in England, their calls, plumage, and markings, the fish and game abounding in the region, their habits, value to the natives, and methods for their capture, and the trees, berries, and fruits of husbandry in this strange country. At the end of a hard winter in the Narragansett country he

4 Williams' Plea, 1677, printed in Carpenter, *Roger Williams*, p. 226.

wrote to the younger Winthrop of a moose killed by the Indians, the skin of which Winthrop could have if he desired.[5]

From his forest-fringed inlet Williams could see the long dugouts of natives skirt the shore or catch the welcome sight of English or Dutch sail. Heralding the dawn of Rhode Island commerce, "John Smith of Warwicke Merchant" and John Throckmorton of Providence began a colonial trade in tobacco, flour, pease, Indian corn, pork, and other foodstuffs on voyages ranging from Long Island to Newfoundland. Throckmorton, homeward bound from Plymouth, ran aground at Sakonnet rocks and lost his first vessel though not the cargo. To transport tools and cloth for barter with the natives and the furs he received in exchange Williams had a large canoe, a shallop, and a pinnace, and was as much at home on the water as in the forest, though on one occasion wind and a rough sea nearly proved his undoing. His "boat not being fitted," he was paddling from Providence when heavy waves capsized the canoe and he was miraculously "snatched" from the jaws of death. During these years Williams noted the appearance of enterprising Dutch fishermen whose boats began to visit Rhode Island shores and he expressed hope that it would stimulate "some English that way." Benedict Arnold, he reported, desired "to buy my shallop and further that work, which I heartily desire. . . . The Natives have taken abundance of sturgeon and cod, and bass this year." In 1649 a Dutch privateer anchored off Newport, and Williams was soon writing to the younger Winthrop that a volatile French member of the crew had gone ashore and made a conquest of the fair sex to the great scandal of Aquidneck.[6]

In the course of his long and affectionate correspondence with the younger Winthrop, Williams relayed word of the king's execution and other great news and discussed religion, politics, agriculture, medical lore, and the latest books from England. The two men set up a joint circulating library and exchanged books and manuscripts.[7] Williams inquired about a tract with levelling tendencies which had drawn his interest: it imported, he wrote, "another high case on foot touching a more equal division of lands" with provision for "younger

[5] *Letters*, N.C.P., VI, 195.

[6] *Ibid.*, 164, 174, 178, 184, 197, 212; *Prov. Recs.*, XV, 53, 55, 59.

[7] *The Medulla* and the *Magnalia Dei*, the *Trial of Wits*, *Eikon Basilike*, Carpenter's *Geography*, and others; see *N.C.P.*, VI, 143, 167, 173, 184, 192, 195, 199.

brethren."[8] One day he informed his friend of the extraordinary news "that the King and many great Lords and Parliament men are beheaded." His sympathies were with Cromwell, not with Charles who "breathed first to last absolute Monarchy and Episcopacy." Rebellion and parliamentary supremacy might seem dangerous and destructive but he believed in the right of revolution: "All that seems weighty in my eyes," he told Winthrop, "are the popular tumults" which royalists attempted to blame on parliament. " 'Tis true it is a dangerous remedy, yet that which God used against Baal's priests."[9]

By the latter part of 1648 intrigues of Rhode Island secessionists and the pressure of the United Colonies brought Williams back into the political arena. In a generous endeavor to win support of the charter, the union party in May, 1648, elected Coddington president, but he rejected the office and eventually Williams took his place as acting president. A former oligarch and for three years treasurer of the Bay colony, Coddington had been one of the wealthy men who Boston townsfolk feared would take all the best land. On leaving the Bay he realized £1300 on his property there, obtained two magnificent estates from the Aquidneck government which he dominated, and established himself as the wealthiest landowner and stock-raiser of the region. No democrat, he had been fighting a rearguard action since 1639 against levellers like Gorton whom he abominated. He had the support of Newport gentry like William Brenton and Captain Partridge and a large following in Portsmouth and now secretly planned to use his influence either with the United Colonies or with the new rulers of England to break the union of Aquidneck with the mainland.[10]

At the end of August, 1648, Williams issued a strong public letter urging the unionists and the Coddington men to arbitrate differences: "Worthy Friends, that ourselves and all men are apt and prone to differ, it is no new thing ... I humbly and earnestly beseech you to be willing to be pacifiable, willing to be reconcilable, willing to be sociable." He feared that dissension would lead to appeals for outside help and result in secession or subjugation of the colony. "To trouble our neighbors of other colonies, seems neither safe nor

8 *Ibid.*, 189.

9 *Ibid.*, 180, 199-200.

10 See study of Coddington's economic interests and aristocratic ambitions in Richman, *Rhode Island*, II, 4-10.

honorable." The only prudent course was for both sides to choose arbitrators and "by one final sentence . . . end all." The unionists supported the proposal, and the following month Williams told the younger Winthrop that he hoped to have him named as an arbitrator.[11] But Coddington's answer confirmed Williams' heaviest fears. Together with Captain Partridge, the Newport magnate negotiated at Plymouth and returned with a proposal to submit to that colony. Randall Holden and another Gortonist visited Plymouth to point out that the scheme was unlawful under the charter but were rebuffed by Governor Bradford. Coddington, however, failed to lure Aquidneck into the Plymouth fold and immediately sailed for England with the intention of getting the charter rescinded.

As Coddington departed, Williams began to have increasing fear that through internal division Rhode Island would be vulnerable to piecemeal dismemberment by the United Colonies. The arrival of Captain Atherton and troops of the Confederacy at Cocumcussot in October, 1648, was an ominous portent of seizure of the lands of the Narragansetts which under the charter were part of Rhode Island. Atherton frankly told Williams of his interest in the region, his thoughts centering for the moment on a plantation at Block Island or the Niantic country. The immediate object of the expedition was to collect payment on the indemnity imposed in 1645 and to charge the sachems with stirring up the Mohawks against Uncas and his Mohegans. Again John Haynes and other magistrates harkened lightly to the siren voice of their crafty ally, paying no heed to sober warnings from Williams who sent word to Connecticut of the grievance of the Narragansetts whose chieftains protested that Uncas and other natives "out of their reach in the English protection" had murdered thirteen of their tributaries in three years "with impunity."[12]

William Arnold came with the confederate troops as interpreter, but the sachems scorned the Pawtuxet renegade because of previous deceptions, and Captain Atherton once more had to turn to Williams. A month earlier when Williams learned that a Mohawk emissary was seeking an alliance with the Narragansetts against Uncas, he feared that the United Colonies would protect their ally and precipitate war. The alliance failed to materialize, and Williams told

---

[11] *Letters*, N.C.P., VI, 149-150, 154.

[12] Haynes to John Winthrop, Jr., 4 *Coll. M.H.S.*, VI, 358; Williams, *Letters*, N.C.P., VI, 156.

Atherton that he was confident the Narragansetts "never intended hurt against the English," though they confessed their enmity to Uncas and intended to present their grievances to the United Colonies when they had paid their wampum. Williams' skill in mediation smoothed the way, and after nearly a week of negotiation at his trading post the soldiers of the Confederation departed "with good content," though not until Williams had spoken his mind about "partiality in the case" and referred Atherton to John Winthrop, Jr., for proof about the character of Uncas.[13] Since 1646 when he founded New London Winthrop had taken the measure of Connecticut's dusky ally and had vented his feelings freely to Williams about his "outrageous carriage."[14]

On May 26, 1649, Williams wrote his New London friend that he had arrived at his trading post "late last night, and wet," after attending the assembly at Warwick where John Smith was elected his successor as president.[15] In subsequent letters Williams betrayed increasing uneasiness at Rhode Island's weakness, Indian unrest, and the devious policy of the United Colonies. After March, 1649, when death removed Governor Winthrop, there remained no powerful figure in the Bay colony likely to trust Williams' judgment on Indian affairs, and thereafter he appealed to the Connecticut worthies, Captain Mason and John Winthrop, Jr., when native explosions appeared imminent. The renegade Pequot, Uncas, out of the inexhaustible cunning of his savage brain, continually devised means to bring down the wrath of the United Colonies upon his Rhode Island foes. Williams heard a rumor in May that the Confederacy was bent on war with the Narragansetts.[16] Richard Smith and his "usual trader," a Narragansett, had put in at Mohegan where Uncas came aboard the pinnace and on a sudden "groaned and cried out that the Narragansett had killed him: the Narragansett man denied it, and Uncas showed a wound on his breast which bled afresh." The subtle Pequot had two fingers of the hapless Narragansett "cut off and sent to Capt. Mason," who obligingly took the man prisoner to Hartford. Williams promptly informed the younger Winthrop, then in Boston, that the Rhode Island sachems professed innocence and had told him

13 For Winthrop's protests to the United Colonies against Uncas, see *Plymouth Col. Recs.*, IX, 101-103.
14 See *Letters*, N.C.P., VI, 152, 153, 155-160.
15 *Ibid.*, 180.
16 *Ibid.*, 181.

that it would have been "childish, now they are so near finishing their payment, to have prevented the English justice against Uncas, which they are in great hopes of." Uncas, they charged, "projected this vilainy" to render them "still odious to the English, and prevent his trial."[17]

A confession, probably bogus, but implicating the Narragansett sachems, was extorted from the alleged assassin. Urging Winthrop to suspend judgment, Williams adduced strong circumstantial evidence to show that the attack could not have been a deliberate plot by the Narragansetts.[18] During Winthrop's absence, Williams wrote in the same vein to Mrs. Winthrop at New London. "I believe nothing of any of the barbarians on either side, but what I have eye sight for, or English testimony."[19] He was confident the Narragansetts were not deceiving him in this instance. Hoping to avert bloodshed, he also conveyed his information to Captain John Mason of Saybrook. On an earlier occasion, Mason naïvely admitted to Williams his general predilection to "favor" Uncas.[20] On June 13 Williams gloomily wrote Winthrop that Mason was ready for the warpath. Mason had acknowledged "loving letters (and tokens, which, upon the burning of his house,) he had received from me," and his letters were "kind to myself" but "terrible to all these natives," especially the sachems. "If nothing but blood will satisfy them, I doubt not but they may have their fill," the doughty captain had written him; "I perceive such an obstinate willfullness, joined with desperate malicious practices, that I think and believe they are sealed to destruction."[21]

Mason was an old Indian fighter and his policy of the big stick was congenial to the commissioners. "The conclusion is therefore ruin," wrote Williams.[22] Mason, he thought, had little understanding of Indian policy, and in another letter he warned Winthrop to be wary of him. Conciliation and fair dealing were not cowardly: "The peace makers are sons of God. . . . Sir, heap coals of fire on Captain Mason's head."[23] Williams continually reiterated his belief that the

---

[17] *Letters*, N.C.P., VI, 175.
[18] *Ibid.*, 176. Williams' evidence throws strong doubt on the usual version of this incident; cf. De Forest, *Indians of Connecticut*, pp. 236-237.
[19] *Letters*, N.C.P., VI, 177.
[20] *Ibid.*, 167.
[21] *Ibid.*, 182.
[22] *Ibid.*
[23] Undated letter, presumably of 1648; *ibid.*, 167.

Narragansetts, if dealt with fairly, would prove good neighbors, and in the end his restraining influence won the day. Ninigret, appearing at Boston, attempted to prove the innocence of himself and Pessicus, but the commissioners refused to believe him. Hostilities were averted by Ninigret's testimony, supported by Williams, that the Narragansetts had never intended to defy the United Colonies.[24] Williams, far more experienced in Indian intrigue than any of the commissioners, remained convinced that Uncas had perpetrated a ghastly hoax and that the celebrated stabbing was self-inflicted. The wound was healed remarkably soon.

What Williams called the "admired partiality"[25] of the United Colonies was visible in two other incidents. The commissioners, so wrathy when the Narragansetts were at fault, made no effort to bring Uncas to book when in August, 1649, his Mohegans attacked the remnants of the Pequots who were subject to Pessicus and Ninigret. In this new crisis the Narragansetts sent for Williams and he found their young bucks thirsting for vengeance, but the sachems took his advice to lay their case before the United Colonies and restrained their men.[26] The commissioners were as little concerned when the Shawomet tribe, which Massachusetts protected, was guilty of depredations. After years in which the shadowy suzerainty of Massachusetts and Plymouth had emboldened Pomham's men to prey on them, the Gortonists finally carried a protest to Plymouth that the natives killed livestock, stole from houses, and even made personal assaults on Warwick settlers.[27] The pretense of orderly restraint in countless small matters by the absentee authorities of Plymouth and the Bay was in the nature of the case an absurdity. The United Colonies issued an ineffectual order to Pomham to take "dew care"; the depredations continued, Pomham defied a Rhode Island injunction to appear in court, and finally in December, 1649, a "great fray" broke out between Warwick men and the Shawomets resulting in minor bloodshed.[28] Williams temporarily composed differences and projected a treaty, but Plymouth and Massachusetts, jealous of any settlement recognizing the rights of the Gortonists,

---

24 *Plymouth Col. Recs.,* IX, 143 ff.
25 *Letters,* N.C.P., VI, 157.
26 *Ibid.,* 185.
27 Chapin, *Doc. Hist. R. I.,* I, 262.
28 *Plymouth Col. Recs.,* IX, 130; *R. I. Col. Recs.,* I, 218.

failed to support him, and Pomham continued on his swaggering way.[29]

In 1650 the Narragansetts fell behind in payments, and early in October Captain Atherton descended with a force of twenty armed men, some mounted. At Atherton's request, Williams relayed a demand for the arrears on the indemnity, three hundred and eight fathom of peage—and more than half as much again to pay for the troops! The sachems answered proudly that they had "ever resolved to pay," but because of the attack on their Pequot tributaries by Uncas and the Mohegans, they "expected satisfaction, and receive none." They were willing to negotiate about final payments, and Williams arranged a rendezvous which, by Atherton's stipulation, was to be attended only by Pessicus and Ninigret, Williams, and Atherton with one or two soldiers. Relying upon the good faith of Williams, the Narragansett chieftains appeared as appointed, suspecting no treachery. But Atherton had played Williams false: secretly the Massachusetts captain "drew up his men . . . round about the Sachems in a hole," outnumbering them twenty to one and "armed and ready with guns." The brave captain then asked Williams to speak to the sachems in the Indian tongue and tell them they were surrounded and that he would take them by force.

"I was betrayed," cried Williams, and turning in blazing anger on the Massachusetts captain, he lashed out at the hazard of lives and blood "for a little money" and cuttingly asked why, if Atherton's cause was just, he need resort to despicable trickery. After long wrangling, Williams brought home to the emissaries of the United Colonies that they were "upon the ticklish point of a great slaughter."

On October 9, sitting in an "Indian house," for his trading post was "filled with soldiers," Williams hurriedly wrote to Winthrop of the incident and of his present hope to save the land from the "plague of war."[30] "I persuaded the Captain to stay at my house four days, and the natives within four days to bring in the peag and I would lay down ten fathom: (as formerly I had done twenty (God knows beyond my ability.)" Williams did not conceal from his old friend his deep indignation. He had told the captain, he said, that he had "desparately betrayed me and himself. . . I hope the Lord will

29 *Letters*, N.C.P., VI, 190.
30 *Ibid.*, 200-202.

show him, and show the Country what dangerous Councils the Commissioners produce: which makes me fear God is preparing a War in the Country." In a second letter eight days later Williams reported that the Narragansetts had paid handsomely and that he had written a petition for the natives asking that the rest of the indemnity be cancelled. Atherton agreed to support the petition and thought Winthrop and several others would. "I was (if not too) warm, insisting on the partiality against the Narragansetts and towards Uncas." Williams described at length the "villainous dealing" of Uncas against Winthrop and New London people, and the captain, now apologetic, told him the whole business was planned from the beginning by the commissioners of the United Colonies who were "resolved to hazard a war upon it." War, Williams insisted, would dispossess many a planter and plantation and bring "blood, and slaughter, and ruin to both English and Indian."[31]

Only the presence of Williams averted war in 1650, and considering the narrow margin of victory in 1676, he eminently deserved the high praise of the younger Winthrop who congratulated him and declared the whole country "obliged to you."[32] Winthrop promptly intervened to pacify the Narragansetts by accepting their peage and cancelling the residue of the indemnity.[33] Three years earlier Williams had been hopeful that "fractions" between tribes would prevent the Indians from combining against the English and offer an opportunity for missionaries "to draw them nearer to civility," but by 1650 he had a foreboding of the eventual conflagration.[34] With men of the stamp of Mason and Atherton in the field and magistrates and commissioners of the Confederation playing off tribe against tribe in the interests of Mammon, postponement of conflict depended upon the delicate balance between cautious older chieftains like Ninigret and embittered younger leaders like Philip. In the face of the imperial policy of the United Colonies there could be no large opportunity in New England for men with the vision of John Eliot, nor any bright outlook for the policy of friendship and race coöperation for which Williams strove in Rhode Island and which the French were developing in Canada with striking success.

[31] Ibid., 203-204.
[32] Ibid., 202.
[33] Winthrop to Atherton, 5 Coll. M. H. S., VIII, 42.
[34] Letters, N.C.P., VI, 186, 202.

A succession of events in 1650 and 1651 once more roused Williams to seek English protection for his struggling commonwealth. While maintaining incessant pressure on the Narragansetts, the United Colonies continued to thwart and weaken the chartered government of Rhode Island, protecting the Pawtuxet secessionists and threatening once more to suppress the Gortonists. In 1648 William Arnold, counting too confidently on defrauding Providence and deceiving Massachusetts, drove the servants of William Field from the latter's land in Pawtuxet. Field sued in the Providence court, Arnold refused to appear, and finally on September 29, 1649, President Smith summoned Arnold and his son Stephen to the colony court of trials.[35] Arnold thereupon produced Williams' original deed to Providence and Pawtuxet which had been in his possession for years and astonished the court by demonstrating that the document gave Providence men no title to Pawtuxet. Copies of the deed and the mutilated condition of the original soon revealed that Arnold had cut out the section recording the Pawtuxet purchase and "pasted the said writing together againe so Cuningly that it Could hardly bee diserned."[36] Had Arnold's brazen fraud succeeded, his secondary deed from Socononoco would have enabled Arnold, Carpenter, and their associates to bar Field, William Harris, and others from their lands and houses in Pawtuxet. Field angrily urged the English penalty of earcropping for forgery or mutilation of records, but old Arnold's ears were spared and in May, 1650, when Massachusetts sent a peremptory order to "forebeare" prosecution, Rhode Island dropped the case.[37] Arnold and Carpenter did not completely pull the wool over the eyes of the Bay magistrates and their attempt to dispossess Harris, Field, and Nathaniel Dickens through court proceedings in Massachusetts resulted in a verdict for the latter.

The infringement of Rhode Island's chartered rights presented increasing menace to the integrity of the colony. Massachusetts in an order of May 23, 1650, summarily upheld the Pawtuxet secessionists in encroachments on Warwick lands and on June 19 formally incorporated Pawtuxet and Warwick in "the county of Suffolke."[38] Williams was presently disturbed by a rumor that a Massachusetts

[35] *Prov. Recs.*, XV, 22 27, 29.
[36] See Chapin, *Doc. Hist. R. I.*, I, 63 and *passim*.
[37] *Mass. Bay Recs.*, III, 196-197.
[38] *Ibid.*, 196-197, 201, 202.

detachment might soon descend to reduce the Gortonists to submission and also the Narragansetts.[39] Verifying the rumor,[40] Atherton's troops arrived in October, and Warwick men, overawed, dared not attempt prosecution of Arnold. On October 26 the Rhode Island assembly resolved to ask Williams to carry their case to England,[41] but unfortunately for the colony the project was not pushed quickly enough and five months later, on April 3, 1651, Coddington obtained a commission in England constituting him governor of Aquidneck for life. On May 22, 1651, Massachusetts sent an official warning to Williams that his plantation must cease attempting to collect taxes from Arnold, Carpenter, and Robert Cole, otherwise the Bay magistrates would intervene "in such manner as God shall put into theire hands." [42] The Rhode Island charter was still a nominal protection of the two mainland settlements, but since the United Colonies now authorized Plymouth to assume jurisdiction in Warwick and Massachusetts challenged the chartered rights of Providence, independence had become precarious.

The opportunism of a small number of Rhode Island land owners and speculators, the meddling policy of the United Colonies, and the blundering action of the council of state in granting Coddington's plea without adequate investigation of his bogus claims[43] to proprietorship of all Aquidneck, had reduced Rhode Island to a situation like that of 1643 when Massachusetts troops came down to harry the Gortonists. In view of the absolutist pretensions of orthodox clergy and gentry, a new harrying of the land was logically to be expected. As early as 1646 the United Colonies made a rigorous order for suppression of "Anabaptisme,"[44] and Rhode Island Baptists like the later Quakers responded by carrying defiance into enemy territory—compounding the abomination by introducing the new mode of baptism by "dipping." In December, 1649, Williams informed John Winthrop, Jr., that Providence and Newport Baptists had been won over to immersion. John Clarke had converted "a great many" at Seekonk in Plymouth territory and "dipped them," and in consequence Williams feared new persecution and had in fact

[39] *Letters*, N.C.P., VI, 198.
[40] *Plymouth Col. Recs.*, IX, 170.
[41] *R. I. Col. Recs.*, I, 231.
[42] *Mass. Bay Recs.*, III, 228; *Prov. Recs.*, II, 53-54.
[43] See Chapter 15, p. 212 and note.
[44] *Plymouth Col. Recs.*, IX, 81.

heard that Massachusetts had threatened action of her own unless Plymouth proceeded "to prosecute at Seekonk."[45] Subsequently Clarke and Obadiah Holmes, indicted by the grand jury at Plymouth, found temporary immunity by placing themselves on the safe side of the Rhode Island boundary. By September, 1651, Massachusetts undertook negotiations with Coddington's regime for extradition of fugitives who found shelter at Aquidneck and began to meditate even more active suppression of Rhode Island plague bearers.[46] Meanwhile the Bay authorities caught three Rhode Island Baptists red-handed and made an example of them to terrorize other itinerant preachers and their would-be auditors.

Clarke, Holmes, and John Crandall of Newport fell into the clutches of the Massachusetts magistrates in July, 1651, while privately visiting an aged Baptist at Lynn who had requested their ministration, and were sentenced to a heavy fine or a severe whipping if they refused payment. Clarke objected that the legal proceedings violated their traditional liberties under English law, to which Governor Endecott retorted harshly that he "deserved death."[47] Obadiah Holmes, adamant in his convictions, refused to pay the fine lest it appear an admission of guilt and blessed God that he was made of the stuff to endure, whereupon John Wilson, minister of Boston church, struck Holmes in fury and called down the "curse of God" upon him.[48] Stripped to the waist and secured in the whipping post, Holmes suffered with stern fortitude while thirty stripes administered with a three-corded whip were laid on his quivering flesh. Two in the crowd of spectators, one an old man who had traveled fifty miles from Seekonk to comfort Holmes in prison, dared to take the victim by the hand and support him as he came trembling down from the whipping post. Sympathy among spectators found no answering compassion among the magistrates. They clapped a fine of forty shillings apiece on the two men who comforted Holmes and sentenced them to a severe whipping in case of default.[49]

Even old friends in England found such atrocities hard to defend, for libertarian ideas were advancing rapidly there and the brutality of New England was widely criticized. From old Sir Richard Sal-

---

[45] Williams to Winthrop, *N.C.P.*, VI, 188.
[46] *Plymouth Col. Recs.*, IX, 215, 220.
[47] John Clarke, *Ill Newes from New-England*, 4 Coll. M.H.S., II, 33.
[48] Holmes's narrative, *Coll. R.I.H.S.*, VI, 362.
[49] *Ibid.*, 366.

tonstall, long since returned to the mother country, came a letter of deep mortification: "It doth not a little grieve my spirit to hear what sad things are reported daily of your tyranny and persecutions in New-England, as that you fine, whip and imprison men for their consciences." English Puritans had hoped "you might have been eyes to God's people here, and not to practice those courses in a wilderness, which you went so far to prevent." Such rigid ways had "laid" New England magistrates "very low in the hearts of the saints."[50]

While the three Rhode Island Baptists were still in prison, Williams wrote to John Winthrop, Jr., in the hope that there might be "some kind of conference" and a merciful conclusion. "The Father of Lights graciously guide them and us in such paths."[51] A little later he wrote again that he had met "Mr. John Clarke, at Providence, *recens e carcere.*" The governor, Endecott, "my much lamented friend," told Clarke that "he was worthy to be hanged."[52] Later when news came of the scourging of Holmes, who was scarred for life by the whip,[53] Williams was so stirred to indignation that he sent a powerful appeal to Endecott.[54] Reminding the Massachusetts governor of their great mutual affection in earlier times, Williams was "humbly bold" to recall the "Humanitie and pietie, which I and others have formerly observed in you," and asked how it could now be "that he that speakes so tenderly for his owne, hath yet so little respect, mercie or pitie to the like consciencious perswasions of other Men?" How could magistrates and clergy "fight against all Consciences opposite to theirs" without running the risk of fighting against truth in some of them:

> Oh remember it is a dangerous Combat for the potsheards of the Earth to fight with their dreadfull Potter. . . . It is a dreadfull voyce from the King of Kings, and Lord of Lords, Endicot, Endicot, why huntest thou me? why imprisonest thou me? why finest, why so bloudily whippest, why wouldest thou (did not I hould thy bloudie hands) hang and burne me?

Williams concluded with an urgent appeal to show more moderation

50 Backus, *The Baptists,* I, 246.
51 *N.C.P.,* VI, 211.
52 *Ibid.,* 213.
53 *Coll. R.I.H.S.,* VI, 367 n.
54 Williams to Endecott, *N.C.P.,* IV, 502-518.

and "more tremblingly to enquire" as to the "holy pleasure." The
letter troubled the dour governor of Massachusetts, although it did
not swerve him from his course. He had the courtesy to reply to his
former Salem friend, hoping to give "satisfaccon as much as lyes in
mee."[55]

In the face of this disastrous succession of events culminating in
the Coddington secession and the Baptist persecution, the amputated
but still functioning government of Providence plantations, of which
Samuel Gorton was now president, resolved to appeal at once to the
council of state. In this proposal Gorton and the assembly, although
legally representing only Warwick and Providence, had the vigorous
support of a majority at Aquidneck. Sixty-five Newport men and
forty-one of Portsmouth joined in a request that John Clarke seek
repeal of Coddington's commission.[56] Impressed by the determination of the unionists, William Arnold on September 1, 1651, hastily
despatched a plea to his northern allies to intervene at once and make
Rhode Island safe for oligarchy.[57] Since Coddington's commission
had "broken the force" of Williams' charter, he believed there would
never be a better opportunity to take over Providence and Warwick.
The need for action was immediate, because Providence men and
the Gortonists were raising two hundred pounds "to send Mr. Roger
Williams unto the Parlyament to get them a charter." Warwick in
fact had already raised a hundred pounds and people there and in
Providence had contributed as much as ten pounds and twenty
pounds a man. Arnold slyly placed his proposal for imperial conquest on the lofty plane of a crusade against sinners, heretics, and
democrats. Since Rhode Island under a new charter would "serve
for an inroade to lett in forces to overrune the whole country," it
was "very unfitt that such a company" should be allowed to maintain
a government: "under the pretence of liberty of conscience about
these partes there comes to live all the scume the runne awayes of the
country." He had heard that a man apprehended for adultery in
Connecticut or New Haven had broken prison and had taken refuge
in Rhode Island and had not been executed, although the woman,
failing to escape, had been put to death. The Pawtuxet renegade,

[55] See Endecott to John Winthrop, Jr., 4 *Coll. M.H.S.*, VI, 153.

[56] See Staples, *Annals,* p. 82; H. E. Turner, "William Coddington," *R. I. H. Tracts,* IV, 41, 48-49.

[57] Arnold to Massachusetts, *R. I. Col. Recs.,* I, 234-235.

whose irreligion and personal morals were notorious in Providence,[58] then struck a chord which he knew would reverberate in magisterial hearts. It was time "there were some better order taken for these partes"; but he begged that his name be kept privy, lest Rhode Island become inflamed against him.

Williams sent word to Winthrop at New London that Rhode Island people had besought him "to endeavor the renewing of their liberties" and that he was departing for England, possibly from New Amsterdam rather than Boston—"you know the reason."[59] This was Williams' last letter from his beloved Cocumcussot. Forced by conscience to sacrifice private to public interest, he sold his trading post to Richard Smith for the paltry sum of £50.[60] In later years Williams was often a visitor among his old Indian friends but he never again reëstablished his trading business or resumed his life in the wilderness.

In October, 1651, Williams petitioned the Massachusetts court for permission to pass "through your jurisdiction as a stranger for a night" to take ship for England. He referred to the letter of 1644 in which eminent English Puritans requested his safe conduct and reminded the Bay magistrates that "ever since the time of my exile I have been . . . a professed and known servant to this colony and all the colonies of the English in peace and war."[61] The petition was granted, and Williams and John Clarke, the latter as agent for Aquidneck, sailed from Boston in November. Meanwhile, the Gortonists served on the United Colonies a dignified and courteous notice of their intentions. Inasmuch as Rhode Island people were excluded from the ports of their neighbors and denied access to supplies, and since the town of Warwick was "bought and sold from one patent and jurisdiction to another" and harassed with impunity by both Indians and Pawtuxet men under countenance of the United Colonies, they were sending an envoy to England to obtain justice. The United Colonies might therefore instruct their agents abroad to answer their accusations.[62]

This was fair warning.

[58] See Williams to Endecott, Dec. 1, 1656, *Pub. R.I.H.S.*, VIII, 145.
[59] *Letters*, N.C.P., VI, 228-229.
[60] Backus, *The Baptists*, I, 452.
[61] Williams to Massachusetts, *N.C.P.*, VI, 231-233.
[62] Arnold, *Rhode Island*, I, 238.

15

COLONIAL DIPLOMAT

THE TURMOIL OF ENGLISH AFFAIRS in the early months of 1652 effectively prevented Rhode Island's agents from pressing their suit to unseat Coddington. Sir Henry Vane was in Scotland; Cromwell, slowly consolidating his power, had but recently won victory at Worcester and he, Vane, and all ranking leaders were now engrossed in the staggering question of a permanent settlement. Williams promptly renewed old friendships with Cornelius Holland and Sir William Masham, both members of the council of state. With their warm support and the decisive influence of Vane, who returned from Scotland in March, Williams and Clarke on April 7 succeeded in getting the Rhode Island petition referred to the committee for foreign affairs.

Meanwhile Williams entered again the brilliant circle of advanced thinkers of whom Vane was the parliamentary spokesman and Milton the great literary champion. Here he met three men, Major Butler, Colonel Danvers, and Charles Vane, with whom he was soon collaborating in public controversy. Williams' most pleasant association was with John Milton. He had been called upon, he related in a letter to Winthrop, "for some time, and with some persons, to practice the Hebrew, the Greek, Latin, French and Dutch. The Secretary of the Council, (Mr. Milton) for my Dutch I read him, read me many more languages."[1] Evidently Milton had discussed with him the startlingly modern educational theories of Comenius. Finding that "Grammar rules begin to be esteemed a tyranny," Williams, who had been tutoring two young men, sons of a member of parliament, proceeded to instruct them "as we teach our children English, by words, phrases and constant talk." In another letter Williams snatched time "near two in the morning" to write from Vane's quarters at Whitehall. Evidently Sir Harry and his guests had talked into the small hours. Williams' reference to old acquaintances of Winthrop's reflected the strange whirligig of fate. Hugh Peter,

[1] *Letters,* N.C.P., VI, 261-262.

former Salem divine who had endorsed the excommunication of Williams, was now eminent at Whitehall and talking toleration. "I have often been with him." Winthrop's brother Stephen was also "a great man for soul liberty." Williams had talked of Winthrop to Vane, "who wishes you were in our colony."[2]

As on Williams' earlier visit, the great conflicts in the nation were a trumpet call to controversy. Revolutionary ardor had swept through the army of saints and dazzled yeomen, artisans, and small tradesmen. Around the campfires of the army, obscure men exchanged heretical and democratic ideas. The old walls had been breached, and a stupefying vista opened on the green pastures of libertarianism in politics and religion. The English Levellers were now in full cry, and aristocratic gentlemen who had set parliament and Puritanism above king were belatedly aghast to find multitudes talking of the plain people above parliament and every man his own priest. Nervous Puritan gentry and clergy pressed parliament to reestablish a state church as a bulwark against "spiritual bolshevism" and prayed fervently that Cromwell and his officers would keep the army from getting out of hand. Already the popular tumult had produced the Agreement of the People, but it remained to be seen how Cromwell would stand on democracy. For the moment he was not yet through with the attempt to reconcile the struggle for popular government with his own imperious sense of high policy and security for the old social structure.

In February, 1652, the orthodox Puritans succeeded in establishing a parliamentary committee for propagation of the gospel and, clinging to the familiar landmark of a state church, attempted to define the degree of latitude to be allowed to dissenters. John Owen and other Independent divines, latitudinarians though they were, complained to parliament of John Biddle's edition of *The Racovian Catechism,* which contained the European doctrines of toleration of Polish Unitarians, with the result that the catechism was ordered to be burned.[3] These same ministers advanced fifteen proposals for an established church which would severely restrict separate worship of dissenters. Any sects which rejected certain specified fundamentals were to be denied toleration, and all people in the nation

[2] *Ibid.,* 234.
[3] S. R. Gardiner, *History of the Commonwealth and Protectorate* (New York, 1897-1903), II, 28.

were to be constrained to pay tithes to maintain ministers of approved churches and compelled to attend Sabbath services either in the established church or dissenting churches which agreed to the fundamentals.[4]

As eight years earlier when they combined with Baptists, Seekers, and left-wing Puritans to defeat Presbyterian intolerance, Vane, Milton, Williams, and their circle now led the battle against the new scheme of Independent intolerance. In rebuttal of *The Humble Proposals* of John Owen and his associates, Williams, collaborating with Major Butler, Charles Vane, Colonel Danvers, and others, published a vigorous protest known as *The Fourth Paper Presented by Major Butler*. It appeared on March 30, 1652, with a preface or "Testimony" signed by "R. W." This preface cut incisively through all proposals for compromise or latitudinarianism and affirmed that real liberty of conscience required complete abandonment of any national church program. Williams referred to a member of the committee for the propagation of the gospel who had declared that he would rather be a persecuting Saul than an indifferent Gallio and quoted Cromwell's quick retort: "I had rather that Mahometanism were permitted amongst us than that one of God's children should be persecuted."[5]

Owen's proposals reflected the vast growth of latitudinarianism, but Vane and his circle envisioned a wider liberty. In the summer of 1652 John Milton composed his famous sonnet to Vane, the concluding lines of which he might equally have applied to his friend from Rhode Island:

> Both spiritual power and civil, what each means,
> What severs each, thou hast learn't, which few have done.
> The bounds of either sword to thee we owe.

England had moved far from the rigid establishment sponsored by parliament and the assembly of divines when Williams was last in England. The Westminster Confession, Presbyterian to the core, had been sanctioned by the assembly but never adopted. Meanwhile freedom had encouraged diversity. Baptist congregations multiplied

---

[4] See summary of the fifteen proposals in Masson, *Milton* (London, 1877), IV, 391-392.

[5] Preface, *The Fourth Paper, Presented by Major Butler* (London, 1652), reprinted by C. S. Brigham (Providence, 1903).

and new sects spawned, Quakers, Diggers, and Fifth Monarchy men in the wake of Ranters, Familists, Seekers, and the early Anabaptists. Skeptical-minded Ranters doubted man's immortality and deified Nature, foreshadowing eighteenth century rationalism. The mystical Quakers with their cry, "Listen to the Lord!" belittled traditional forms and ceremonies, satisfied with nothing but the indwelling spirit. Impatient zealots of the Fifth Monarchy with the militant spirit of old Islam sought immediate overthrow of false religion—by the sword if needs be—and the final establishment of the kingdom of saints as foretold in the Bible. In the face of this amazing growth of new sects, Anglican and Puritan alike stood aghast and scandalized. Meanwhile, in the center of all controversies loomed Cromwell, personally favoring the large *de facto* religious liberty that had come into existence, yet propelled in the opposite direction by the national church party in parliament and still more radically by Colonel Harrison and Fifth Monarchy men of the army. Despite the efforts of Vane and Cromwell, the rump parliament sponsored Owen's fifteen proposals and began to embody them in a series of resolutions.

Roger Williams had his own large remedy for these troubled seas of religious contention, the same that he had given eight years earlier in *The Bloudy Tenent* only to have the book despised and "burnt by the Presbyterian party (then prevailing)."[6] It had not been forgotten, and in 1647 Samuel Richardson asked a pointed question: "Whether the priests were not the cause of the burning of the book, entitled 'The Bloudy Tenent,' because it was against persecution? And whether their consciences would not have dispensed with the burning of the author of it?"[7] In a bulky and impetuous volume of 1652 Williams once more engaged in "skirmishes against the priests,"[8] but this time his book was "received with applause and thanks by the army" and by members of parliament who recognized that there could be no reconciliation "or living together" except by toleration.[9]

In 1647 Cotton had published two tracts, one of a personal character justifying Williams' banishment, the other a fat tome entitled

<hr />

[6] Williams to John Cotton, Jr., 1671, *N.C.P.*, VI, 353.
[7] *The Necessity of Toleration*, reprinted in *Tracts on Liberty of Conscience* (E. B. Underhill, ed., London, 1846), p. 270.
[8] Williams to Gregory Dexter, 1652, *N.C.P.*, VI, 235.
[9] Williams to John Cotton, Jr., 1671, *ibid.*, 353.

The Bloudy Tenent Washed White in the Blood of the Lambe.
In characteristic seventeenth century style Williams aimed his final
blast at Cotton under the lumbering title, *The Bloody Tenent Yet
More Bloody: by Mr. Cottons endevour to wash it white.* This
was Williams' last broadside against the "Fig-leave Evasions and
Distinctions" by which Cotton sought "to hide the nakedness" of
persecution.[10] He twitted Cotton with desiring "to have the word
persecuting changed for the word punishing." But wasn't this ever
the dissimulation "of all that ever persecuted or hunted men" for
conscience? "And for the washing of this bloody Tenent in the
blood of the Lambe, Time hath and will discover that such a Blacka-
more cannot be washed."[11] And was the insistence of New England
ministers on compulsory church attendance unrelated to their fear
of "thin" congregations if free worship were granted?[12] A clergy
which levied tribute by forced payment of tithes tended to become
"rich and lordly, pompous and princely" and stagnate intellectually.[13]
Boldly exposing the arrogance of class, Williams attacked the
"monopoly" on public office by the oligarchy of saints and declared
that those who pretended to be "Christs Stewards" maintained themselves by "oppression."[14] Expressive of his faith in the downtrodden,
he castigated the spiritual and class snobbery which assumed that
rational judgment was a monopoly of the privileged few. Even
"the best and wisest" were prone to "intrap, intangle, and bewilder
themselves" and might well learn from their own fallibility to be
"lesse bitter in their Judgements and Censures on the poore Under-
lings and Outcasts."[15]

With wrathful utterance Williams pursued the doctrines of uni-
versality and absolutism through all their "Winding Staires and
back dores,"[16] exposing relentlessly the arrogant contempt for mankind betrayed by those who assumed that decency and humanity
solely depended upon compulsory acquiescence to one doctrinal
formulation and who naively conceived that infallible truth could
be prescribed by mortal men and inward regeneration imposed from

10 *Bloody Tenent More Bloody*, N.C.P., IV, 61, 474, 524.
11 *Ibid.*, 57, 58.
12 *Ibid.*, 375.
13 *Ibid.*, 30, 381-382, 403-404.
14 *Ibid.*, 104, 364, 365.
15 *Ibid.*, 467-468.
16 *Ibid.*, 528.

without.[17] Such men cried for mercy when oppressed and denied it to others when ascendant.[18] English Independents now ejected Anglicans and Presbyterians from their livings and drew a magic circle, bidding the people to "walke at Libertie (to wit, within the Conjured Circle) so far as they please."[19] When Williams surveyed the mental torment and human tragedy wrought by instruments of intolerance and the ravages of trampling hosts in the wars of religion, his warm rhetoric mounted in inspired and pulsating indictment of imperious doctrines that could brook no rival. Force usurps the place of reason, "burnes up the holy Scriptures, and forbids . . . any tryall or search, or (truly) free disquisition to be made by them," compels the most able and diligent to "pluck forth their own eyes" and read by the "Cleargies Spectacles," and works murderous and malignant ruin "which no Uncleannes, no Adulterie, Incest, Sodomie, or Beastialitie can equall, this ravishing and forcing . . . the very Soules and Consciences of all the Nations and Inhabitants of the World."[20]

Frantic and ambitious men insisted that compulsory uniformity was a source of strength and social stability, but history demonstrated that religious freedom brought political security and economic gains. Holland prospered as a "confluence of the persecuted" and its toleration drew boats and trade, "and that so mightily in so short a time, that Shipping, Trading, wealth, Greatnesse, Honour" fell like a garland from heaven.[21] With prophetic vision Williams perceived that freedom of worship was a prerequisite in any permanent solution of the Irish question. What made the Irish "so inraged and desperate?" The "Lawes against their Consciences and Worships"; no wonder Catholics rose to cast off their "yoakes."[22] Why, if Catholics acknowledged the Pope only in spiritual affairs and pledged civil obedience, need they be oppressed more than others?[23] Men had yet to learn that civil turbulence and bloodshed provoked by the rival ambitions of religious factions would decline only when free speech and free worship won acceptance. The "most noble and

[17] *Ibid.*, 207-209, 226, 234, 326, 439, 504, 508 f.
[18] *Ibid.*, 425, 498, 522.
[19] *Ibid.*, 525, 527.
[20] *Ibid.*, 495-496.
[21] *Ibid.*, 9, 407.
[22] *Ibid.*, 312, 313, 497-498.
[23] *Ibid.*, 312; see also 11, 316-317, 327.

inner part," the spirit, "minde and conscience of man, that is indeed the man," must be unchained.[24] Only when "free Conferrings, Disputings and Preachings" took the place of coercion could mutual understanding be generated and the rent fabric of society repaired.[25]

Williams' acquaintance with non-Christian peoples through direct contact with American Indians, his interest in Turks, Jews, races and creeds in the far corners of the world, had given him more than an inkling of the scientific approach of the modern anthropologist. Reflections upon heathen civilizations and variations in social patterns reinforced his belief in freedom and diversity.[26] He repeatedly emphasized the world view and the simple fact of political and religious heterodoxy. The "best Historians and Cosmographers" had shown that the world was divided into thirty parts, and only five of the thirty parts were "acquainted" with "the sound of Christ Jesus."[27] It was clear from history that divine will left different peoples free to order their own civil affairs according to their lights.[28]

Once more Williams struck a resounding blow for the cause of democracy. Earlier in 1644 his radical political views had won esteem in the army but had contributed to the burning of his *Bloudy Tenent*. Robert Baillie, quoting verbatim Williams' famous democratic statement, had scathingly attacked it as a monstrosity of political conceit, the subjection of kings and parliaments "to the freewil of the promiscuous multitude."[29] With flaming conviction Williams now reaffirmed his revolutionary doctrine. Kings of the earth used power "over the Bodies and Goods of their Subjects, but for the filling of their paunches like Wolves."[30] Defending anew the pacific and humane virtues of republicanism and free heterodoxy, Williams stripped coercive orthodoxy, legitimacy, and divine right of the shimmering garments of sanctity and revealed their barbaric imperial logic, employment of "Civill Armes and Forces to the utmost" and constant pressure for "universal Conquest" to establish "Rule and Dominion over all the Nations of the Earth."[31]

---

24 *Bloody Tenent More Bloody*, N.C.P., IV, 439, 440.
25 *Ibid.*, 247, 316, 476.
26 *Ibid.*, 222, 238, 242.
27 *Ibid.*, 161-162.
28 *Ibid.*, 71, 244, 447.
29 *Dissuasive*, pp. 125, 150-151.
30 *Bloody Tenent More Bloody*, N.C.P., IV, 402.
31 *Ibld.*, 337.

Williams perceived the same dire stringency in the stern demand of Fifth Monarchy men for a Mosaic code in place of English law. He had seen Cotton's Judicialls.[32] Reliance on the Pentateuch for law "awaketh Moses from his unknowne Grave, and denies Jesus yet to have seene the Earth." It denied men the power to make their own laws. A just God, "though he be Justice it selfe," could not be imagined to impose one indefeasible "universal strictnes" upon the whole world.[33] Williams' democratic faith had emancipated him; he thrust divine law into the realm of a philosophic abstraction, identified with ethics. Magistracy is of God only in the sense that marriage is, "being an estate meerly civil and humane, and lawfull to all Nations of the World, that know not God."[34] Government is secular and its proper function is to secure each individual in the "naturall and Civill Rights and Liberties" which are "due to him as a Man, a Subject, a Citizen."[35] Having blasted the entrenchments of aristocracy and orthodoxy with these explosive definitions, Williams flung anew the marshalled force of the democratic challenge. The "free Inhabitants" of the world, even among the heathen, are the "Choosers and Makers" of the "Servants of civil Justice."[36] A civil ruler, "whether succeeding or elective," is "but a Minister or servant of the people" who "make the laws, and give the Magistrate his commission and power."[37] The people are "the Original of all free Power and Government" and can set up their "owne severall Lawes and Agreements . . . according to their severall Natures, Dispositions and Constitutions, and their common peace and well-fare."[38]

In April, 1652, Williams published the *Hireling Ministry None of Christ's,* a small pamphlet attacking the orthodox agitation for tithes to maintain approved ministers and arguing the reasonableness of voluntary donations, the system currently sponsored by extreme sectaries like George Fox and republican leaders who revolved in Vane's radical junto. Williams enlarged the issue to the great question of free churches in a free state. "I desire not that liberty to my-

[32] *Ibid.,* 287.
[33] *Ibid.,* 484-489.
[34] *Ibid.,* 282.
[35] *Ibid.,* 276, 365, 414.
[36] *Ibid.,* 281-282.
[37] *Ibid.,* 187, 198-199.
[38] *Ibid.,* 28-29, 487.

self, which I would not freely and impartially weigh out to all the consciences of the world beside." It was the "absolute duty" of the government to maintain "absolute freedom," whereby each division of people in the British Isles could establish whatever system of maintenance they freely chose.[39] A few weeks later, in May, 1652, another of Vane's circle, John Milton, gave noble expression to similar sentiments in his famous sonnet to Cromwell:

> . . . much remains
> To conquer still; Peace hath her victories
> No less renowned than War: new foes arise,
> Threatening to bind our souls with secular chains.
> Help us to save free conscience from the paw
> Of hireling wolves, whose Gospel is their maw.

In April, Williams also published a non-controversial tract, *Experiments of Spiritual Life and Health,* dedicated to Lady Vane. He had written it during a winter among "the naked Indians of America" by the flickering fires in their "wild houses" and sent it to Mary Williams, then convalescing from illness, as a "handfull of flowers . . . for thy dear selfe, and our dear children."[40] This small work stressed the inescapable inwardness of regeneration and urged cultivation of true piety by "doing good to men" and having compassion for the "affected or miserable." Here was embodied the hopeful humanism of a Seeker who regarded outward ordinances as inventions of men and held to the devout faith that inner regeneration alone was the road to salvation. This tract revealed how far Williams had swung from strict Calvinism. The saving message of the New Testament tempered the wrath of an angry God.[41] Through a doctrine of man predicating human perfectibility and freedom of the will, Williams identified himself as the spiritual kin of Arminians and pietists who found the inwardness of religion the heart of the matter.

During these months Williams in company with others of Vane's brilliant circle spoke out stoutly for readmission of the Jews into England. In the pamphlet embodying Major Butler's fourth proposal, Williams made his stirring plea, oft quoted by later Americans,

[39] *Hireling Ministry,* p. 19.
[40] *Experiments* (Rider ed.), pp. iv, 2.
[41] For Williams' handling of the angry God theme, see *ibid.,* pp. 56-57.

to break down the "superstitious wall of separation (as to civil things) between us Gentiles and the Jews" and give the outcasts "without their asking" free and peaceable habitation. English incivilities and inhumanities against Jews cried to heaven. The *Hireling Ministry* resolutely reiterated the same opinion.[42] With such support Cromwell in the next few years went as far as he felt himself able, and although Jews were not admitted on the free basis which Williams desired, numbers of them immigrated with the lord protector's connivance and the force of the age-old proscription was permanently broken.

Meanwhile Williams interested himself in the case of Sir Thomas Urquhart, the eccentric and erudite Scots translator of *Rabelais*. Captured at the battle of Worcester, September 3, 1651, the famous Knight of Cromartie now languished in prison at Windsor Castle. Williams' efforts to procure a parole earned a generous tribute from the old royalist, who in his epilogue to *Logopandecteision,* published in 1653, acknowledged "thankfulness to that reverend preacher, Mr. Roger Williams of Providence in New England, for the manifold favours wherein I stood obliged to him above a whole month before either of us had so much as seen other." Williams presented his case to "the most special members both of the Parliament and Councel of State." Sir Thomas desired to meet him "to testifie the affection I did owe him," but Williams delayed meeting

> . . . till he had, as he said, performed some acceptable office, worthy of my acquaintance; in all which, both before and after we had conversed with one another, and by those many worthy books set forth by him, to the advancement of piety and good order, with some whereof he was pleased to present me, he did approve himself a man of such discretion and inimitably-sanctified parts, that an Archangel from heaven could not have shewn more goodness with less ostentation.[43]

As a result of Williams' efforts, Urquhart obtained his release in July, 1652.

In the spring of 1652 Williams wrote to Mrs. Sadleir, daughter of Sir Edward Coke, that he was presenting her a copy of his

---

[42] For Williams' tolerant attitude and extracts from his writings, see R. B. Morris, "Jewish Interests of Roger Williams," *Am. Hebrew,* Dec. 9, 1921, p. 138.

[43] *Pub. R.I.H.S.,* new ser., VIII, 135-136; Urquhart, *Works* (Maitland Club ed.), pp. 408-409.

Experiments, a tract in simpler style than his early sermons, for he had long since discovered the "vanity and soul-deceit of such points and flourishes." Williams' purpose was kindly and his book non-controversial, but he could not resist a reference to his sorrowful flight twenty-two years before and the present reversal of fortune which had brought him "many friends and divers eminent," including Cromwell himself who several times had been pleased "to send for me."[44] Mrs. Sadleir replied tartly that her reading was restricted to the Bible, "the late King's book," and solid Anglican books like Hooker's *Ecclesiastical Polity,* Bishop Andrewes' sermons, and Jeremy Taylor's works; and she therefore returned Williams' tract "with thanks."[45] Not to be downed so easily, Williams promptly sent her his mammoth *Bloody Tenent More Bloody,* informing her that he was already seeking the books she mentioned and asking her to cast a "judicious and loving eye" on the one he now sent.[46]

Mrs. Sadleir's judicious eye got no further than Williams' title page: "When I . . . saw it entitled 'The Bloudy Tenent,' I durst not adventure to look into it." She returned the book, wishing to be troubled "no more in this kind," and signing herself: "Your Friend in the Old and Best Way."[47]

The good lady was soon troubled. Williams in reply questioned the soundness of cleaving to old ways and shutting the mind to new: "I am far from wondering at it, for all this I have done myself," until learning no longer to swallow "without chewing" or submit blindly to tradition and custom. His desire to be open-minded had led him to read the books Anne Sadleir mentioned—even one of Bishop Laud's!—but he still thought Protestants and Catholics too much given to "merely formal, customary, and traditional professions," whereas a "true order of ministry, baptism" was as nothing compared to "true regeneration and new birth." In a postscript he recommended Milton's answer to the king's book and a volume by one of her own authors, which he found excellent. "I mean the 'Liberty of Prophesying,' "—Jeremy Taylor's celebrated plea for broad toleration within the church.[48]

[44] Williams to Mrs. Sadleir, *N.C.P.,* VI, 237-240.
[45] *Ibid.,* 241.
[46] *Ibid.,* 242.
[47] *Ibid.,* 244.
[48] *Ibid.,* 245-249.

This was too much for the daughter of the fiery and irascible old Sir Edward Coke: "Mr. Williams,—I thought my first letter would have given you so much satisfaction, that, in that kind, I should never have heard of you any more; but it seems you have a face of brass, so that you cannot blush."[49] She trembled when she read his aspersions upon the late martyr king, "and none but such a villain as yourself would have wrote them." She cited chapter and verse, including *Romans* XIII: 1-2, the injunction to obey the powers that be, which were ordained of God—favorite text of royalism and divine right and likewise the text on the title page of the Massachusetts *Book of Lawes* of 1648. Anne Sadleir scorned his recommendation of Milton's rebuttal of the king's book. If she were not mistaken, he was the same man who had written a tract urging the lawfulness of divorce: "and, if report says true, he had, at that time, two or three wives living. This, perhaps, were good doctrine in New England; but it is most abominable in Old England."[50] God's judgment was plain in striking that man with blindness. As for Jeremy Taylor's book for toleration, "I say, it and you would make a good fire." She closed with the acid suggestion that if Williams now turned "from being a rebel" to "fear God and obey the king," she might yet meet him in heaven; meanwhile she wished him "in the place from whence you came" with an ocean between them.[51] Mrs. Sadleir preserved Williams' letters as damaging evidence, in the pious hope that someday Tyburn might "give him welcome."[52]

Throughout the summer of 1652 the council of state was critically absorbed in relations with the Dutch, and the Rhode Island petition of April 7 lay in abeyance. In May the explosion came when Van Tromp's fleet met Blake in the Downs. For five months Rhode Island was ignored while Vane was busy with naval affairs. At last, on September 8, Williams wrote to his old friend Gregory Dexter of "interim encouragement" from the council. A final determination would be long delayed, since "our adversaries" threaten an appeal to parliament "in case we get the day before the Council." Williams had often longed "for my old friend" as printer for his recent tracts.

---

49 *Ibid.*, 249.
50 *Ibid.*, 251.
51 *Ibid.*, 249-252.
52 See *ibid.*, 253.

He also dearly hoped that Mary Williams could join him, for "joyful I should be of her being here with me."[53]

A major object of Williams' mission was accomplished sooner than expected. Clarke's published narrative[54] and Williams' testimony before the council exposed the duplicity of Coddington's bogus claim that he had discovered and purchased Rhode Island for himself. Since Williams had written the Aquidneck deed and signed it as one of the two English witnesses, his contradiction of Coddington's contention was conclusive,[55] and on October 2, 1652, the council ordered Coddington's commission vacated. But the business was only half done. Confirmation of the old charter hung in the balance, and Edward Winslow from Plymouth and Edward Hopkins and George Fenwick from Connecticut, all three now in high favor with Cromwell, were presenting claims to the Narragansett country. Unless the charter was confirmed, Rhode Island might yet be parcelled out to the United Colonies.

During these protracted negotiations, Williams had the satisfaction of witnessing the growing triumph of toleration. In December, 1652, Richard Baxter, one of the moderate Presbyterians, led the way toward interdenominational coöperation among Presbyterians, Independents, and even moderate Anglicans.[56] The rise of sectarianism and the hatred of the old clerical domination had made impossible—saving a restoration of the monarchy—a return to the old State Church and the policy of persecution. Rapidly growing sects like the Baptists now had some pretense to respectability, and John Clarke aptly remarked in his Baptist tract for toleration, published in 1652, that old England was becoming new while "New England is become Old."[57]

The rapid extension of freedom inevitably begot religious prodigies which scandalized the nation, and on July 25, 1652 occurred one of the incidents which eventually led Williams to

[53] *Letters,* N.C.P., VI, 235-237.

[54] See 4 *Coll. M.H.S.,* II, 24-25.

[55] Voluntary choice of Clarke as agent by Aquidneck *ipso facto* disproved Coddington's profession to represent a majority; see Williams, *Letters,* N.C.P., VI, 154, and Staples, *Annals,* p. 82. For the duplicity of Coddington, see *Cal. State Papers, Colonial, 1574-1660,* I, 390; Chapin, *Doc. Hist. R. I.,* II, 24-25, 29; and H. E. Turner, "William Coddington," *R. I. H. Tracts,* IV, 41, 47-49.

[56] See S. R. Gardiner, *Commonwealth and Protectorate* (New York, 1897-1903), II, 325-326.

[57] See title page, *Ill Newes from New-England.*

impugn the Quakers for sensational "incivilities." While a preacher at Whitehall was discoursing on the Resurrection, a woman completely nude appeared in the church and ran through the congregation to the pulpit, crying, "Welcome the Resurrection!"[58] Roger Williams was never to forget such outbreaks of the Quakers; and although George Fox opposed the payment of tithes as vigorously as he, and spoke for religious liberty, the Rhode Islander never attained to a sympathetic appreciation of the father of the Inner Light who, no doubt to Williams' chagrin, was rapidly winning over many English Seekers.

While free worship became a lusty, bawling infant, the newborn child of democracy sickened and died. Had poor men, asked the Levellers, fought only to give power to men of estates? Give the plain people the vote, replied officers like General Ireton in the army debates, and what would restrain them from seeking economic equality and confiscating property?[59] King and peers were purged from the government, but the army command and lawyers, merchants, and pushing country gentry in parliament retained enough sense of the dynamics of power to halt short of universal suffrage and new elections and operated the commonwealth as a nominal republic under protection of the military. "A nobleman, a gentleman, a yeoman," declared Cromwell, "that is a good interest of the land and a great one." With the levelling principle he could not agree; "for what was the purport of it but to make the tenant as liberal a fortune as the landlord?"[60] The great inconsistencies of the Puritan revolution were coming to light. There could be no reconciliation of the new doctrine of liberty with Puritan doctrines of rule by the saints or the old parliamentary doctrine of rule by the possessing class. By 1652 rumors of corruption spread so far as New England,[61] and meanwhile General Harrison's stern Fifth Monarchy men and Cromwell himself chafed increasingly at the restraints of parliament. The day of dictatorship was not far off.

On April 1, 1653, Williams wrote home to his colony, hoping that William Dyer had arrived with the documents which the council had

[58] Gardiner, *Commonwealth and Protectorate*, II, 24.

[59] See A. S. P. Woodhouse, *Puritanism and Liberty* (London, 1938), pp. 57-58, 74-79, and *passim*.

[60] Cited by C. H. Firth, *Oliver Cromwell* (N. Y., 1909), pp. 248, 249.

[61] See Briscoe letter, 3 *Coll. M.H.S.*, I, 32-34.

drafted in answer to "the petition Sir Henry Vane and myself drew up." Although in these documents the council revoked Coddington's commission, the Dutch war and the opposition of Connecticut and Plymouth still prevented official action to reunite Rhode Island under the old charter. Sir Arthur Haselrig, influential in the council, had thrown his weight in behalf of Colonel Fenwick, his son-in-law, and the Saybrook patentees, who alleged a claim to Rhode Island territory. Winslow and Hopkins, "both in great place," were rallying their friends in parliament and council and had support from many of the "priests, both presbyterian and independent."[62] Evidently Williams' second tract on the Bloody Tenent had given comfort to the enemy.

Within three weeks the hope of Williams for Rhode Island and of Levellers for England met a heartbreaking check. Resolved to give the people "not what pleases them" but what to his mind was "for their good," Cromwell took over the government, dismissed the council, and dissolved parliament by threat of force. Neither Sir Henry Vane, Cornelius Holland, nor Sir William Masham were members of the new council formed on May 3. With parliamentary leaders driven into involuntary retirement, Cromwell moved steadily toward his high destiny as uncrowned king. In the summer of 1653 John Lilburne, arch Leveller, was clapped in prison for championship of free government, though he had been enthusiastically acquitted by a London jury. Cromwell did, indeed, make one last compromise with constitutional republicanism in the Instrument of Government, but when this, too, failed, he became protector in name and dictator in fact. Thereafter military might prevailed, and almost the only voice that continued to protest was Sir Henry Vane's.[63]

Eventually Williams carried back to New England tales of opposition to the protector "as an usurper" and he wrote to Winthrop of men who had been put in prison for public criticism of the new regime.[64] Sympathizing with Vane, who declared the protector plucked up liberty by its very roots, Williams privately criticised Cromwell for making Vane a virtual prisoner.[65] He also disliked the

---

[62] Williams to Providence and Warwick, *N.C.P.*, VI, 254-255.

[63] See T. C. Pease, *The Leveller Movement* (Washington, D. C., 1916), pp. 348-351.

[64] *Letters*, N.C.P., VI, 260.

[65] *Ibid.*, 373.

imperialism of Cromwell and saw little excuse for war with the Dutch.[66] Dictatorship and divine right monarchy were alike alien to Williams' mind, but he nevertheless admired the man who was striking such stout blows for toleration. The friendly relation between the two continued, and the protector found time for "many discourses" with him. Williams "told Oliver" his foreboding of recurrent bloodshed between Catholics and Protestants till toleration prevailed, to which Oliver "much inclined."[67] Cromwell, perhaps already dreaming of conquest of Spain's rich overseas possessions, regarded New England colonies as "poor, cold and useless."[68] But he gratified Williams by approving protection of the Narragansetts and liberty for their pagan worship.[69]

Within two months after establishment of the protectorate, Williams made up his mind to return home. Since arrival in England, he had received eighteen pounds from Providence, besides five pounds paid to his wife, and was short of funds.[70] He had several "offers" in England but refused them, having no mind to forsake Rhode Island.[71] The compelling reason for returning before conclusion of his negotiations was the growing distraction in Rhode Island. The colony sorely missed John Clarke and Roger Williams, the two strongest peacemakers in the union party. The irreconcilable faction of Coddington had taken advantage of the uncertain status of the old charter, and meanwhile the Dutch war had precipitated a bitter conflict between the mainland and Aquidneck over the issue of privateering.

Before his departure Williams established friendly relations with Henry Lawrence, president of the council.[72] With the possible exception of Sir Gilbert Pickering, who in 1644 had signed the letter to Massachusetts requesting safe conduct for Williams, the councillors knew little of Rhode Island or the facts of the case. Sir Anthony Ashley Cooper, the future Lord Shaftesbury and demagogic leader of the Whig party under Charles II, was generally a supporter of toleration, and the other members, mainly drawn from the military,

---

[66] *Bloody Tenent More Bloody,* N.C.P., IV, 9-10; *Letters,* N.C.P., VI, 273.
[67] *Letters,* N.C.P., VI, 311.
[68] *Ibid.,* 285.
[69] *Ibid.,* 270.
[70] *Prov. Recs.,* XV, 63.
[71] *Letters,* N.C.P., VI, 269.
[72] *Ibid.,* 261.

were practical men and presumably disposed to act without prejudice. In February, 1654, Williams left the negotiations in the capable hands of John Clarke, and made a last visit to Sir Henry Vane. Just as he departed for Portsmouth to take ship, the Rhode Island petition won favorable attention and was referred to committee. On March 8, after hearing the claims of Hopkins, Major Bourne and other agents of the United Colonies, the council decided tentatively in Rhode Island's favor, and Henry Lawrence immediately despatched word to Williams at Portsmouth "that the Council had passed three letters as to our business."[73]

"Road Island," wrote Mason to Winthrop, "had like to have procured very great priviledges, but the current is stopt."[74] Williams, however, was the proud bearer of letters from the council which substantially fulfilled the object of his mission. But the turbulent conditions and rife spirit of disunion in Rhode Island were to put Roger Williams to his greatest test.

[73] *Cal. State Papers, Colonial, 1574-1660,* I, 414; *N.C.P.,* VI, 261.
[74] 4 *Coll. M.H.S.,* VII, 417.

16

PRESIDENT WILLIAMS

ROGER WILLIAMS ARRIVED AT BOSTON at the beginning of summer, 1654, and received permission to pass through Massachusetts. He brought with him an order of the council directing the Bay colony to grant him freedom of passage on any later occasions. This the magistrates ignored.[1]

Though the Rhode Island agent bore to his own colony the precious documents essential to restoration of union, there was no flattering welcome for him as in 1644. During his absence the mainland government of Providence and Warwick had virtually collapsed, and in May, 1652, Samuel Gorton retired from the presidency in disgust. The Coddington interregnum produced even greater disruption on the Island. The impulse for popular government had grown since the former years of Coddington's supremacy, and the self-appointed proprietor of the Aquidneck plantations discovered that not even his commission from England commanded respect. Rebellious citizens, impatient of law, rose in armed force, threatened Coddington, and ordered his court to disperse. The governor resorted to the desperate expedient of asking the Dutch for a detachment of soldiers to overawe the populace.[2] Early in 1652 enraged citizens resorted to the lawless procedure of vigilante justice. In pursuance of a court action, Captain Partridge, right-hand man of the governor, took forcible possession of the house of one of the inhabitants, whereupon a howling mob came with "guns and swords and stafs,"[3] dispossessed the captain and hung him out of hand.

Warned by this episode, Coddington took a hasty vacation in Boston and only dared return after signing a confession at the dictation of the Islanders that he had no more title to Aquidneck than any other purchaser or freeman.[4] Subsequently when William Dyer

---

[1] See *Letters,* N.C.P., VI, 297, 304.

[2] *Documents Relating to the Colonial History of New York* (Albany, 1853-1883), I, 497.

[3] Coddington to Winthrop, 4 *Coll. M.H.S.,* VII, 284.

[4] *R. I. H. Tracts,* IV, 23.

arrived with the council's order rescinding Coddington's commission, factionalism mounted so high as to defeat all efforts for reunion under the old charter. In May, 1653, assemblies on the mainland and the Island convened simultaneously and held elections, each government claiming to represent the colony. A faction in Providence and Warwick opposed to the mainland assembly took part at Newport, with the result that two sets of officers attempted to exercise authority in Providence and Warwick.[5] In June, 1653, the Warwick-Providence government drew up a remonstrance, protesting that Aquidneck hostilities against their Dutch neighbors were like "to set all New England on fire."[6] Meanwhile Pawtuxet men again refused to pay taxes levied by Providence, and the Bay colony by threat of intervention forced Providence to desist.[7] Orderly government and public spirit in Rhode Island had reached its lowest ebb.

Warned of this discouraging prospect, Williams had armed himself with a letter of reproof from Sir Henry Vane. He now made copies of the letter in his own hand and circulated them in the four towns of the colony.[8] How was it, asked Vane, that his old Antinomian friends had fallen into such divisions, tumults, and injustice? "Are there no wise men amongst you? No public self-denying spirits, that at least, upon the grounds of public safety, equity and prudence, can find out some way or means of union . . . before you come a prey to common enemies. . . ." When the council endorsed "your freedom," it supposed a better use would be made of it. But ugly distempers in the body politic should not be incurable; "I hope better things from you," concluded Vane, and recommended that all parties choose representatives and hold a common meeting to restore union. Coming from Sir Henry Vane, great statesman of the English commonwealth and old and respected friend of the colony, this reproof was cutting and effective.

Despite this telling use of Vane's powerful appeal, Williams' initial effort failed to bring his fellow-settlers to reason. He attempted to hold a "conference tending to reconciliation," but the mainland settlements, alienated by the Easton and Dyer party of Aquidneck which had authorized privateering against the Dutch,

[5] *R. I. Col. Recs.*, I, 264, 265.
[6] *Ibid.*, 270.
[7] *Mass. Bay Recs.*, IV, 149; Arnold, *Rhode Island*, I, 247.
[8] Vane to Rhode Island, Feb. 8, 1654, *N.C.P.*, VI, 257-258.

stood on local rights and refused to confer until they had settled upon a policy in town meeting.[9] Williams thereupon appealed directly to Providence in a stirring and incisive public letter.[10]

"I am like a man in a great fog," he declared. Apparently the way forward was blocked, but if he moved backward he would lose all the ground gained in his long years of endeavor "to keep up the name of a people, a free people, not enslaved to the bondages and iron yokes" of neighboring colonies, nor oppressed by barbarous Indians or unruly factions "within ourselves." First to settle in "these wild parts," he had placed his life in jeopardy and diminished his estate by countless efforts to pacify the Indians and by long public service, including nearly five years spent in England "to keep off the rage" of neighboring colonies "against us." What benefit had he reaped?

"I have been charged with folly for that freedom and liberty which I have always stood for; I say liberty and equality, both in land and government." He had been told that he labored for a licentious and contentious people; he had endured sharp words from persons who had hoped that he "might never have landed" and had been taunted by others with gratuitous intimations that he had failed in "maintaining the charter and the colony." In indignant retort, Williams reminded the citizens that they had fetched him from a profitable employment to undertake a high and costly public work and then left him stranded without funds. Yet by private earnings and loans from friends abroad he had paid Rhode Island's debts and come home "with your credit and honor," after grappling successfully "with the agents and friends of all your enemies round about you." Williams closed his letter with a ringing appeal to rise above the narrow spirit of local patriotism and proposed that the Providence town meeting resolve on a joint conference with the other towns to iron out difficulties by open discussion. If "aught remain grievous," four arbitrators could be chosen and the matter definitely settled.

Williams' persuasive power won Providence, and with this assurance he soon had a promise of coöperation from the other towns. "We have had some gusts amongst us as to our whole Colony and civil order," he informed Winthrop. "By the good hand of the Lord they were persuaded to choose twenty-four Commissioners (six out

9 *Letters,* N.C.P., VI, 264-265.
10 *Ibid.,* 263-266.

of a town) to reconcile."[11] At a conference held at Warwick, August 31, Williams and the friends of union carried the day, and the twenty-four commissioners signed articles of agreement, reuniting the four towns. Because of the strong feeling against the Easton government, the commissioners decided to start with a clean slate and called a special election to be held September 12. They also voted that the code of laws and other enactments antedating the Coddington interregnum should remain in force.[12] Thus by a substantial agreement upon Williams' program, the dangerous spirit of disunion which had flourished for three years met its first noteworthy check.

Four days prior to the meeting of the commissioners, Williams contrived to get the town of Providence to send an answer to Sir Henry Vane. As its language betrayed, this communication was as much an object lesson to local malcontents as an answer to Vane. The document was signed by the town clerk but composed by Williams and written in his hand.[13] The letter admitted that Vane's "sharp and bitter arrows" had justly found the mark. The recent distractions had been caused by the overweening ambition and covetousness of some of the citizens: ". . . possibly a sweet cup hath rendered many of us wanton and too active, for we have long drunk of the cup of as great liberties as any people that we can hear of under the whole heaven." Rhode Island had been spared the bloody civil conflict of England and had escaped both the iron yoke of "wolfish bishops" and the "new chains" of Presbyterian intolerance; "nor in this colony have we been consumed with the over-zealous fire of the (so called) godly christian magistrates. Sir, we have not known what an excise means; we have almost forgotten what tithes are, yea, or taxes either, to church or commonwealth." Such freedom tended to render men wanton and forgetful. It was hoped, however, that Vane would hear no more complaints of the men of Providence or of the colony, and that "when we are gone and rotten," posterity would read in the town record Vane's "pious and favorable letters . . . and this our answer, and real endeavor after peace and righteousness."[14]

At the special election of September 12 Williams was chosen

11 *Letters*, N.C.P., VI, 283.
12 *R. I. Col. Recs.*, I, 276-279.
13 Backus, *The Baptists*, I, 293.
14 *Letters*, N.C.P., VI, 268.

president as the man most capable of consolidating popular support. The freemen also elected an able body of assistants including Randall Holden of Warwick, Thomas Harris of Providence, and Benedict Arnold of Newport. Benedict Arnold, formerly one of the secessionists of Pawtuxet, had come to think better of Rhode Island and her charter and in 1653 renounced subjection to Massachusetts and moved to Newport. His change of front was a welcome symptom of the new spirit of harmony.

Hardly was the new government inaugurated when Indian troubles once more drew Williams' attention. Ninigret, sachem of the Niantic tribe affiliated with the Narragansetts, had received a challenge to war from a Long Island sachem who was under the protection of the United Colonies. Ninigret, whom Williams described as "proud and fierce," was not the man to refuse a fight and promptly took the warpath, returning with fourteen captives. Taking affront, the United Colonies forced Ninigret to return his captives. Subsequently, under cover of peace, the Long Island Indians, so Williams wrote, "pretending to visit Ninigret, at Block Island, slaughtered of his Narragansetts near thirty persons, at midnight."[15] In spite of this treacherous attack by the allies of the confederation, Williams heard rumors that the United Colonies had "meditations of war" against the Narragansetts.[16] Ninigret, summoned to Hartford, refused to attend and declared that the Long Island Indians had slaughtered sixty of his people and the son of a sachem. In his rebuff to the United Colonies, he asked proudly: "If your governor's son were slain, and several other men, would you ask counsel of another nation how and when to right yourselves?"[17]

Fearing an invasion by the United Colonies and a war in the interior of Rhode Island, Williams wrote a long letter to the Bay court urging sober second thought. Though the sword might be necessary on certain occasions, "all men . . . ply to windward, to maintain their wars to be defensive." Why shouldn't it, in fact, "be not only possible, but very easy, to live and die in peace with all the natives of this country"?[18] Williams reminded the Bay of the legal rights of Rhode Island Indians, who had been granted freedom from

[15] Williams to Massachusetts, Oct. 5, 1654, *N.C.P.*, VI, 275.
[16] *Ibid.*, 269.
[17] Quoted in Arnold, *Rhode Island*, I, 253.
[18] Williams to Massachusetts, Oct. 5, 1654, *N.C.P.*, VI, 271.

outside interference by the recent order of Cromwell and his council. Persistent animosity of the United Colonies toward the Narragansetts, in defiance of this order, savored of persecution. Recent Massachusetts tracts had publicized the work of John Eliot and others in their "glorious conversion of the Indians of New England," but in some of them the Narragansett tribes were "publicly branded, for refusing to pray and be converted."[19] The Rhode Island sachems, Williams informed the Bay, had asked him to petition "the high Sachems of England" that they might not be forced to change their religion or be subject to invasion by the English. "For they said they were daily visited with threatenings by Indians that came from about the Massachusetts, that if they would not pray, they should be destroyed by war."[20] This had been the grounds for the action of Cromwell's council in ordering the United Colonies to respect the rights of the Narragansetts. England was ringing with praises of Eliot's work in converting the Indians—"I speak not ironically,"—and flattering notice of the conversions had been taken in the pulpits in England, and churchwardens had gone from house to house "to gather supplies for this work."[21] Yet was there not a paradox in "the clashings of these two, viz.: the glorious conversion of the Indians in New England, and the unnecessary wars and cruel destructions of the Indians in New England"?[22]

In any case, Williams contended, war would be unjust and catastrophic. The Narragansetts had been good neighbors, maintained peaceable commerce with the English, and had been "long confederates with you."[23] Williams knew of not a single case in which they had stained their hands "with any English blood, neither in open hostilities nor secret murders." Though they were barbarians, the only offenses charged against them concerned mere "matters of money, or petty revenging of themselves on some Indians, upon extreme provocations."[24] It would be folly, then, to invite the "plague of war," the course of which was ever "wonderful fickle," bringing calamities, taxes, ruin of commerce, and heavy loss of life, and a pity if, "for the sake of a few inconsiderable pagans," all the

19 Williams to Massachusetts, Oct. 5, 1654, *N.C.P.*, VI, 271-272.
20 *Ibid.*, 270.
21 *Ibid.*, 271-272.
22 *Ibid.*, 272.
23 *Ibid.*, 271, 274.
24 *Ibid.*, 274.

gracious work of planting in the wilderness should rashly be destroyed.[25]

This strong plea for peace came too late. Four days after Williams wrote his letter, Massachusetts sent troops under Major Willard to wreak vengeance on the Niantics. Ninigret's men, however, fled into the swamps, eluded Major Willard, and the Massachusetts forces returned empty-handed, to the great chagrin of the United Colonies. Williams' endeavors now began to have effect. Before Willard left, Williams conferred with him and found that the Bay court had not yet met and accordingly had not formally considered his plea for peace. To Willard, who had not seen his letter to the Bay, he presented a copy. He also talked with the soldiers. Some of them admitted that "the Narragansetts had yet killed no English," but they accused them of killing "two hundred of Mr. Winthrop's goats." The death of the goats seemed to them nearly as good a *casus belli* as the blood of an Englishman. Rhode Island's great peacemaker thereupon wrote to Winthrop that his "private loss" of a few beasts was less crucial than the hazard of the lives of peaceable Indian neighbors and fellow countrymen and the provocation of permanent hostility in the hearts of the Narragansetts.[26]

Winter was approaching, not a good season for an energetic campaign, and Massachusetts belatedly recognized the force of Williams' pleas and the prudence of peace. With the Bay opposed to continuance of war, the other colonies were compelled to desist and hostilities ended. During the winter, Williams had many consultations with the Indians and found that they made "absolute denial" of the much-touted slaughter of the goats, "excepting three or four," killed by the Pawcomtucks, who had renounced subjection to the Narragansett sachems. "Your great trial, loss and hindrance I am exceedingly grieved at," he wrote to Winthrop; but during the winter he had ferreted out the actual truth. The white servants on Winthrop's island, with the convenient conscience of Englishmen on the make, had sold the goats for their own private profit and charged the loss to the account of the Narragansetts. "They say that some English whom you trusted there, not only gave Ninigret one goat, but they have known divers given or sold to English or Dutch pinnaces." Williams had distrusted this Indian testimony until "conferring with

[25] *Ibid.*, 272-273, 276.
[26] Williams to Winthrop, Oct. 9, 1654, *ibid.*, 277.

some English further, I find it undeniable from many English witnesses, that many goats have been sold (and some at cheap prices,)
by some whom you have trusted, to many vessels."[27]

This information exploded the *casus belli* of the goats. Once
again Williams checked the imperial arrogance of the United
Colonies who had condemned the Narragansetts without a hearing
and flagrantly violated the orders from England. The evidence in
his letter stripped naked the racial bigotry which continually stung
the natives by assuming the trustworthiness of the white man's
testimony even when contradicted by the word of a sachem. Not
only had dishonest Englishmen rather than natives been actually at
fault, but, as Williams' letter went on to relate, no iniquity ever
charged upon the Narragansetts equalled the enormity of a crime
recently perpetrated against them by certain whites. In this revolting
affair, a Dutchman and some English members of his crew, including "one Samuel, a hatter, and one Jones, a seaman, and an Irish-
man," had foully desecrated the grave of a sister of Pessicus and
mangled her body. These Narragansetts, who had never yet taken
an English life, now trooped down to Warwick, where the Dutchman and his crew were tarrying, and grimly demanded justice. The
sachems, accompanied by "four score armed men," were so incensed
"as to talk often of men's lives, and of fighting." Williams held
a "solemn debate" with them and only with great difficulty kept them
from bloodshed, giving assurance that they would have justice either
in Dutch or English courts.[28]

In this letter of February, 1655, Williams also informed Winthrop of his progress in adjusting differences within the colony;
"yet the spirits of some have not been so reconcileable." Among the
malcontents were his own brother, Robert Williams, and Thomas
Olney of Providence, and Easton, Dyer, and a number of citizens
of Newport. "We enjoy liberties of soul and body, but it is license
we desire."[29] This indictment of the colony was scarcely an exag-
geration. What Rhode Island democracy needed was a man who
could infuse strength into the government and simultaneously appeal
to the better nature of the inhabitants. Forced to deal with deeper
currents of disaffection than any other governor of a New England

---

[27] Williams to Winthrop, Feb. 15, 1655, *N.C.P.*, VI, 280-282.
[28] *Ibid.*, 280.
[29] *Ibid.*, 283, 287.

colony during his lifetime, Williams did his conscientious best to fill this rôle. Where he could, he chose the path of conciliation so congenial to his talents. In adjusting differences by mutual agreement and mediation, he had no peer in the English colonies, whether in Indian relations or in disagreements between party factions. There were, nevertheless, several occasions during his administration when conciliation might be taken as a sign of weakness or a compromise with principle, and in these instances Williams took a stronger line.

During the winter, the new president of the colony met one of his severest tests in riots which broke out over the question of military training. Rhode Island, friendly with the Narragansetts but fearful of the consequences of the policies of the United Colonies, had initiated the usual colonial practice of compulsory militia service. On November 8, 1654, Providence, making its first attempt to establish periodic musters of the "train band," chose military officers in a town meeting over which Williams presided.[30] Since militia service imposed an unaccustomed burden and violated an old Baptist scruple against the bearing of arms as un-Christian, it is not surprising that some of the townsmen objected. Basing their remonstrance upon natural rights and religious liberty, these conscientious objectors, Thomas Olney, William Harris, John Field, Robert Williams, and several others, circulated a paper asserting, "That it was blood-guiltiness, and against the rule of the gospel, to execute judgment upon transgressors, against the private or public weal."[31]

Thomas Olney, who for a time officiated as a Baptist minister in Providence, might logically refer to the Baptist doctrine of pacifism, but Roger Williams perceived in the conclusion of the remonstrance nothing but anarchism. With the inconsistency inherent in philosophies of a higher law, Williams proclaimed natural rights in the name of democracy, to overthrow monarchy or the oligarchy of class, but objected to invoking them against democracy itself.[32] As president he felt it his duty to condemn the "tumult and disturbance" and the "pretence" of violation of conscience and accordingly issued a public letter to Providence which is perhaps best known of all his writings.

[30] *Prov. Recs.*, II, 76-77.
[31] Backus, *The Baptists*, I, 297.
[32] For a stimulating appraisal of inconsistencies in the theory, see B. F. Wright, *American Interpretations of Natural Law* (Cambridge, 1931), pp. 327-345.

He had never spoken or written for "an infinite" freedom of conscience which would place individual rights above the rights of society, to the sacrifice of the common welfare. To clarify his definition of civil and religious liberty, he likened human society to a ship at sea on which Catholics, Protestants, Jews, and Turks were all embarked together. All may worship or not as they please, but if any refuse help toward common charges or defense, or defy "the common laws and orders of the ship, concerning their common peace or preservation"; or if any mutiny against their officers or "preach or write that there ought to be no commanders or officers, because all are equal in Christ, therefore no masters nor officers, no laws nor orders, nor corrections nor punishments . . . I never denied, but in such cases, whatever is pretended, the commander or commanders may judge, resist, compel and punish such transgressors, according to their deserts and merits."[33]

Though this elevated religious freedom as a natural right beyond the reach of governmental power, it did not place liberty of speech and press in the same exalted category. Williams' definition denoted no limitation on freedom of thought, but his language, if narrowly construed, would sanction prosecution of public advocates of anarchism on the grounds of sedition against the government. Williams has been charged with breaking with his own principle, and it has been suggested that the idea of individualism in politics, as a corollary to that of freedom of conscience, was better understood by Williams' fellow citizens than by the founder of the colony himself.[34] This is untenable. Williams did not violate his own principle, for his earlier definitions of civil liberty were consistent with that of 1655. Nor did the bulk of Rhode Island freemen have a different principle; the code of laws of 1647, endorsed by the whole colony and squarely based on Williams' philosophy, stressed obligations as well as rights.

The anarchist interpretation of civil liberty brought Williams to the nucleus of a big question, never completely decided. The wavering line between lawful expression of discontent and words provocative of open violence remained so tenuous even three centuries later as to invite demands for defense of democracy in a fascist manner. Under later American theory of constitutional limitations, rights were reserved by the individual to himself, but

[33] Williams to the Town of Providence, *N.C.P.*, VI, 278-279.
[34] Richman, *Rhode Island*, II, 68-71 *et seq.*

the practice still conformed to the more realistic theory enunciated
by Williams. In actuality civil liberties have been privileges exercised under restraints prescribed by law. "Equally fundamental with
the private right is that of the public to regulate it in the common
interest."[35] This was substantially the basis for Williams' position in
1655 and clearly in line with Rhode Island law. Nevertheless Williams and Rhode Island, exploring the ways of democracy in days
when it was struggling for existence, set a stricter limit on freedom
of expression than Thomas Jefferson thought necessary for public
safety. Under the Jeffersonian formula, the agitations of anarchists
and other radicals were a proper cause for punishment only when
civil violence was an imminent or actual consequence. The range of
court discretion is enormous, but by applying the test of "clear and
present" danger, modern judicial liberality, at its broadest, sanctions
freedom of speech and press short of actual breach of peace by inci-
tation to open resistance.[36]

The Rhode Island pacifists, with the inconsistency so common
to anarchist movements, condemned the government for sanctioning
force and then carried this conscientious objection to the point of
"risinge or takinge armes" in opposition to Williams' government.
As president, Williams, though himself no friend of war, believed
it advisable to have a militia to bring Indian offenders like Pomham
in for trial and impress the United Colonies and local secessionists
with the determination of his government to defend democracy
within Rhode Island boundaries. His public letter apparently quieted
the agitation but did not convince the conscientious objectors. Three
months later at the annual elections Williams was reëlected president,
but a leading Providence pacifist, Thomas Olney, was returned as
assistant. Debate ensued over Olney's part in the recent "risinge or
takinge up of armes to the oposeinge of authoritie." Williams and
the assistants ended the matter by naming two Portsmouth representatives to "treate" with Olney and declare the "minde" of the
court to him. Olney seems to have satisfied them as to his loyalty
and was thereupon formally "engaged" as assistant.[37] A few days
later when a "great debate" over the same question broke out at a

[35] Nebbia *v.* New York (291 U. S. 502, 1934).
[36] Zachariah Chafee, *Freedom of Speech* (N. Y., 1920) and *An Inquiring Mind* (N. Y., 1928).
[37] *R. I. Col. Recs.*, I, 303, 307.

Providence town meeting, Williams' policy of conciliation again triumphed, the town voting that, since Olney had been duly elected, "for the publike union and peace sake it should be past By and no more mentioned."[38]

In theory, Rhode Island's president defined advocacy of anarchism as a breach of peace. In practice, his administration exhibited a keen respect for individual rights and the democratic process.

[38] *Prov. Recs.,* II, 81.

17

LIBERTY WITHOUT LICENSE

IN THE EIGHT MONTHS OF HIS FIRST TERM as president, Williams accomplished a great task in drawing Rhode Island out of the headstrong particularism and ugly personal bickering which had racked the colony during his absence in England. His reëlection in 1655 and again in 1656 for a third consecutive term, constituted a mandate from the people. Rhode Island, needing a unifying philosophy and a popular leader, now fully appreciated the services of the man who could rally factions to lay aside private grievances and combine for the common good. Much remained to be done. The Arnold clan at Pawtuxet, protected by the Bay colony, obstructed the orderly process of government, Coddington and his faction were still irreconcilable, and meanwhile a new malcontent, William Harris, fell under the spell of the doctrines of anarchism. Before Williams laid down his office for the last time in 1657 he was compelled to draw still more clearly the distinction, as he saw it, between liberty and license.

The legislation passed during Williams' last two years as president exhibited a steady tendency to strengthen the central authority. By an enactment of May, 1655, the assembly liberated the central government from financial dependence upon contributions from the towns. The commissioners or assistants were to determine the amounts to be raised for general taxes and were empowered to appoint colonial officials to see to the collection.[1] Dealing another deadly blow at the particularism of the towns, the assembly in 1656 asserted the supremacy of the laws of the central government and ordered that no colonial enactments be "obstructed or neglected under pretence of any authoritie of any of the towne charters."[2]

The Williams administration, in the process of strengthening the central authority, restricted the unmitigated freedom of individuals where it seemed likely to run into license. Rhode Island had long been called by her enemies a refuge of rogues, and William

[1] R. I. Col. Recs., I, 306.
[2] Ibid., 333.

Arnold in 1651 merely echoed orthodox mythology when he described
the colony as a sewer, draining off "all the scume" of the country.
"That State that will give Liberty of Conscience in matters of
Religion," the Simple Cobbler had written in 1647, "must give
Liberty of Conscience and Conversation in their Moral Laws, or
else the Fiddle will be out of Tune, and some of the strings crack."[3]
Nathaniel Ward and his brethren airily assumed that religious
freedom brought license in all things and that Rhode Island, lured
on by this false marsh light, would mire herself foully in immorality
and lawlessness. Williams and his associates now set out to prove
these critics mistaken.

While orthodox Puritan settlements submitted each newcomer
to a rigorous inquisition of his faith and morals before admitting
him as an inhabitant, Rhode Island gave asylum to all sorts and
conditions of men. This frontier freedom might easily permit repeti-
tion of incidents like the desecration of the grave of Pessicus' sister.
The Williams administration, though avoiding the orthodox Puritan
remedy of minute surveillance of private lives and morals, determined
to make gross violators of English *mores* reckon with the force of
the colony's law. The assembly of May, 1655, placed liquor dealers
under a license system, laid an excise tax on intoxicants, and fixed
a maximum price to protect consumers.[4] One of these regulations,
to prevent the "great mischiefe" of Indian drunkenness, restricted
sales to a native to a quarter of a pint of wine or liquor a day, an
amount small enough to ensure temperance. Other enactments strove
to make up for the laxity of the four towns in failing to provide
prisons and stocks.[5] Because strong language had flowed so freely
in the recent period of dissension, a new law placed verbal incivilities
in the category of breaches of the peace. On first complaint, a
"notorious and customarie swearer, and curser," was to be put on
probation. If he then defaulted, he was to be admonished and for a
third offense was to sit two hours in the stocks or pay a fine.[6]

There was also new legislation on moral questions. In case of
adultery, for which the code of 1647 had provided no express
penalties, whipping and a fine were now prescribed.[7] A month later,

[3] Nathaniel Ward, *The Simple Cobbler*, Force's Tracts, III, no. 8, p. 9.
[4] *R. I. Col. Recs.*, I, 307-309.
[5] *Ibid.*, 310-311.
[6] *Ibid.*, 314.
[7] *Ibid.*, 311-312; *cf. ibid.*, 173.

at the session of June, 1655, new laws were passed to curb loose living and solicitation of women, empowering magistrates to inflict "some moderate corporall punishment."[8] If complaints were found false, the magistrate could punish the false accuser. Another law provided adequate punishment for robbing a grave.[9] Brawlers in open court were to be held to strict account.[10] Legislation of 1656 prohibited tippling after nine o'clock in public houses and held masters of families accountable for the "licentious courses" of servants or sons who were under age.[11]

These enactments do not denote a growing harshness in Rhode Island justice. The penalties were moderate compared with those of either the mother country or Massachusetts and Connecticut and merely amplified earlier provisions in the code of laws. Some of the enactments of Williams' administration represent a distinct liberalization of the code. In October, 1656, with Williams presiding, the court made the penalties for grand and petty larceny less severe.[12] The most notable liberality was in the law of divorce, passed in May, 1655, radically extending the grounds for divorce to include cases where a couple had separated because of mere incompatibility.[13] Williams, who presided, had become converted to the views of his friend, John Milton, and undoubtedly was responsible for passage of the law. Williams, as president, authorized the first divorce under the new law, granting John Coggeshall liberty to contract a new marriage; apparently as an afterthought prompted by Elizabeth Coggeshall's petition for the "same equall libertie," the court gave the divorced wife similar permission![14]

During his second term, Williams made rapid progress in healing the scars left by the Coddington usurpation. A letter from the lord protector, read before the assembly on June 28, 1655, instructed the colony "to proceede in your government" under the charter of 1644, thereby putting a full stop to any question by the United Colonies or Rhode Island factions of the lawfulness of Williams' administration.[15] President Williams made good use of the letter

[8] *Ibid.*, 318.
[9] *Ibid.*, 319 f.
[10] *Ibid.*, 321.
[11] *Ibid.*, I, 330, 332.
[12] *Ibid.*, 350; cf. *ibid.*, 174.
[13] *Ibid.*, 312.
[14] *Ibid.*, 314, 319.
[15] *Ibid.*, 316-317.

from his "verrie lovinge friend, Oliver. P." Immediately after its reception, the law against loose living was passed, on the score that "we have certaine information" that Cromwell had heard complaints of Rhode Island morals. A law against "Ringleaders of Factions" also slid through, on the basis of the "expresse command" in Cromwell's letter to provide against "intestine commotions." In the future, ringleaders found guilty by the general court were to be sent to England for trial by the council of state.[16] In appreciation of Cromwell's beneficence, Rhode Island sent overseas an indigenous gift. In October the lord protector received a letter forwarded from Falmouth by a sea captain, together with "a young deer that came from Mr. Williams, President in Providence Plantations in New-England."[17]

On February 21, 1656, Williams wrote to John Winthrop, Jr., that the "fire between Mr. Coddington and others" was now coming "to public trial. . . . I fear this year will be stormy."[18] The storm came, but not from the quarter Williams expected. Coddington, bowing to events, accepted office as a commissioner from Newport and appeared at the Warwick assembly in March. The Williams administration was anxious for conciliation, but suspicions were rife. On request of the assembly, Coddington made a formal submission: "I William Coddington, doe freely submit to the authoritie of his Highness in this Colonie as it is now united, and that with all my heart."[19] The assembly then seated him and sent word to John Clarke to drop charges against him in England.[20] There were still some grievances outstanding. Upon complaint that "there are gunnes in the Indians hands like unto those Mr. Coddington brought over," the enterprising magnate of Newport was asked to account for the disposal of his guns.[21] To smooth the way to better feeling, the assembly expunged from the records certain actions which "might seem prejuditiall" to Coddington and others and dropped presentments which had been preferred by both sides in the recent partisan warfare.[22]

[16] R. I. Col. Recs., I, 318-319.
[17] Coll. R.I.H.S., XXIV, 128.
[18] Letters, N.C.P., VI, 299.
[19] R. I. Col. Recs., I, 327.
[20] Ibid., 328-329.
[21] Ibid., 332.
[22] Ibid., 332-333.

The only remaining obstacles to a vigorous united government were the Arnold clan at Pawtuxet and the pretensions of the United Colonies to exterritorial jurisdiction in Rhode Island. On November 15, 1655, Williams fired an opening gun in a renewed campaign to wrest Pawtuxet and the Indians of that neighborhood from subjection to Massachusetts. In a lengthy communication to the Bay he dealt with four outstanding issues.[23] The first was an action for damages to the amount of two thousand pounds which the town of Warwick had preferred against Massachusetts before Cromwell's council. While abroad, he and Edward Winslow had nearly reached a settlement out of court, and he now suggested that arbiters chosen by both sides proceed at once to a final settlement. The second matter was the "insolencies" and thievery of the Indians at Warwick and Pawtuxet who, when called to account, "pretend your name," escaping with impunity because "they know you favor us not."

The third difficulty was the similar immunity of the Arnold clan. They had lately professed "a willingness to arbitrate" the question of land titles, but said "they dare not for your sakes," which was mere pretext inasmuch as they obeyed neither Massachusetts' laws nor Rhode Island's and paid taxes in neither colony. Massachusetts should consider "how unsuitable" it was to obstruct orderly proceedings in Rhode Island and how unequal "for people to be compelled to order and common charges, when others in their bosoms, are by such (seeming) partiality exempted for both." Two of the four Pawtuxet families were willing to reunite with Rhode Island, including Zachariah Rhodes, who was a Baptist and therefore "(potentially) banished by you." William Arnold and William Carpenter were both "very far, also in religion, from you, if you knew all."[24]

The fourth matter was the question of common defense. The danger to Rhode Island, "being a frontier people to the barbarians," was greater than that of other colonies. Although it was a vital interest of Massachusetts to strengthen Rhode Island as the first line of defense, she had forbidden Rhode Islanders to purchase arms and munitions within her jurisdiction. The law should be repealed. Moreover both colonies should take stronger measures to prevent the sale of munitions to potential enemies. The natives "all the land

[23] *Letters*, N.C.P., VI, 293-296.
[24] *Ibid.*, 295.

over, are filled with artillery and ammunition from the Dutch, openly and horridly," and from the English "by stealth. . . . For myself . . . I have refused the gain of thousands by such a murderous trade, and think no law yet extant, among yourselves or us, secure enough against such villainly." [25] He was sending word of this traffic in arms to the lord protector and his council where it was not likely to make a favorable impression.

This letter to the Bay court met with no response, but Rhode Island's president, making settlement of the Pawtuxet and Warwick questions a major objective of his administration, corresponded with Governor Endecott in the spring of 1656 and finally obtained agreement on a conference with the Massachusetts court. [26] Preparing to present the case in person, Williams despatched another letter to the Bay, [27] stressing the unfortunate results of dual jurisdiction, the annual loss to Warwick from Pomham's depredations, and the increasing danger of bloodshed from this "intermingled cohabitation." Not all the English towns of New England put together suffered as much molestation "as this one town and people." The Pawtuxet men opposed his plan for reunion, professing fear of retribution, but he pledged Rhode Island to admit them as freemen with full colony privileges. He repeated his objections to the embargo against Rhode Island in powder and arms and urged repeal as obviously to the interest of Massachusetts, since Rhode Island was "your thorny hedge on this side of you" and ought to be strengthened.

Five days later at Boston Williams conferred with the magistrates who once had banished him. [28] Upon return to Rhode Island, where he was reëlected president on May 20, he announced to the assembly that Massachusetts favored settlement of the Pawtuxet and Warwick questions and agreed to his proposal of arbitration with the Arnold clan. He requested, in conformity with his pledge to Endecott, that the Pawtuxet men should be offered full privileges as freemen of the colony. The assembly endorsed this settlement, although stipulating that the arbitration take place within three months. [29]

[25] *Letters*, N.C.P., VI, 296.
[26] *Ibid.*, 299.
[27] *Ibid.*, 300-303.
[28] *Ibid.*, 304-305.
[29] *R. I. Col. Recs.*, I, 339 f.

The arbitration did not actually take place within the specified time, but before Williams left office he convinced Massachusetts that the situation was intolerable. On August 6 he drafted a public letter, one copy of which he directed to Providence and the Pawtuxet secessionists and another to Massachusetts. George Palmer, accused by the Arnold clan of seducing a Providence girl, gave evidence to the Rhode Island president before witnesses of the moral turpitude of the Pawtuxet secessionists. Some of them had known "and concealed a longe time" from both Rhode Island and Massachusetts "a Buggery committed by Richard Chasmore on his heifer." Once the matter was public property, these same Pawtuxet men implicated themselves by helping "Long Dick" Chasmore to make his escape. The copy of this letter which Williams sent to the Massachusetts governor also contained evidence that the Pawtuxet allies of the Bay "make a trade of selling powder and shotts to the barbarians."[30]

On September 27 Williams sent further word to Endecott about immorality at Pawtuxet.[31] "Sir, while matters are undecided betweene yorselves and us concerning Patuxit we can neither proceed with them without yor offence, nor winck at them without great scandall." He had heard further testimony about the nefarious trade with the Indians, particularly William Carpenter's "powder selling." He had issued a warrant for the fugitive Long Dick.

In the next three months Pawtuxet behavior caused Governor Endecott additional chagrin. Long Dick, after escaping to the Dutch, returned for his cattle. When Williams issued warrants for his arrest, one of the subjects of Massachusetts, Zachariah Rhodes, helped him make a second escape and subsequently got his cattle away for him. Since the Boston magistrates still exercised ostensible jurisdiction, Williams suggested they also investigate another matter, the "no small presumptions of old Arnolds uncleannes with his maide and a powder trade driven by his son Stephen." As a result of correspondence with the Dutch governor concerning Long Dick, the culprit had returned and "surrendred himselfe to me at my howse." Williams had bound him over for trial. As Rhode Island's president, he was accountable to the general court and to

---

[30] Williams to "Neighbors," Aug. 6, 1656, *N.E.H.G.R.*, XXXVI (1882), 78.
[31] Williams to Endecott, 1656, *Pub. R.I.H.S.*, VIII, 144.

"his Highnes if I suffer Such Crimes unquestioned before my face." The Bay magistrates perhaps quieted their consciences somewhat more readily, on the ground of "want of Easie Inspection and Informacion."[32]

The Pawtuxet news so affronted the magisterial sense of rectitude that Massachusetts dispatched officers to apprehend Long Dick and bring him to Boston. This in turn provoked a tempest in Providence, temporarily disrupting the friendly relations Williams had established with the Bay. A group of Providence citizens, including Arthur Fenner, town deputy, determined to prevent the Bay colony from interfering with the course of Rhode Island justice and called an unauthorized town meeting. The result was vigilante action by a mob which rescued Long Dick from the Massachusetts officers. Williams immediately issued a letter in his official capacity as president, rebuking Fenner and the townsmen for "disorderly and dangerous courses." They had violated the democratic process by summoning an unlawful town meeting and arrogating power not entrusted to them. They had virtually compounded a felony in helping a prisoner escape and had complicated delicate negotiations between the two colonies.[33]

Williams, recalling the recent lynching of Captain Partridge, dreaded the demoralizing effect of vigilante action, regarding it destructive of democracy itself. Believing that orderly political procedure must be upheld if democracy was to survive, he backed up his verbal lashing of local officers and townsmen by issuing presentments against Arthur Fenner, Thomas Harris, William Wickenden, Thomas Angell, Samuel Bennett, his old friend Gregory Dexter, and his son-in-law, John Sayles, who had married Mary Williams in 1652. These he charged under the recent law against "Ringeleaders in new devisions in the Collony." When the first of these cases came before the court of trials on March 13, 1657, a few weeks after the mob action at Providence, the Rhode Island president did not appear to make out his accusation and the court accordingly found the defendants innocent.[34] The other cases came up at the session of October 16, and again Williams absented himself and the de-

[32] Williams to Endecott, Dec. 1, 1656, *Pub. R.I.H.S.*, VIII, 145-146.

[33] Williams to Fenner and the Inhabitants of Providence, Feb. 24, 1657, *Proc. R.I.H.S., 1883-1884,* p. 79.

[34] *R. I. Court Recs.*, I, 27.

fendants were cleared.[35] Apparently Williams intended merely to give forceful warning of the necessity of lawful procedure and regarded a court summons as sufficient humiliation for the offenders.

The Providence riot strained relations with the Bay colony. Roger Williams, as president, was not to have the pleasure of ending the friction over Pawtuxet, but in little over a year after his retirement from office his work bore fruit in the reunion of Pawtuxet and Rhode Island.[36]

During his last months in office, Williams faced other perplexing cases of defiance of governmental authority. It was the ill fortune of his administration to be confronted with the only notable anarchist opposition in early Rhode Island history. Inasmuch as he had taken command in a period of turbulence, following the Coddington hiatus and before Rhode Island democracy had simmered down into a more orderly notion of self-government, it fell chiefly to him to see Rhode Island through her growing pains. His administration was dogged by a considerable resentment of increasing governmental power and by a contrary insistence on unfettered individual liberty. Later colonial governors had royal commissioners of the king to fall back upon, in dealing with defiance of authority. Roger Williams labored alone and relied upon reason, not force.

Among the malcontents was Catherine Scott, one of the earliest Baptists in Providence and a woman preacher. It is probable that she had begun to imbibe Quaker ideas, for two years later she went to Boston to protest against the cropping of Quaker ears, returning with the scars of a Massachusetts lash. While Williams was president, she carried her religious zeal to the point of open contempt of authority and espousal of something like philosophic anarchism. In the same category was Rebecca Throckmorton, who also eventually became a Quakeress. Two others were Robert West and Ann Williams, whose husband, Robert, had been one of the conscientious objectors of 1655. On March 13, 1657, Catherine Scott and the other three were summoned to the court of trials under a presentment by the president as "Comon Aposers of all Authority."[37] Again Williams did not appear, and the court accordingly dismissed

[35] *Ibid.*, 33, 34.
[36] *Coll. R.I.H.S.*, II, 206-212; *Mass. Bay Recs.*, IV, Part I, 333.
[37] *R. I. Court Recs.*, I, 26.

the charges. Williams dealt likewise with William Coddington, who was presented at the same time for "Contempt of the order of the Collony."[38] Williams' peculiar method of calling forcible attention to obligations under the law was apparently based on a sound judgment of the character of the offenders. In the years following there was no further trouble either from the Baptist anarchists or the prosperous magnate of the Island who eventually served as president of the colony for a number of terms.

Meanwhile a more serious case appeared on the docket. William Harris, presented for "open Defieance under his hand against our Charter, all our Lawes," and against "parliment the Lord protector and all government," became increasingly bellicose and boasted he would maintain his anarchistic writings "with his blood."[39] The president thereupon issued a second warrant transferring the case to the general assembly. Williams did not appear at the assembly in May and apparently hoped that a summons to the highest Rhode Island court would wean Harris from anarchism. Harris stuck to his guns. The general court continued the case to an adjourned session at Warwick and summoned Williams to appear. At the adjourned session, July 4, Harris by order of the court read his book attacking authority, and then Williams read his accusation and a reply to Harris' defense of anarchy. The commissioners concluded that Harris "much bowd the Scriptures to maintaine, that he that can say it is his conscience ought not to yield subjection to any human order amongst men." Uncertain of the law in such a case, the court gave a preliminary finding that the behavior of the accused was both "contemptuous and seditious" and ordered the evidence, including Harris' book, sent to English authorities. William Harris and his son were heavily bonded to the amount of £500.[40]

Since the legal evidence is not now available, one can scarcely form a considered judgment as to the merits of the Harris case. From scattered references—all *ex parte*—it would appear that Harris, suddenly discovering a tender conscience about paying "Rates," circulated to the four towns of the colony a manuscript in which he assailed "all Civill Government" and predicted that people soon would "Crie out No Lords, No Masters." In his bowing of scripture,

[38] *R. I. Court Recs.,* I, 26.
[39] *Ibid.,* 25; Arnold, *Rhode Island,* I, 263.
[40] *R. I. Col. Recs.,* I, 364, 365.

Harris represented his opponents as the house of Saul, destined to grow "Weaker and Weaker (which . . . his booke interprets to be Civill Governors and Governments)," whereas against these the house of David, *i.e.,* "William Harris and his Saints," was growing "stronger and stronger." Among other counts, Harris was accused of attacking all punishments and prisons—by implication, the efforts of the Williams administration to improve the penal system—and of stigmatizing officials and lawmaking assemblies as "Hypocrites, Satyrs, Owles (Courts of Owles), Dragons and Devills."[41]

The projected trial of Harris on the charge of treason never materialized. The ship which was bearing the evidence to England foundered and all papers were lost. After twelve years of contemptuous isolation in the woods at Pachaset following his disfranchisement at Providence, Harris did not take kindly to the increasing insistence of the colonial authorities upon greater strictness and orderly procedure. Nevertheless he learned a lesson from his trial and immediately turned from contempt of law to the practice of law, proving far more adept in pleading the doctrine of vested rights than in expounding scriptural allegory. Perhaps Roger Williams and the court would have done well to tolerate William Harris in his anarchy, for in his law and order phase, Harris rent the colony with his lawsuits. Nor was Williams to have any peace while Harris lived.

Williams did not attend the court of election in May, 1657, and was not a candidate for reëlection. Doubtless he had incurred some resentment by his measures, although it is noteworthy that Fenner, Dexter, Angell, Sayles, and others with whom he had difficulties were soon his close associates in opposition to the fraudulent land schemes which William Harris concocted. In letters to John Winthrop, Jr., Williams occasionally spoke of reluctance to continue in office. By serving in the critical years from 1644 to 1647 and 1654 to 1657, he carried the colony through its most difficult period. One of the few men in the English colonies bred to the ministry who became a magistrate, he was never by preference a politician or administrator. His great contributions along political lines lay in three things: his brilliant understanding and persuasive power as inter-

[41] *Prov. Recs.,* XV, 122.

preter of Rhode Island democracy; his capacity to still local con-
tentions by trenchant appeal to the larger patriotism of his fellow
citizens; and his diplomatic finesse in negotiations about the charter
and in interchanges with the United Colonies in defending Rhode
Island's territory and authority. In these three fields, Roger Williams
had no peer.

18

THE NEMESIS OF ORTHODOXY

UNDER WILLIAMS' LEADERSHIP THE DISCIPLINING of radical sectarians and raw agrarian democracy in the Rhode Island wilderness
proceeded apace; common men proved their capacity to govern themselves and ambitious men like Coddington and the Arnolds bowed to
the will of the people and learned to abide peaceably by the democratic
process. By 1658, when Pawtuxet was regained, Rhode Island had
passed substantially through the ordeal of unification. Meanwhile,
midway in Williams' administration, the colony passed with ease
through an eventful test of its tolerance and broadened the precedent
it had set for the American credo. Along about the year 1656 alien
refugees, non-Christian, bred to the Talmud, began to come to the
colony; and hard on their heels came men and women bred to the
English language and English ways but who did strange violence to
both and were abominated above all others in the English world—
radical sectarians who were to become the nemesis of New England
orthodoxy.

Williams, who recently in Cromwell's England had declared it the
duty of magistrates to raze the wall of separation which shut Jews
off from ordinary civil relations with Christians,[1] had in his capacity
as chief magistrate the duty and pleasure of welcoming the first Jewish refugees in the English colonies. The liberality of Rhode Island
cut squarely across the old racial grooves worn deep by centuries of
persecution. Technically still excluded from England despite the
connivance of Cromwell, honored only in the one small haven of the
Dutch Netherlands, these aliens of despised creed were hated and
oppressed everywhere by Christians whose religion, now triumphant,
had sprung from that of the ancient Hebrew. "What then is to be
done to this depraved, damned people," asked Luther, and the great
German reformer sanctioned the burning of their synagogues and the
burning of their homes. Williams' old patron, Sir Edward Coke,
renowned as a champion of liberty under the law, found it in his

[1] See Chapter 15, p. 208f.

heart and in his law to deny Jews the ordinary protection of English courts; they were infidels, perpetual enemies, and had no rights enforceable at law.[2]

The first Jews in Rhode Island came from Holland and from Spain's American colonies. Forbidden in Catholic countries to marry by Hebrew rites, compelled to assume Christian names, and, particularly in the realms of Philip II, subject to insufferable persecution, multitudes of Jews swarmed into the tolerant commercial centers of the Netherlands. Spanish Jews who sought refuge in the far off lands of Mexico and Peru found themselves facing anew the *autos-da-fé* from which they had fled. By the middle of the century several thousand emigrated to Brazil, placing trust in Dutch control, but the reconquest of Brazil by the Portuguese in 1654 delivered them again into the hands of persecutors.[3] Refugees once more, some twenty of these in 1655 arrived in New Amsterdam, the last promising Dutch outpost in the new world, only to find Peter Stuyvesant adamant against their admission. Several of the émigrés, hearing of hospitable plantations but a little way up the coast, found a welcome from President Williams and a final home in Rhode Island. An order from the West Indies company overruled Governor Stuyvesant and Jews began to settle in New Amsterdam; but public worship was a monopoly of the Dutch Reformed church, and Jews like other dissenters were restricted by law to services in their homes. By 1658 word had circulated of greater liberality in Rhode Island, and in that year fifteen families of Dutch Jews made the voyage from Holland to Newport where they soon established Jeshuat Israel (Salvation of Israel), earliest overseas Hebrew congregation under the English flag.[4]

Safe among tolerant neighbors who recognized and respected one's right to be different, Rhode Island Jews revived the cherished customs they had been forced to abjure, those coming from Spain and Portugal then and in the eighteenth century finding liberty at last to

[2] Samuel W. McCall, *The Patriotism of the American Jew* (N. Y., 1924), pp. 56-58, 64.

[3] *Ibid.*, 69-72; Lewis Browne, *Stranger than Fiction* (N. Y., 1925), p. 272.

[4] For the beginning of Jewish migration see Charles P. Daly, *The Settlement of the Jews in New Amsterdam*, ed. Max J. Kohler (N. Y., 1893); McCall, *The Patriotism of the American Jew;* and especially, Max J. Kohler, "The Jews in Newport," *Pub. American Jewish Historical Society*, no. 6 (1897), pp. 62-73, and R. B. Morris, "The Jewish Interests of Roger Williams," *American Hebrew*, Dec. 9, 1921.

renounce Christian names and Catholic rites. Michael Lopez changed his name to Abraham and remarried his wife according to Jewish ceremonies.[5] Newport's reputation for social tolerance attracted more émigrés, including some from Curaçao in 1694 and some hundreds from Spain and Portugal after 1750. Elsewhere in New England a few stragglers penetrated. Although not persecuted, they were not wanted, David Campanell, "a Jew from Rhode Island," being warned out of Boston in 1726 and a few others receiving similar warnings.[6] The readiness of Williams' colony to harbor refugees won her no credit from Puritans of the confederation, and at the close of the seventeenth century Cotton Mather could find it in his heart to characterize Newport as "the common receptacle of the convicts of Jerusalem and the outcasts of the land."[7]

"I have desired," Williams declared to Cromwellian England, "to labor in Europe, in America, with English, with Barbarians, yea, and also I have longed after some trading with the Jews themselves, for whose hard measure, I fear the nations and England have yet a score to pay."[8] Friendly and interested, an accomplished linguist as fluent in Dutch and Hebrew as in Indian dialect, he could converse with the newcomers in their foster language or their own tongue, and in 1671 he commended the manners of the Jews, comparing them favorably with those of some of his own countrymen who had turned rabid Quakers. The immigrants justified his confidence that a sound conscience was "found in all mankind." Friendly relations and good will sprang up between the English settlers and the newcomers, and in 1685 when the estates of Mordecai and Abraham Campanell, Rachel Mandes, and others were sequestered—on the charge of "alienage,"—the Rhode Island assembly intervened: "we declare, that they may expect as good protection here, as any stranger" so long as obedient to law. This mutual confidence continued, and several years later Abraham Campanell was licensed as a freeman.[9] In the eighteenth century, able and cultivated émigrés like Aaron Lopez became

[5] See article by Mrs. Caesar Misch, in T. W. Bicknell, *The History of Rhode Island* (N. Y., 1920), II, 629.

[6] Leo M. Friedman, *Early American Jews* (Cambridge, 1934), p. 9.

[7] Quoted by Max J. Kohler, "The Jews of Newport," *Pub. Am. Jewish Hist. Soc.,* no. 6 (1897), p. 65 f.

[8] *The Hireling Ministry,* p. 176.

[9] *R. I. Col. Recs.,* III, 160; T. Durfee, "Gleanings from the Judicial History of Rhode Island," *R. I. H. Tracts,* v. 18, p. 134 f; Kohler, "The Jews in Newport," *Pub. Am. Jewish Hist. Soc.,* no. 6 (1897), p. 38.

merchant princes in Newport, introducing the new manufacture of sperm oil and candles, furniture factories, and rope walks, accounting in no small part for the golden age of Newport commerce.

Rhode Island's remarkable defiance of the time-encrusted tradition of Christian intolerance toward Jews was perhaps, at the time, no more striking than her attitude toward the "cursed sect" of Quakers. The reception of the first Friends at Boston and New Amsterdam insured their hearty welcome in Williams' colony, and before Rhode Island people had seen a Quaker, they were aroused to indignation as tales began to drift in of the beginnings of the most savage persecution the colonies had seen. In July, 1656, when Mary Fisher and Ann Austin landed at Boston, their supply of Quaker tracts was burned and the two women were "stripped stark naked" and examined for "tokens" of witchcraft, much like strangers inspected by the priests or medicine men of primitive tribes for signs of evil powers. The women were no sooner ejected than William Brend and seven more Quakers appeared in Boston where they were promptly imprisoned. To the "Strangers and outcasts" in Boston jail came a letter from Samuel Gorton. "The report of your demeanour . . . as also the errand you come upon hath much taken my heart." The rulers of Massachusetts had long attempted to deceive and "tyrannize," and Rhode Island people, though lying as "buried" in their remote corner of the earth, were "grudged at, that we have this present burying place." If the prisoners desired refuge in his colony, Gorton would help them transfer from the ship in which they were to be deported.[10]

When Virginia and tolerant Maryland gave the first Friends a harsh reception, it is not surprising that Massachusetts Puritans and Dutch Calvinists did likewise. Following the landing of some Quakers at New Amsterdam in August, 1657, two horrified Dutch ministers sent home a report of the activities of several Quaker women who "began to quake and go into a frenzy, and cry out loudly in the middle of the street that men should repent, for the day of judgment was at hand. Our people not knowing what was the matter ran to and fro while one cried 'fire' and another something else."[11] One of the Quakers went to Long Island where many

---

[10] *Coll. R.I.H.S.*, II, 16-17.

[11] *Ecclesiastical Records of the State of New York* (Albany, 1901-1916), I, 400.

refugees from the rigors of New England Puritanism had settled, and there rapidly made converts. Seized by the Dutch, the Quaker was sentenced to hard labor and, upon refusal to work, nearly beaten to death. Governor Stuyvesant, after imprisoning the other Quakers in a "filthy dungeon," deported them. "We suppose they went to Rhode Island," wrote the two alarmed Dutch clerics, "for that is the receptacle of all sorts of riff-raff people and is nothing else than the sewer of New England."[12]

The Dutch clerics guessed correctly. William Brend, Christopher Holder, John Copeland, and others of the party put in at Newport where they and later Quakers made an astounding number of converts, including not only the rank and file but prominent men like Coddington and Walter Clarke. Brend invaded Providence, and there Catherine Scott, sister of Anne Hutchinson, John Throckmorton, and other Baptists who, as conscientious objectors, had recently perplexed President Williams, embraced the new faith. There was good reason why Rhode Island should prove fertile soil. Her people like the Friends proclaimed the right and necessity of religious liberty, inclined toward pacifism, scrupled at oaths, objected to tithes and "hireling ministries," and denounced pretensions of priests to a monopoly of understanding of divinity and truth. The colony's radical social psychology, based on a democratic doctrine of man assuming the rational capacity of ordinary citizens and affirming the dignity of human personality, had long ago prepared its inhabitants for a confident conviction that true religious apprehension was within reach of the lowliest of men. The "priesthood of all believers" was no new doctrine in Rhode Island; and to many older residents, Separatists, Baptists, and Seekers, it was no hard matter to accept belief in the "inner light."

The invasion of these "ravening wolves of dissent" struck terror in the rulers of the realms of orthodoxy. Indomitable and indefatigable, the ardent apostles of the inner light carried their message with a flare for sensationalism, invading every sanctum of the saints, proclaiming their new faith and God's judgment on their persecutors, ready to lay down their lives with the confident fatalism and serenity of spirit of a Mohammedan warrior. Massachusetts had never coped with a people like these, and the oligarchy of the Bay, ingrown and

[12] *Ibid.,* 399.

isolated, dreading the innovations which had so greatly changed England, struck blindly at the heretics, moving yet farther from the noble Puritanism which had given expression through Milton to the *Areopagitica*.

In contrast to the Friends with their free, individualistic, and mystical spirituality, their belief that revelation was personal and unfolding, and their intoxicated vision of the brotherhood of man, Puritans of the confederation assumed that divinely revealed truth was intelligible to and in charge of the clergy and magistracy of God's chosen people and that this truth was largely static. Already uneasy in the face of the individualism implicit in Puritanism, ortho-dox leaders were horrified by the pungent and cleansing philosophic anarchism in which Quaker thought had its roots. A religion so personal, so free, struck fundamentally at authoritarian theology and might by its contagion win converts by the thousands. Such spiritual individualism augured political repercussions. There was something dangerously democratic in a people who scorned dis-tinctions of class and sex and wore hats in the august presence of magistrates and kings. The doctrine of the brotherhood of man was propaganda for equalitarianism. Well might Governor Endecott suspect that men who denounced tithes would agitate against limi-tations on the right to vote and hold office. After the appearance of the first Quakers, Massachusetts demanded and the confederated colonies enacted stringent legislation to muzzle and eject the daring invaders. In September, 1658, the panic-stricken United Colonies proposed the death penalty and stigmatized Quaker doctrine as per-nicious and "devilish": it produced not only seditious breaches of peace but turned "the hearts of the people from their subjection to government."

Meanwhile, in September, 1657, five months after Williams re-tired from the presidency, the confederation brazenly demanded that Providence Plantations cease giving sanctuary to Quakers. Despite their own "prudent care" in fortifying their gateways by sea, Rhode Island had opened a postern gate to their great annoy-ance. Laws against heretics would "fall short" so long as Quakers from Rhode Island "have opportunitie to creep in amongst us." Toleration in Providence Plantations was injuring orthodoxy in other colonies, giving heretics "meanes to infuse and spread theire accursed tenates." The "contagion" was dangerous, and the confederacy warned Rhode Island to eject her Quakers "and for the future prohibit theire cominge amongst you." Upon performance of this "request" depended the decision whether "Intercourse" by way of trade "may bee with safety continued between us."[13]

This cool summons to join the united front of red-baiters and heresy-hunters was received by Roger Williams and other citizens with scorn. The court of trials was then meeting at Providence, headed by the new president of the colony, Benedict Arnold, once esteemed by Massachusetts as a Pawtuxet ally, and including among its members Williams' friend, Arthur Fenner, and Randall Holden, the Gortonist who many times had snapped his fingers in audacious defiance of the magistrates of the Bay. The ex-president, Williams, was not a magistrate, but there is small doubt that the father of Rhode Island had a hand in drafting the court's masterly answer of October 13. The irony of the demand that Rhode Island people desert their dearest principles and turn persecutors was not lost on their leaders and they made the most of the opportunity. Their reply was sagacious, dignified, and deft. With unspoken but obvious allusion to orthodox revilement of Providence Plantations as the sewer of New England, they called attention to their regulations for extradition of fugitives from justice and other measures to preserve "just and equal entercourse" between colonies. Urbanely silent as to their own views of persecution, they affirmed a generally cooperative spirit but mentioned an impediment to ejection of Quakers: "We have no law among us, whereby to punish any for only declaring by words, etc., theire mindes and understandings concerning the things and ways of God." Curiously this deficiency had been a kind of protection; Rhode Island found that "in those places where these people . . . are most of all suffered to declare themselves freely, and are only opposed by arguments in discourse, there they least of all desire to come."[14]

The authors of the Rhode Island reply, thinking perhaps of President Williams' recent experience with Providence anarchists, had some apprehension lest Quaker teaching tend toward the "cutting down" of government, but they made it clear that if Quaker individualism produced abuse of civil rights, they would simply punish the abuse, not suppress civil liberty. As a few short years would

[13] *R. I. Col. Recs.*, I, 374-376.
[14] *Ibid.*, 376-378.

show, this reply might well be accounted a landmark in the contest for liberty in New England, but its immediate effect was to incense the stewards of the Lord. The threat of economic sanctions had not been idle, and Rhode Island soon complained through her agent, John Clarke, against the stoppage of trade in essential commodities, particularly the denial of access to "the concourse of shipping."[15]

Resolutely in the years following, Rhode Island held to her course in spite of pressure and fulfilled her destiny as the gateway of New England dissent. From the security of her soil, flaming evangelists stormed in again and again on the citadels of orthodoxy, Mary Clark proceeding to Boston where she received twenty stripes, Humphrey Norton to New Haven whence he returned with the scars of the lash and the letter H branded on his hand, and others to Plymouth to be similarly thrashed and ejected. Such treatment and increasingly severe laws against Quakers merely brought renewed incursions. Sarah Gibbons, flogged in Plymouth and deported to Rhode Island, entered Massachusetts, only to be forcibly returned with additional welts disfiguring her back. Immediately John Rous, Christopher Holder, and John Copeland, already once scourged in the Bay, again crossed the Rhode Island line, submitted to the ordeal of the corded whips of Massachusetts jailors, and returned with their right ears cropped.

As such incidents multiplied, conscientious Rhode Island residents, some of them Quakers, likewise entered forbidden territory and braved persecution in order to testify against it. Catherine Scott of Providence, for protesting at Boston against brutality towards Quakers, received ten lashes and a warning from Governor Endecott that a hanging might be her next answer. A Newport convert, Hored Gardner, was similarly moved to testify and likewise scourged in Boston. Mary Dyer accompanied two other Quakers to New Haven and bore witness against the branding of Norton until silenced and ejected. To New Amsterdam went a Providence cobbler, William Wickenden, spreading the Baptist gospel, and a little later a Providence Quakeress, wife of Francis Weeks, where both were persecuted and deported.[16] Rhode Island, reported the Dutch clergy, "is

---

15 *Ibid.*, 396-399; R. P. Hallowell, *The Quaker Invasion* (Boston, 1887), p. 171.
16 *Eccles. Recs. of the State of N. Y.*, I, 361-362; R. M. Jones, *The Quakers in the American Colonies* (London, 1911), p. 225 n.

the *caeca latrina* of New England," whence errorists and enthusiasts "swarm to and fro sowing their tares."[17]

The death penalty, adopted by Massachusetts on the recommendation of leading citizens like John Hull and the Boston ministers, Wilson and Norton, failed to stop the incursions from Rhode Island. Four Quakers defied even this extremity and paid with their lives. Just before one of these hangings the magistrates received a heartbroken plea from William Dyer imploring them to spare his wife; but Mary Dyer, the story of whose "monstrous" birth still had vicious currency in the Bay,[18] refused to promise not to return and, twice banished, once as an Antinomian, now again as a Quaker, went with quiet dignity to her doom.

Though thus an innocent accessory to one of the most brutal persecutions in colonial history, Rhode Island by giving sanctuary to dissent contributed powerfully to the discrediting of coercive uniformity and rule by the saints. Roger Williams' prediction that a religion which feared competitors and trusted to the sword would betray its own weakness and lose spiritual appeal was now verified. Whipping the Quakers, with such "cruelty," wrote James Cudworth of Plymouth, and the patience of the victims, gained "more Adherence to them, than if they had suffered them openly to have preached a Sermon."[19] For their sympathy with the Quakers, prominent men like Cudworth, John Brown, and Arthur Howland of Marshfield, an elder, were disfranchised. Isaac Robinson, son of the famous Pilgrim minister, became an avowed convert. Despite confiscations of property and suppression of civil liberty, Quaker meetings continued at Sandwich, Falmouth, Duxbury, and Scituate. Northward among the coastal towns of Massachusetts the efforts to root out the heresy likewise failed. John Chamberlain of Boston, the Southwicks of Salem, Lydia Wardwell of Hampton, and other converts clung stubbornly to their new faith in the face of repeated floggings, and the courts became clogged with cases of recusancy and surreptitious attendance at Quaker meetings. After the hanging of William Leddra in 1661, expediency compelled the magistrates to desist from the foolhardy determination to enforce the death penalty.

[17] *Eccles. Recs. of the State of N. Y.*, I, 409, 433; see also pp. 410, 426, 427, 444.
[18] See entry in John Hull's Diary for Sept. 26, 1658.
[19] Cudworth to Brown, 1658; printed in R. P. Hallowell, *The Quaker Invasion* (Boston, 1887), p. 164.

Connecticut, reported barren ground by the Quaker John Rous, was troubled by few converts to the new sect, and these few under Winthrop's lenient policy generally suffered minor disabilities, though as late as 1672 Coddington complained of Connecticut's recusancy fines and confiscation of Quaker property.[20] To his old friend, Winthrop, Roger Williams wrote in warm congratulation for the humane treatment accorded Norton and Rous: "I rejoice, Sir, that your name . . . is not blurred, but rather honored, for your prudent and moderate hand in the late Quakers' trials amongst us."[21] Under the Cart and Whip act brutalities continued in Massachusetts, in one case Anne Coleman being stripped to the waist and lashed so severely as to split the nipple of her breast,[22] but persecution after 1661 represented a rear guard action. Congeries of devoted Quakers were firmly rooted at Shelter Island and half a dozen settlements on Long Island, at Nantucket, in scattered Plymouth towns, at Salem and northern towns of the Bay, with individual Quakers even in Boston itself. Magistrates were now dealing not with itinerant missionaries but their own people. The monopoly of the orthodox church was broken, and the permission of dissent which Williams had demanded at Salem in 1635 must perforce at last be recognized.

In spite of the intercession of Charles II, die-hard oligarchs were still able to exclude dissenters from political rights, but New England orthodoxy had shot its bolt. The principle had been established that a dissenter might come and stay. A revived and hostile Stuart power in England forced circumspection, and simultaneously the New England regime confronted declining prestige among its people at home. In the years following 1657 Bay clerics like Increase Mather beat a retreat on still another battlefield and, compromising with expediency, lowered requirements for church membership. An intimation of internal decay, the Half-Way Covenant slowly undermined the sacerdotal process by which Visible Saints were elevated above their fellows.

[20] Rous to Fell, quoted in Jones, *The Quakers*, p. 72; Coddington to Winthrop, 4 *Coll. M.H.S.*, VII, 288; see also Underhill to Winthrop, *ibid.*, 192.

[21] Williams to Winthrop, Feb. 6, 1660, *N.C.P.*, VI, 308.

[22] George Bishop, *New England Judged* (London, 1703), p. 430.

19

THE NARRAGANSETT LAND FEVER

THE RESTORATION OF CHARLES II on May 8, 1660, marked the disintegration of the great revolutionary movement in which Roger Williams had played a part on both sides of the Atlantic. The demand of plain people for regular parliaments, equal electoral districts, and manhood suffrage was to be heard no more for over a century. The movement to make the people sovereign, already outlawed under Cromwell, had lost its first major battle in England; and peers and middle-class gentry and merchants were no less determined than the king that never again should the reins of power fall from the proper hands. Sir Henry Vane went to the block, too dangerous a republican to receive a pardon, but Denzil Holles, Anthony Ashley Cooper, and many pushing gentry of the old Puritan party, made their peace with royalty, kept lands won from cavalier families in the revolution, and laid the foundations for the great Whig clique of the eighteenth century. The Anglican establishment became a political pawn. Simultaneously Louis XIV set the European pattern for a century to come, exploiting the religious establishment in the interests of the new despotism, forging a formidable alliance against liberty to criticize or agitate for reform.

In New England the economic drift and calculating spirit of the new era was imperceptibly preparing for the emergence of the Yankee from the Puritan mould. The growing toleration of dissent and the appearance of land engrossers like Richard Wharton betokened a new generation in which zeal ran a little colder but in which hunger for wealth and position no whit abated. Ere long the Massachusetts saints were to be plagued by Edward Randolph, imperial sleuth of Charles II; and meanwhile Samuel Maverick, a royal commissioner, observed that the New England oligarchy "begin to thinke and feare that the major part of the people will not stand by them."[1]

Rhode Island, though sparsely populated by "poore despised Peas-

[1] *Coll. N.Y.H.S.*, II (1869), 128.

ants that lived so remote in the woods,"[2] was not to escape the trend of the times. Roger Williams, his major work complete by 1658, was to be drawn again and again from his beloved privacy to service in town and colony in struggles against forces he feared as hostile to the interests of Rhode Island democracy. The ambitious speculative ventures of the New England squirearchy and the intervention of the revivified and capricious royal power presented a double menace. Williams' humble experiment remained a standing witness to the validity of liberty of conscience and a threat to intolerant orthodoxy, but its democratic program failed to become vital as a germinal force popularizing democracy in other plantations. By the end of Williams' lifetime popular rule in his own commonwealth was itself on the defensive, struggling against the erosion of economic forces, the engrossment of open land by proprietary companies, and the pervasive imitation by Rhode Islanders of English notions of class and family. By 1683 when Williams died, William Harris, introducing English custom, had harked back to aristocratic feudalism, leaving his estate bound in entails to the fourth generation.

Just as Williams retired from the presidency, speculative interest in the Narragansett country set in motion a series of conflicting proprietary enterprises. Richard Smith, Jr., of Cocumcussot claimed Hog Island, enlisted Plymouth support, and contended that the island lay outside of Rhode Island jurisdiction.[3] In September, 1658, with the approval of the United Colonies, Massachusetts annexed the Pequot lands west of the Pawcawtuck River and claimed a strip on the east side extending ten miles into Rhode Island.[4] Meanwhile in 1657 the Pettiquamscut partners, John Hull of Boston in a strange association with three Newport men, to whom Benedict Arnold and William Brenton were later joined, began to purchase a series of tracts, some of them as large as seven and twelve miles square, along the southern shoreline of the Narragansett country.[5] At the same time well-to-do Newport men including Coddington, Benedict Arnold, and later William Brenton and Francis Brinley acquired Dutch Island and the great tract on Conanicut Island lying in Narragansett bay southeast of Richard Smith's trading post.[6] None of these pur-

---

2 Rhode Island petition to Charles II (1665), *Coll. N.Y.H.S.*, II (1869), 155.
3 *R. I. Col. Recs.*, I, 373.
4 *Mass. Bay Recs.*, IV, Pt. 2, 353.
5 *Coll. R.I.H.S.*, III, 275-276.
6 *Ibid.*, 52, 54, 55; *R. I. Col. Recs.*, I, 403; III, 21.

chases were made with consent of the colony, and to put a stop to them the Rhode Island assembly in 1658 reinforced the earlier law of 1651 by declaring all future Indian purchases void unless expressly authorized.

Meanwhile, counting on Massachusetts support, the Richard Smiths, father and son, and Humphrey Atherton, who in 1658 became superintendent of Eliot's praying Indians, conceived a plan to wrest from Rhode Island its unoccupied south country and exploit it as a rich principate along larger proprietary lines. Long ago, as commander of Massachusetts troops sent to cow the Narragansetts, Atherton had made no bones to Williams of his ambition for a Narragansett plantation. The elder Smith, originally a Plymouth man and never a dissenter from New England orthodoxy, was one of the few Rhode Island settlers who in 1643 aided the Massachusetts expedition against the Gortonists and since that time had encouraged Eliot in his efforts to convert Rhode Island Indians to Puritan congregationalism. In the summer of 1659 Atherton, the Smiths, and a group of Massachusetts partners joined in the scramble for land, defying Rhode Island law and purchasing two extensive tracts overlapping Gortonist purchases north of Smith's trading post and extending southward along the bay about twelve miles, taking in some of the richest land in eastern New England.[7]

This was but the beginning of one of the most brazen pieces of land jobbery in early New England history. The Atherton company soon became an enterprise in which eminent leaders of the United Colonies held a private interest. Meanwhile the Narragansetts, inflamed by the mortal offense of Uncas, who jeered at the ignominious death of Miantonomu, and by the invidious partiality of a peremptory order of the Confederacy to refrain from retaliating on the Mohegans, got out of hand, and some hot-headed braves fired shots into a Connecticut house, symbolic of their long-suppressed resentment.[8] Any letters of Williams relating to this incident have perished and we have only the *ex parte* report of the United Colonies. The commissioners saddled Ninigret with an indemnity of five hundred fathom of peage and ninety-five more for the slaying of a Connecticut Indian. As security for the wampum, the agents of the Confederacy, headed by George Denison and Thomas Stanton,

[7] *R. I. Col. Recs.*, I, 464; III, 227.
[8] *Coll. R.I.H.S.*, III, 52, 53, 60.

inducted the Narragansetts into the mysteries of an English mortgage. Two weeks later, on October 13, 1660, the Atherton company
—now expanded by the strategic admission of Stanton and George
Denison, Daniel Denison, Simon Bradstreet, Josiah Winslow, and
other leading men in the Confederacy—decoyed the mystified
sachems into a second mortgage on all unsold Narragansett land,
promising in return to pay off the first mortgage and to give the
tribe six months to meet the obligations on the second. After expira-
tion of the time limit the company foreclosed and induced two
uncomprehending sachems to go through the pantomime of convey-
ing possession by turf and twig.[9]

When the royal commissioners of Charles II held hearings on the
Atherton company affairs a fantastic story was written into their
records. The records were subsequently lost at sea, but the hearings
revealed that the sachem who signed the original Atherton deeds of
1659 was merely a younger brother of Pessicus and lacked power
to convey the lands. It was also "proved" that he was "seduced,
being made drunk, and kept so for some dayes" at the time the sale
was made. The royal commissioners also learned that Governor
Winthrop of Connecticut was made a partner in the company without
his knowledge and that the object in granting partnership to Major
Winslow of Plymouth and other officers of the United Colonies was
to create a vested interest which would insure support of the company against Rhode Island. Furthermore the Indians never knew
what "mortgaging meant," and when they asked when the peage
was due, they were deliberately deceived and put off until the time
had expired and their lands stood forfeit.[10]

New England Puritans might have misgivings about the restoration of the Stuart monarchy since it spelled the defeat of Puritanism
in England, but for the Puritans associated with the Atherton company it opened an inviting avenue for sanctifying the fraudulent
deals with the Narragansetts. While seeking a charter from Charles
II, Connecticut pressed for eastward extension of its jurisdiction in
a determined drive to eject Massachusetts from the Pequot country
and Rhode Island from the Narragansett lands. Falling in with
this scheme, the alert speculators of the Atherton company bom-
barded John Winthrop, Jr., Connecticut's agent in London, with a

[9] 5 *Coll. M.H.S.*, IX, 12, 25, 29, 32, 106; *R. I. Col. Recs.*, I, 465.
[10] *Coll. N.Y.H.S.*, II (1869), 90-91.

series of letters urging the alluring opportunity of claiming not only the whole south country but if possible extinguishing Rhode Island as a colony on the grounds that it was a "receptacle" for "all malefactors" that "run away from other Colonies" and encouraged "vileness of opinions and corruptness of manners" which were a "cutting vexation" to neighboring plantations.[11]

In seeking to obtain the Narragansett country, Winthrop exploited a twisted interpretation of Williams' patent of 1644, apparently considering that appropriation of the area would work no great injury to Rhode Island which had only begun to expand in that direction.[12] In 1662, aided by Connecticut's prudent provision of a lavish slush fund—particularly useful in an age when even honest Samuel Pepys saw no wrong in taking private douceurs for benefits conferred in his capacity as civil servant,—Winthrop won his charter. Soon afterward he wrote in chagrin to an Atherton partner of a "great wrong" perpetrated by Rhode Island in suddenly interposing, endangering his costly triumph precisely when the charter was about to be sealed.[13] John Clarke had petitioned for a royal charter to replace Rhode Island's irregular parliamentary patent and asked that Winthrop's charter be recalled since it "swallowed up" half of Rhode Island.[14]

Lord Clarendon and imperial-minded Charles smiled on Rhode Island as a useful offset to the dour intolerance and truculence of New England saints, and Winthrop, diplomatically veering with the wind, saved his charter by arranging an arbitration on the question of the Pawcawtuck boundary and jurisdiction over the lands staked out by the Atherton company.[15] The award validated Rhode Island's claim to the Pawcawtuck, and John Clarke's charter of 1663 accordingly interpreted the boundary in language which constituted an amendment of the Connecticut charter. The royal government, however, badly bungled the settlement. The arbitral award favored Winthrop and his Atherton partners by authorizing them to decide for themselves whether to submit to Rhode Island or Connecticut! The company could and inevitably did assert allegiance to Connecticut, while that colony in turn could and did, by literal interpretation

11 5 *Coll. M.H.S.*, IX, 29, 43, and *passim;* Arnold, *Rhode Island*, I, 379-383.
12 5 *Coll. M.H.S.*, IX, 33.
13 *Ibid.*, 34.
14 *Coll. N.Y.H.S.*, II (1869), 44.
15 Williams to Mason, *N.C.P.*, VI, 341-342.

of its charter, claim the whole Narragansett country despite the language of the Rhode Island charter.

How far sanction by Charles and his council of this anomalous arrangement was influenced by two extraordinary new Atherton partners, Captain John Scott, a disreputable Long Island adventurer who suddenly turned up in London as lobbyist for the company, and Thomas Chiffinch, a notorious Whitehall pimp and master of the arts of political corruption, will never be known. Before returning to Connecticut, Winthrop sent word home that his Narragansett partners had "taken a good way" by employing Scott to petition the king; if Scott succeeded, it would undoubtedly give Connecticut the "advantage."[16] The imperial authority's blundering ignorance of New England conditions and the corrupt influence of Scott and Chiffinch resulted in a royal communication of 1663 entrusting protection of the interests of the Narragansett speculators to the tender care of the United Colonies. Clarke's charter, confirmed seventeen days later, added to the legal confusion since Rhode Island could claim that it countermanded this royal order.[17] Thus, because of the Atherton interests, no definitive settlement was made on the boundary question or jurisdiction over the Atherton lands, and Connecticut and Rhode Island were thereby committed to a conflict which was to retard a sound expansion of Rhode Island's town system, undermine her democratic social structure, and embitter her relations with the orthodox colonies for more than half a century.

During these years Roger Williams strove ineffectually against the rising tide of speculation. As a Providence commissioner at the court of November, 1658, he no doubt strongly supported the act which made it illegal to submit lands to another jurisdiction and the law forbidding purchases from the natives without consent of the colony.[18] Six months later the court drafted him to treat with Plymouth concerning the controversy over Hog Island raised by Richard Smith, Jr.[19] In the summer of 1659 when his services were requested as interpreter for the Narragansett speculators, he warned Atherton against illegal purchase of Rhode Island territory, refused to interpret, and indignantly rejected the brazen proffer of a share

[16] 5 *Coll. M.H.S.*, VIII, 79.

[17] *R. I. Col. Recs.*, I, 466, 518; II, 1. Arnold, *Rhode Island*, I, 383.

[18] *R. I. Col. Recs.*, I, 401, 403.

[19] *Ibid.*, 409, 420.

in the enterprise.[20] In August, a few weeks later, he served with Gorton and others on a committee which drafted a strong protest against the Atherton company and the Massachusetts annexation of the western Narragansett country. Williams and his associates made the unanswerable legal argument that the "pretended" Atherton purchase violated a Rhode Island law the principle of which was insisted upon by each of the United Colonies and that the Massachusetts annexation of territory east of the Pawcawtuck represented open defiance of Williams' charter and an order from the Lord Protector, both of which overrode the fictitious Massachusetts claim based on the Pequot conquest.[21]

Two days later, while intervening in a controversy in which Aquidneck freeholders were arrayed against Coddington, Benedict Arnold, and their partners who claimed Conanicut as a private proprietary, Williams urged the colony to unite to the "great End" of subduing the wilderness "to English Industrie and Civilitie," warned against entanglement with outside speculators, and declared that the principles of Massachusetts "destroy our Liberties and tear up our very Foundacion and Constitution."[22] He never lost his warm regard for John Winthrop, Jr., but his letters revealed how sorely he was troubled by Winthrop's participation in the Narragansett speculation. In two letters of 1660 Williams frankly confessed Rhode Island's alarm and his own regret that Winthrop would be an absentee proprietor, though he expressed the hope that his friend's influence as an Atherton partner would remove the cause for alarm.[23] In a letter to Providence citizens Williams was more blunt, warning them of a report that Connecticut was seeking royal consent to "enslave" Rhode Island.[24]

During this same period Williams was gravely concerned over another speculative venture. William Harris, who "came out of the woods" in 1656 to launch an anarchist attack on taxes in the name of conscience, suddenly swung to the other extreme and in 1659 initiated in Providence an unscrupulous land mongering scheme in the name of private rights and vested interests. The immediate stimulus arose from Harris' insecure title to the lands which he had occupied

[20] N.C.P., VI, 342-343.
[21] R. I. Col. Recs., I, 421; 5 Coll. M.H.S., IX, 10-12.
[22] Coll. R.I.H.S., XXVII, 85-92.
[23] N.C.P., VI, 308, 312.
[24] Pub. R.I.H.S., VIII, 160.

at Pachaset west of the Pocasset river and at Toskeunke where the Pawtuxet river dipped southward into the tract purchased by the Gortonists. As early as 1642 the Indians complained of the "intrusion" of Pawtuxet men into territory not conveyed in Williams' grant.[25] By a deed from local chieftains, Harris in 1657 attempted to fortify his title and establish the southern boundary of Pawtuxet as reaching eight miles inland up the Pawtuxet river.[26] This deed while purporting merely to "confirm" Williams' Indian deed of 1638 would, if valid, more than double the extent of Pawtuxet by setting the boundary four miles west of the line as described by Canonicus and Miantonomu. Neither Williams nor the Gortonists, five of whom had been early settlers in Providence and several of them among the original thirteen partners of Pawtuxet, agreed with Harris' contention as to the boundary[27] and accordingly Warwick settlers began to cut grass at Toskeunke. Harris studied his law books, contemplating a suit for trespass, and realized he would lose his case unless he could "antedate and prevent . . . the blades of Warwick" by proving a grant from the Indians prior to the Gortonist purchase of 1643.[28]

Lean, sharp-featured, cantankerous, but astute and inordinately ambitious, Harris devoted his tremendous nervous energy and cunning brain to a brilliant stratagem. If successful, it would give him and his Pawtuxet partners a valid claim not merely eight miles into the hinterland but twenty miles, establish priority of Harris' title over the Warwick claimants, and win strong Providence support by reinterpreting the bounds of the town so as to make the local public domain the largest in Rhode Island. An arbitration paved the way for confederation of Harris with the old Pawtuxet secessionists, Arnold, Carpenter, and Rhodes, the arbitral award on June, 1657, supporting the Harris contention that Pawtuxet extended west of the Pocasset river.[29] Harris promptly urged his Pawtuxet partners to divide the unoccupied land, declaring, "I am, Allwayes Ready, to devide, because, by devitione, of the same, Each man, shall posses, his Owne."[30] Soon afterward William Field, a Pawtuxet partner,

25 *Simplicities Defence,* Coll. R.I.H.S., II, 66 and note.
26 *Harris Papers,* p. 48.
27 *Ibid.,* pp. 53-55, 60-61, 312.
28 Williams, *Letters,* N.C.P., VI, 392.
29 *Prov. Recs.,* XV, 94.
30 *Harris Papers,* p. 50.

joined with Harris and Arnold in an unsuccessful attempt to extend the Providence-Pawtuxet boundary westward.[31] Meanwhile in December, 1658, the Arnold clan abandoned its alliance with Massachusetts, and Harris, Arnold, and Thomas Olney, now close confederates, got Providence to certify, as part of the "town evidence," a memorandum of 1639 purporting to record Miantonomu's permission for grazing, "for our use of Cattle," up the Pawtucket and Pawtuxet rivers "without limmets."[32] Five months later Field, Olney, Arthur Fenner, John Sayles and other Providence representatives obtained permission of the Rhode Island assembly to remove Indians "within the bowndes" of the town "as expressed in their towne evidence" and to purchase three thousand acres more if still "straytened."[33]

Within two weeks Harris was negotiating with the drunken sachem who conveyed the original Atherton purchases. For £9 10s. the sachem signed a new deed ostensibly "confirming" the memorandum of 1639. But this new document contained more than a mere restatement of Miantonomu's permission for grazing "up the Streames": by the legerdemain of the Harris phrasing, the dead Miantonomu was made to grant the land itself in outright conveyance for "plowing . . . farmes, and all Manner of plantation whatso Ever," reaching inland "Twenty full Miles."[34] To give color of legality to the fraud, Harris in the next six months procured the services of the Richard Smiths in the Narragansett country and obtained the signatures of the great sachems to an additional "confirmation," although in this case to quiet the suspicion of the chieftains the deed made no mention of extension upstreams as far as twenty miles and contained a pledge against removal of any natives without their consent and satisfaction.[35] Thus fortified with a bogus title antedating the Gortonist purchase, Harris, Carpenter, Rhodes, and Field sued Warwick for trespass and on March 13, 1660, won their case, thus obtaining court validation of the new "confirmations" of the memorandum of 1639.[36] A few days later by means of this legal sanction and the dazzling bait of an enlarge-

[31] Prov. Recs., XV, 76.
[32] Ibid., IV, 71.
[33] R. I. Col. Recs., I, 418.
[34] Prov. Recs., V, 297.
[35] Ibid., 300. See also third "confirmation," ibid., 303.
[36] Harris Papers, pp. 53, 55-56.

ment of town lands by several hundred thousand acres, Harris and
his confederates got the Providence purchasers to accept the new
deeds and agree to extend the northern Pawtuxet line mid-way
between the Pawtucket and Pawtuxet rivers westward twenty
miles![37]

If the twenty-mile scheme succeeded, the fortunate individuals
who held one or more of the thirteen shares in Pawtuxet stood to
aggrandize themselves beyond the dreams of avarice. Harris, who
acquired the Holliman share in addition to his own, could lay claim
to two-thirteenths of the vastly enlarged Pawtuxet tract. He held
also his original Providence share, soon supplemented it with a half
interest in Way's right, and sought also to obtain validation of the
Verin right.[38] His chief confederates likewise played for high stakes
and seized the speculative opportunity to add to their swollen holdings. Carpenter, another of the original thirteen purchasers of Pawtuxet, shrewdly acquired the Pawtuxet shares of Throckmorton and
Greene on the eve of the great coup and later acquired Cole's. He
also loaded up on Providence shares, hastily buying four between
1659 and 1663 and holding six by 1675.[39] Rhodes, possessing one
Pawtuxet share, bought a second in the nick of time, 1659, and in
the next four years bought at least five Providence rights, most of
them in the undivided land west of the seven-mile line.[40] Thomas
Olney, Sr., sold his Pawtuxet right but by previous acquisition of
four Providence shares stood to gain handsomely.[41]

Dissension soon broke over the Pawtuxet and Providence boundaries as citizens realized the full implications of the Harris
maneuver. Asked to explain the boundaries, Williams denied that
Pawtuxet extended west of the Pocasset. In sworn testimony of
October 8, 1660, Thomas Olney, using a circumlocution, called the
aged father of the town a liar: "Roger Williams doth now deny"
what he once admitted as to the "bounds of patuxcet."[42] Meanwhile
the natives, beginning to perceive the fraud, "cried Commootin,
lying and stealing," and the great sachem Pessicus declared that

37 *Prov. Recs.*, II, 125.
38 *Ibid.*, III, 40; IV, 95; XIV, 75.
39 *Ibid.*, I, 71, 74, 76, 85, 101-102; IV, 21; XIV, 275; XV, 75, 96.
40 *Ibid.*, I, 68, 86; V, 56, 77, 78; XVII, 82.
41 *Ibid.*, I, 64; IV, 31, 32; VI, 63; XIV, 82, 87-88.
42 *Harris Papers*, p. 57.

"the twenty miles" confirmed by the Harris deed was "a meer deception."[43]

Never one to buy up holdings in order to speculate upon later settlers and sensitive as ever on the point of exploiting the Indians, Williams on October 27 made a statesmanlike proposal to protect native rights and settle the land question on a democratic basis. Earlier encroachments by William Field[44] and others upon Indian lands beyond the proper western boundary could be legalized as in the past by compensating the natives, a work in which Williams would gladly help. Meanwhile to "quench contention" over land and accommodate those "who want," he proposed a new plantation near Providence as "an effectual endeavor for true public good." Shrewdly evaluating the speculative and exclusive impulse in the older established settlements like Providence, Williams was seeking a democratic land system and conceived of a series of new plantations founded on the principle of his early "fellowship." The undivided land of the proposed settlement should be distributed by an open, expanding town fellowship, each new comer to pay the fixed rate of thirty shillings apiece and receive admission as a purchaser with a right to the land equal to that of the original purchasers. He offered "gratis" his services "in hope that such as want may have a comfortable supply amongst us, and others made room for, who may be glad of shelter also."[45]

Since a new purchase for a separate plantation would forestall the speculative scheme to enlarge the boundaries, the Pawtuxet confederates, who had taken care to capture most of the town offices, immediately named Harris, Olney, and Arthur Fenner on a committee to reply. Denying that the Harris deeds stretched the boundaries, they tartly declared that if they accepted Williams' plan they or their posterity would "Smart for it, and wee conceive herein that wee doe Truley understand what your Selfe doth not."[46] Though he failed to win support for a more democratic land system, Williams won a partial victory over the Pawtuxet speculators. Sobered by his warning that new purchases with compensation to the

---

[43] *Ibid.*, p. 311; *Prov. Recs.*, XV, 164.

[44] As early as 1648 both Williams and the natives protested against Field's occupation of land beyond the boundary without compensation; *R.I.H. Tracts*, XIV, 46.

[45] *N.C.P.*, VI, 314-315.

[46] *Prov. Recs.*, II, 135.

natives were imperative in order to stop the Cowesets and Nipmucks from "running" to Massachusetts, Providence made Williams head of a committee to negotiate purchases.[47] During the winter he was racked with "old pains and Lamenesses," at times unable "to rise nor goe nor stand," but recovering, he negotiated four purchases with local chieftains and arranged payments which eventually totaled "near" £250 "in their pay."[48]

Williams' four new deeds were drafted in language completely ignoring the Harris "confirmations," made no reference to the twenty-mile claim, and conveyed the land to the "town of Providence."[49] It was thus possible for Williams and his supporters to deny the Pawtuxet speculators any right in the new territory other than their share as townsmen in Providence. Attempting to strengthen their claim that the existing Providence purchasers and the Pawtuxet partners were joint and exclusive proprietors of the new town lands, the Harris men demanded that Williams give "an Asurance" or confirmation of the town evidence.[50] He complied and the town accepted it, but he drafted his confirmatory deed in language which flatly contradicted the "upstreams" contention and reasserted the original Providence principle of equality in land and free admission of after comers.[51] Early in 1662 Williams' one-time servant, Joshua Winsor, sent a petition to the town meeting recalling agreement by the Combination to make equal divisions of land "unto all the inhabitants" including after comers. This petition protested the actions of certain "wicked men" who had "crept" in and were "robing" the town. Harris, Olney, and Field were falsely "deludeing the inhabitants" by calling Williams' new purchases a confirmation "by vertu thereof to monopolies" choice land through claiming a "patuxet share."[52]

Thus by the new purchases and Williams' confirmatory deed his party re-opened the boundary question and won supporters against the monopolists. Before long Arthur Fenner and William Wickenden, who at first fell into Harris' "bewitching traps," turned against the Pawtuxet leader, who in a rage denounced Fenner as a "false

[47] *Prov. Recs.,* III, 2; *N.C.P.,* VI, 315.
[48] *Pub. R.I.H.S.,* VIII, 147; *N.C.P.,* VI, 390.
[49] *Prov. Recs.,* V, 283-286.
[50] *Ibid.,* XV, 88.
[51] *Ibid.,* V, 306-309.
[52] *Ibid.,* XV, 81.

fellow, Rouge and Rascall."[53] Harris and his confederates were still sufficiently powerful to prevent repeal of the order to run the boundary to the twenty-mile line. Lacking an outright majority and playing for time, Fenner, Dexter, and others of the Williams party were equal to the occasion and blocked every effort of the Pawtuxet men to get the town's consent to survey the boundaries and run the Pawtuxet line westward.[54] Until the line was run, none of the speculators could win the fruits of their monopoly. In the end Williams' views on the Pawtuxet question were to prevail.

[53] *R.I.H. Tracts,* XIV, 33-34.
[54] *Prov. Recs.,* III, 59; XV, 105. *Harris Papers,* pp. 73-74.

20

DEMOCRACY ON THE DEFENSIVE

IN AN ERA WHEN ENGLISH POLICY MARKED the reassertion of the aristocratic ideal, when the merry monarch granted large slices of American territory to absentee proprietors and the strange spectres of palatines and landgraves flitted along Carolina shores, the Rhode Island charter of 1663 was an anomaly, carrying on the republican heritage of the Puritan revolution. In substance the charter reproduced the cardinal features of Williams' revolutionary patent of 1644 and accorded Rhode Island larger scope for self-government along democratic lines than any other royal grant to an American colony. Specifying a governor, deputy governor, and ten assistants as colonial officers, the charter provided that these and the deputies should sit in "general assembly" at Newport in May and October, exercising the powers of admitting new freemen and making and repealing all laws. This increased the number of assistants, who acted as councillors and executive aids of the governor, but did not set them apart as an upper chamber with a "negative voice" on legislation coming up from the deputies. Thus, with no sharp separation of powers between legislative and executive officers, an assembly that was unicameral, and a governor without a veto, the charter left the assembly omnipotent, subject to the will of the freemen to whom was reserved the right to elect all representatives and major officers on an annual basis. Echoing the language of Williams' patent, the charter authorized the assembly to modify English precedent, making laws as seemed "meete" according to "the nature and constitutione of the place and people there."[1]

Approving the Rhode Island request to "hold forth a livelie experiment" with a "civill state," the charter provided that no person should be "called in question" for any scruples of conscience which did not "actually disturb the civill peace."[2] Clarendon and the king's councillors, according to Williams, were "startled" at this "extraor-

[1] *R. I. Col. Recs.*, II, 7-9.
[2] *Ibid.*, 4-5.

dinary" grant, so sharply at variance with parliament's Clarendon
code, but were compelled to bow to the royal will; and thereby set the
first great English precedent for the absolute principle of religious
freedom, "any lawe, statute, or . . . custom of this realme, to the
contrary."[3] Inclined to "wink" at overseas toleration even of Jews
and anti-Christians, Charles extended to his colonies a wider liberty
than he dared demand in England.[4]

The liberality of the Rhode Island charter provided not only a
larger measure of home rule than any other colony but included a
constitutional protection of the rights which Roger Williams had
long sought to defend against the United Colonies: security of the
Narragansetts from punitive expeditions or invasion by other colonies without Rhode Island's consent, legal right of Rhode Island
people to the liberties and immunities of English subjects in any
English dominion, freedom to trade at Boston or elsewhere and
peaceably to "passe and repasse" through the New England colonies
despite any law "or sentence" of those colonies to the contrary.[5]
Thus by organic royal act the orthodox embargo against Rhode
Island was illegal and decrees banishing Williams and his associates
inoperative. Hailing these hard-won privileges, freemen from all
quarters of the colony assembled on November 24, 1663, at "a very
great meeting" at Newport. The charter was read and then "held
on hygh . . . to the perfect view of the people." Two days later
Pessicus and Ninigret, informed of the new guarantee of their
security, returned thanks to King Charles.[6]

With Rhode Island's right to the Narragansett country and Block
Island now apparently unassailable, popular resentment against Connecticut and Massachusetts interlopers reached a high pitch, and
during the winter Williams wrote to Governor Winthrop of Connecticut that many in the colony were "hott and dry." Winthrop replied
that he was glad to see "that the winter of your age hath yet warme
affections for your old freinds." Though Williams' head had
"growne white," there was "candor in the heart" brighter than the
snow which covered the hills. "Your wise moderation I know doth

[3] *Ibid.*, 6; *N.C.P.*, VI, 345-346.
[4] *N.C.P.*, VI, 346. See secret instructions to the royal commissioners, *Col. Docs.
of N. Y.*, III, 57-61.
[5] *R. I. Col. Recs.*, II, 15, 17, 18, 20.
[6] *Ibid.*, I, 509, 513.

well helpe to ballast in gusts and too high sailes." Winthrop closed
with warm regards to "Mrs. Williams, and all yours."[7]

At a meeting in March, 1664, the new government was formally
instituted, Williams taking the office of assistant. After serving
again in May, when he was reëlected, he wrote to Winthrop somewhat in the spirit of an old patriarch with forebodings about the
new temper of the times. The rising generation in New England,
aping the rest of the world in worship of the old trinity, "Profit,
Preferment, Pleasure," was making land "as great a God" as gold
was with Spanish colonists. Though he privately regretted being
drawn again into political service, Williams would contribute his
"poor mite" in behalf of the "public interest of the whole of New
England" and not the private interest of "this or that town" or group.
Rhode Island's claim to the Narragansett country by the charter
had so taken the people that the assembly impetuously proposed to
arrest "old Mr. Smith" because of his secession to Connecticut, but
Williams had been able "to stop that council" and had substituted
a friendly negotiation to persuade Smith and his partners to submit
peaceably to Rhode Island. If Winthrop, Major Mason, and their
associates would "help on such work," differences between the colonies could readily be settled.[8]

Later in 1664 Williams had a hand in boundary negotiations with
Plymouth and also an adjustment with Massachusetts by which
Westerly, settled by Rhode Island Baptists, and Block Island, settled
by Massachusetts Puritans, were recognized as subject to Rhode
Island, but he was disappointed in his hope that Governor Winthrop
would induce the Atherton partners and Connecticut to accept Rhode
Island jurisdiction in the Narragansett country. Connecticut repudiated the Winthrop-Clarke arbitration, stood on the priority of
its charter, and claimed the whole region east to Narragansett bay.
Because of this action Williams felt compelled to take sides against
his Connecticut friends and served on a committee to run the western boundary and on another to reply to Connecticut. Meanwhile,
he and John Clarke headed a committee to "look over" the body of
laws "and put them in a better forme" if they were inconsistent with
the charter.[9]

<hr />

[7] 4 *Coll. M.H.S.*, VI, 529, 532.
[8] *N.C.P.*, VI, 319-320; *R. I. Col. Recs.*, II, 44-49.
[9] *R. I. Col. Recs.*, II, 40, 49, 64, 67-77, 82.

The code of 1647 and later laws were brought into line and reënacted. The code as reënacted did not include an anti-Catholic law; by a curious mistake of compilers, such a law appeared in eighteenth century statute books as of the year 1663 although neither then nor later ever passed by a Rhode Island assembly.[10] It was found that royal liberality in the charter did not sanction the system by which a majority of the freemen had the power to repeal unpopular laws, and accordingly the assembly put an end to Rhode Island's experiment with direct democracy.[11] The king's command, presented by the royal commissioners in 1665, compelled one other alteration conducive in the long run to the retrogression of Rhode Island democracy. The colonial suffrage which had been liberalized in 1658 to permit any freeholder to vote was qualified with the ominous requirement that voters must be of "competent estates" and "civil conversation."[12] By this test the suffrage was to be narrowed in the eighteenth century.

In March, 1665, the royal commissioners, making an honest attempt at just settlement of intercolonial disputes, gave Rhode Island jurisdiction over the Narragansett country until the king should determine the boundary question, declared the Atherton deeds voidable on condition the Narragansetts paid 1,055 fathom of wampum, and ordered Pomham and his tribe to evacuate Warwick Neck and cease despoiling the settlers. Infinitely more liberal and judicious than later corrupt royal agents like Edward Cranfield or authoritarian bureaucrats like Lord Bellomont, the commissioners dealt handsomely with Rhode Island. It proved a hollow victory. The crown neglected to settle the boundary question, and three years later Connecticut and Rhode Island were again embroiled over possession of the Narragansett country. The Atherton partners retained their rich holdings on the west shore of Narragansett bay. Pomham, persuaded by Williams and the commissioners to remove, agreed to £20 satisfaction from Warwick, but trading on the friendship of John Eliot and support from Massachusetts, accepted the gratuity and then stayed on the Neck, a plague to Warwick settlers until he cast his lot with the losing side in King Philip's war.[13]

[10] *Ibid.*, 36-37. S. S. Rider, "Origin of the clause in the laws of R. I. (1719-1783) disfranchising Roman Catholics," *R. I. H. Tracts*, 2nd ser., no. 1.
[11] *R. I. Col. Recs*, II, 27. See Lobingier, *The People's Law*, pp. 85-86.
[12] *R. I. Col. Recs.*, II, 110, 113.
[13] *Ibid.*, 134-138; *Coll. R.I.H.S.*, XI, 81 ff.

In the decade following these proceedings Williams served once as a deputy, May 1667, and two terms as assistant, 1670-1672, but otherwise largely withdrew from colonial politics. His religious zeal had never cooled. A half century after Williams' death Callender recalled that he "used to uphold a public worship" at Providence, "as many now alive remember," and went once a month for many years to hold services in the Narragansett country.[14] Richard Smith, Jr., who had inherited in 1666 at his father's death, offered his house for these monthly meetings and reported that "Mr. Williams . . . precheth well and abell, and much pepell comes to here him to theyr good satisfaicion."[15] Williams valued the friendship of the Narragansett trader because of a common interest in Indian labors, but he never could stomach the incongruity of professing concern for Indian souls while debauching them with rum for the sake of beaver and in 1669 he commented caustically upon Smith's long practice of selling the natives liquor.[16]

Ominous changes in Rhode Island society, particularly the tensions between new settlers, mostly small farmers or humble folk, and the men who sought to intrench themselves behind the protection of vested rights as proprietors and speculate on after comers and rising land values, increasingly disturbed Williams. But Rhode Island democracy, though driven imperceptibly on the defensive, remained a living reality, and Williams, in a public letter of 1666 occasioned by a Warwick dispute over the burden of taxes, expressed anew his flaming faith in the democratic process. More specifically than in any other surviving document from his hand, Williams summed up here the democratic privileges which Rhode Island enjoyed and which her people should cherish: the inestimable jewels of peace and liberty, civil rights protected by law, freedom of worship, and the organization of popular consent by the process of elections and broad representation. "All the World," he proclaimed, "lies round about us drie and barren of such Liberties."[17]

In town affairs the aging father of Rhode Island continually exerted a benign and active influence, aiding Dexter and Fenner in the long battle to keep the town lands open to all comers on equal

---

[14] *Coll. R.I.H.S.*, IV, 111.
[15] D. B. Updike, *Richard Smith,* The Merrymount Press, (Boston, 1937), p. 97.
[16] *N.C.P.*, VI, 332-333.
[17] *Pub. R.I.H.S.*, VIII, 148-149, 153.

terms. Inveterate champion of vested rights, Harris quoted the proverb "firste come first served" and fought strenuously to uphold town votes dating back to 1662 by which no more purchasers were to be admitted.[18] Refusal to admit newcomers and humble folk to equal rights instituted a class division, and men like Williams and Dexter felt strongly that there was no excuse for it in view of the new enlargement of the town lands. Thomas Clements appeared at town meeting on June 3, 1667, with a piece of dynamite, a bill entitled a "Sovereign Plaster" written by himself and Dexter. It called for repudiation of the Harris "upstreams" confirmations, affirmed the enlargement of the town lands a strictly new purchase made by the "diligence" of "neighbor Williams," and declared for the principle that "all men that have payd Eqall shall have Eqall," whether quarter right men or not.[19] To forestall this attack, ruinous to their Pawtuxet scheme, Harris, who was moderator, and Carpenter threw the meeting into an uproar by depriving Williams' party, which now constituted a majority, of the "libertie to vote for officers."[20] Fenner, an assistant in the colony, promptly called a separate town meeting in the same room and this proceeded to elect officers and vote approval of the Sovereign Plaster.[21] Fenner, Williams, and others drafted two complaints to central authorities and characterized Harris as a firebrand of ungovernable temper who on one occasion had thrown a "poore mans wife over a fence of 4 rayles twice"![22] The assembly upheld Fenner and discharged Harris from office as assistant, reproving him as a man prone to act in a "deceiptfull manner."[23]

Having lost a majority in Providence, Harris became impatient with town meeting democracy and appealed to Governor Nicholls of New York to appoint a special court drawn from other colonies to vest him in his rights by judicial decision.[24] Nothing came of this and in the next two years Harris staved off defeat by devices which once more produced turmoil reaching the proportions of a colonial question. In 1668 Williams drafted a town appeal to the central

18 *Harris Papers*, p. 76; *Prov. Recs.*, III, 11, 16, 48-49.
19 *Prov. Recs.*, II, 72-75; III, 105.
20 *Harris Papers*, p. 80.
21 *Ibid.; Prov. Recs.*, III, 102-106.
22 *Prov. Recs.*, XV, 117; *Harris Papers*, pp. 77-82.
23 *R. I. Col. Recs.*, II, 208.
24 *Harris Papers*, p. 86.

authorities, charging Harris with bringing local government to a standstill through his Machiavellian maneuvers to obtain "a great Lordship of Land."[25] In 1669, in an exchange of peppery letters with young John Whipple, a Harris partisan, Williams forcefully exposed the "upstreams" fraud, declared Dexter's proposals in the Sovereign Plaster "honest, equall and peaceable," and declared that the "consent" of a majority of purchasers in town meeting should determine land disposal and bind the minority.[26] Harris, however, befuddled the town meeting by resorting to English common law as a protection of property against democracy. Contending that a vote in town meeting did not constitute lawful judgment by his peers and that "due form of law" in this case required judicial process, Harris temporarily triumphed, procuring a declaration that Dexter's Sovereign Plaster was "voyd," since it was "illegal."[27] Nevertheless Williams' party soon won the battle on one of Dexter's proposals, all quarter right men after 1673 obtaining a full right in the new town lands equal to that of the first settlers.[28] Meanwhile colonial authorities unravelled the political tangle in Providence in 1670, settling an election dispute between Harris and Fenner by naming Williams as colonial assistant.[29] Since Providence would run the line no farther west than the Pocasset river, the Pawtuxet partners were still blocked in their ambitions, and Harris realized that his only hope of defeating Williams and the majority in Providence and winning his long series of lawsuits against Warwick men lay in an appeal to the king for judicial settlement by a special commission composed of magistrates drawn from the other New England colonies. After 1670 Harris became a supporter of Smith and the Atherton partners, making himself and his claims favorably known to leading dignitaries in Connecticut, Plymouth, and Massachusetts.

Just as Williams became assistant a storm broke over the Narragansett country. In 1668 Connecticut inhabitants at Stonington asked their colony to assume jurisdiction east of the Pawcawtuck in order to defend the town's right to the "Pequot" lands and protect Stonington children from the deplorable example of the Baptists at Westerly; "parents hartes bleed" while their little ones

[25] *Prov. Recs.*, XV, 122, 124 n.
[26] *R. I. H. Tracts*, XIV, 25-45; *N.C.P.*, VI, 327-331.
[27] *Harris Papers*, p. 93; *Prov. Recs.*, III, 149..
[28] *Prov. Recs.*, III, 247; IV, 202.
[29] *R. I. Col. Recs.*, II, 255, 287-293, 302.

are "daylie tempted" to fall into "riotous, wanton, luxsurious" lives. The three Stonington men who drafted this petition, Stanton, Denison, and Richardson, were Atherton partners.[30] Reviving its claim under Winthrop's charter, Connecticut took a threatening tone and her envoys, one of whom was Fitz-John Winthrop, met a Rhode Island commission on June 14, 1670, and insisted that the eastern boundary of the colony was Narragansett bay. Prior to this fruitless meeting Governor Winthrop, mortified at his colony's repudiation of his agreement with John Clarke, forcefully dissented from Connecticut's position. After the meeting Fitz-John Winthrop, expressing prevailing sentiment, demanded that Connecticut take over the Narragansett country and reduce the "impertinent brutes" at Pettiquamscut to "Conecticot civility."[31] At this juncture Williams sent a powerful appeal to Major Mason, assistant in Connecticut, and Thomas Prince, governor of Plymouth, urging a joint effort at disinterested settlement. The legal points presented by Connecticut, he said bluntly, were a mere smoke screen for vested interests of individuals; a "depraved appetite" for land had become "one of the gods of New England."[32] Moved by this appeal, Mason sent Williams' letter to Fitz-John Winthrop and the other Connecticut envoys and urged them to surrender the Connecticut claim, reminding them that much of the Narragansett country was "barrane" rocky upland or swampy lowland, not worth the danger of bloody conflicts nor the cost to "hundreds of poore men" who would never receive "benefitt by it."[33] In spite of these efforts a Connecticut force of fifty men marched to Smith's settlement at Wickford and named Atherton supporters as local officers. Thus the battle began in earnest, to last many years during which both colonies arrested, fined, and imprisoned rival officers and their adherents in the Narragansett country.

Richard Smith, Jr., and William Harris, playing a double game in this critical situation, were in league with Connecticut although both held places of trust under the Rhode Island government.[34] On February 24, 1672, Williams accused Harris before the Rhode Island court of disloyalty. Harris had opposed a "rate to send an

---

[30] *Conn. Col. Recs.*, II, 530, 533; 5 *Coll. M.H.S.*, IX, 29, 31.
[31] 5 *Coll. M.H.S.*, IX, 78
[32] *N.C.P.*, VI, 333-351.
[33] *R. I. Col. Recs.*, II, 348-350.
[34] Updike, *Richard Smith*, pp. 30-31, 86-87; *R. I. Col. Recs.*, II, 375, 413.

agent for England" and written a defense of Connecticut's charter
in which he named the Seekonk river and Narragansett bay as the
lawful boundary, thus placing even Providence and Warwick inside
the Connecticut line![35] Harris went to jail to await trial. The
Arnold administration overreached itself by passing a rigorous
measure to punish tax agitation and another to confiscate the property of "plotters" who aided Rhode Island's enemies, and in consequence the Quaker party in a strange alliance with supporters of
Harris and Smith won the election in May. The soundness of Rhode
Island democracy was demonstrated when the new assembly immediately repealed the repressive law against tax agitators as an infringement of the "libertyes of the people." Hoping for a peaceful
adjustment with Connecticut, the assembly named Williams on a
board of conciliatory commissioners to reopen negotiations. The
pro-Connecticut assistants, Richard Smith and Francis Brinley,
obtained release of Harris, who became a deputy from Providence,
and in October these three procured an act validating the title of
the Atherton partners.[36]

Hard on the heels of the Quaker triumph at the polls, George
Fox made a whirlwind tour of Rhode Island towns, rousing large
throngs to tremendous enthusiasm. Williams, equally zealous in his
own Seeker faith and a rationalist who had ever been distrustful
of the inner light, yearned to cross lances with the famous founder
of the sect and sent a challenge to meet in debate. Rhode Island
Quakers suppressed Williams' letter until their great champion had
departed, but in August, 1672, three fiery Quaker orators, John
Burnyeat, William Edmundson, and John Stubs, converged on
Rhode Island and met the white haired father of the colony in a
dialectical tournament lasting four days. Strengthened by zeal, Williams, now nearly seventy, rowed all day with his "old bones,"
reaching Newport at midnight before the morning appointed. A
highly partisan audience of Baptists and Gortonists on one side and
Quakers on the other gathered to cheer on their respective champions. William Harris capitalized on the occasion by charging
Williams with approval of the execution of Charles I and handed
Edmundson one of Williams' Civil War tracts with the citation

---

[35] R. I. Col. Recs., II, 429-430; Harris Papers, pp. 104-106.

[36] R. I. Col. Recs., II, 454-456, 460, 465, 477-478; Williams to United Colonies,
1672, 2 Proc. M.H.S., III, 258-259.

marked. Harris, Williams asserted afterwards, "cares no more for the Quakers than the Baptists" but merely curried favor with them to advance his private interests.[37] Thomas Olney, a Harris man but a Baptist, intervened at various points in behalf of Williams, as did also Samuel Gorton and his followers, Greene and Holden. Such support was salutary, for the Quakers were interrupting Williams' discourses and heckling him to such an extent that at various times leading Quakers, Governor Easton, Deputy Governor Cranston, and even Coddington appealed for fair play. Angered by derisive cat calls, "Old man, Old man," and a whisper that was circulated on one of the days of debate that he was drunk, Williams in turn resorted to invective, raked up the instances in which deluded Quaker women had gone naked in public, and went so far as to suggest "moderate" legal penalties against Quaker "incivilities," for example their uncourteous refusal to take off their hats! Both sides claimed a triumph but neither side added to their stature, though against the unmannerly character of the debate the historian of democracy might point to the advantage of public discussion as a sane alternative to the policies of repression prevailing elsewhere.[38]

Ironically the Quaker government in Rhode Island passed pacifist legislation and scrupulously respected native rights, only to confront the greatest Indian war in New England history. War scares had developed as early as 1667. The Rhode Island government investigated Major Mason's charges that Ninigret was involved in a conspiracy and found the sachem innocent. Nevertheless Captain Wait Winthrop and Connecticut forces in 1669 violated the royal injunction in the charter and invaded the colony to deal directly with Ninigret.[39] Williams, though afflicted by "age, lameness, and many other weaknesses,"[40] retained his old keenness in penetrating the intricacies of native intrigue and sought to restrain the colonies of the Confederation from goading the Narragansett sachems or King Philip and the Wampanoags into unnecessary war. In 1667 he reported suspicious actions of Philip but warned the belligerent Plymouth magistrates that their Indian informer was unreliable. In subsequent years he investigated other rumors and on a critical

---

[37] Williams to United Colonies, *ibid.*
[38] *George Fox Digged*, N.C.P., V, 59-61, 115-116, 239, 306-316, and *passim.*
[39] *Conn. Col. Recs.*, II, 550.
[40] *N.C.P.*, VI, 362.

occasion when Philip was summoned to Plymouth remained as a hostage among the Wampanoags.[41] As war clouds lowered darkly over the land in 1675, Williams corresponded with Major Mason and other leading magistrates in New England and on June 25 remarked to Winthrop that his "old bones and eyes" were "weary with travel and writing" to the governors of Rhode Island, Massachusetts, and other colonies. On June 23 commissioners headed by Captain Hutchinson, an Atherton partner, appeared at Williams' house with an official Massachusetts request for aid in negotiations with the Narragansetts. He guided them to the heart of the Narragansett country and arranged a parley at which the sachems professed to "hold no agreement" with Philip. The commissioners, at Williams' urgence, promised to right old wrongs suffered at the hands of Uncas and the United Colonies, and in turn the Narragansetts pledged a strict standard of neutrality. As Williams despatched his report to Governor Winthrop he received the fearful tidings that the Wampanoags led by Philip had "slain five English of Swansey." Plymouth was in arms and the war was on.[42]

Within a few days Williams began to realize that the United Colonies had been too late in their overtures to the Narragansetts. Ninigret and the older sachems sought to hold their men in check, but Pessicus admitted "he could not rule the youth" in his tribe and advised his Rhode Island friends "to stand upon their guard." Williams, while ferrying young Canonchet across the bay in his "great canoe," warned him that war was suicide, but found this proud and warlike son of Miantonomu, while friendly to himself, inclining toward Philip.[43] Scenting blood and inflamed by the Wampanoags, young Narragansett braves remembered the dastardly murder of their great sachem, humiliating treaties and debts imposed upon them, the partition of their lands by fraud and force, and other items in their long score against the United Colonies. Such dealing, wrote Gorton in these months of crisis, had made "the Sachims afraid, least by this meanes in short time they shall be spued out of the country, for want of land."[44] In the same vein Williams declared later that "one great occasion" of the war was the stealing of native

[41] *Plymouth Col. Recs.*, IV, 165; V, 76; X, 353; Backus, *The Baptists*, I, 418.
[42] *N.C.P.*, VI, 363-370.
[43] *Ibid.*, 371, 375-376.
[44] 4 *Coll. M.H.S.*, VII, 631.

lands.[45] This and the old policy of the orthodox Puritan magistrates in detaching tribes from subjection to their great sachems and of orthodox missionaries in teaching their dusky charges "not to obey their heathen princes"[46] now bore its bitter fruit. Only a few years before, Williams had protested strongly against Massachusetts maneuvers which had detached the Nipmucks from allegiance to the Narragansetts, and pointing out that the king had expressly denied New England power "to alter the Indians' laws," urged the policy of respecting even a "barbarous order and government."[47] Humane Rhode Island Quakers, Baptists, and Gortonists had kept the peace with the formidable Narragansetts for forty years by according them the stature of human beings and insisting on their rights to their own worship and customs. Imperious orthodox Puritans had no such concept of race relations, and in consequence Rhode Island, though ruled by pacifist Quakers striving desperately for neutrality, became a battleground in which the smoking ruin of pioneer homes and the grisly witness of the heads of slaughtered settlers impaled on poles marked ever more widely the range of the furious conflict.

The very slender margin of the ultimate victory for the English makes clear today the wisdom of the pleas by Williams, Gorton, Richard Smith, and Governor Winthrop of Connecticut to leave the Narragansetts alone and trust to the older sachems to keep a large proportion of their warriors from joining Philip. On July 12 Winthrop urged Major Savage to employ Williams and Smith in further negotiations.[48] A Massachusetts and Connecticut army with a troop of horse and another of infantry now invaded Rhode Island in violation of her charter, employed Smith as interpreter "on behalf of Connecticut," rashly threatened the Narragansetts and forced them to sign a treaty rigorous in its terms and obliging the sachems to confirm "all former grants" of lands. Three of the commissioners had a personal interest in the Atherton company. Subsequent pressure to surrender refugee Wampanoags, chiefly women and children, goaded increasing numbers of Narragansetts to join Philip, and on November 2, 1675, the United Colonies declared war.[49]

[45] N.C.P., VI, 394.
[46] Coll. N.Y.H.S., II (1869), 84.
[47] N.C.P., VI, 326-327.
[48] 5 Coll. M.H.S., VIII, 171-172; N.C.P., VI, 370, 374-376; Updike, *Richard Smith*, pp. 110-113.
[49] Coll. R.I.H.S., III, 79-83, 167-171.

On December 18, a combined Plymouth, Connecticut, and Massachusetts force of over one thousand men stormed the Narragansett stronghold in the "Great Swamp Fight," winning at heavy cost and then leaving Rhode Island to the mercy of savages howling for revenge. From the Rhode Island mainland white women, children, and many of the men fled to security at Aquidneck around which circled armed patrols in boats, successfully guarding Portsmouth and Newport. Warwick and Pawtuxet were burned to ashes, and Providence, though garrisoned, was twice attacked and largely destroyed. After the savage second attack Williams found his home in ruins and only about twenty of one hundred and twenty-three houses left standing. The Massachusetts court, hearing of his misfortune and considering "how readyly and freely at all times he hath served the English Interest," temporarily suspended his banishment, offering sanctuary on condition he vented none of "his different opinions." But Williams, now a septuagenarian, remained as joint captain with Fenner in command of the courageous Providence men who "staid and went not away."[50]

Early in 1676 Williams received one of the last letters of Connecticut's governor, who died on April 5. Winthrop thanked him for his kindness in sending a "little volume of poetry" and remarked on Williams' skill in penetrating the "darke corners" of Indian machinations, signing himself "Yours according to ancient friendship *Semper idem*."[51] In August, 1676, Mary Williams left her refuge at Aquidneck, returning to her husband in a sloop of their son Providence who was then ferrying Indian captives to Newport where they were distributed as indentured servants for short terms like white servants. Rhode Island, unlike the United Colonies to whom John Eliot addressed a spirited but fruitless condemnation of slavery,[52] did not bind captured Indians to long years of servitude in scattered colonies or ship them to the foul slave marts of northern Africa; and to prevent any violation of the earlier Gorton act, the assembly passed a law in March, 1676, "that noe Indian in this Collony be a slave."[53] In the elections of May, 1677, the wartime reaction against Quaker pacifism produced an overturn, and the

---

[50] *Plymouth Col. Recs.*, X, vi; *Prov. Recs.*, VIII, 12; H. W. Preston, "Defenders of Providence," *Coll. R.I.H.S.*, XXI, 56 ff.

[51] 4 *Coll. M.H.S.*, VI, 306-307.

[52] *Plymouth Col. Recs.*, X, 451-453.

[53] *R. I. Col. Recs.*, II, 535.

Arnold administration, back in power, promptly revised without wholly abolishing the Quaker provision exempting conscientious objectors from military service. William Harris lost his place as assistant and was never again elected to a colonial office. Roger Williams was elected assistant but because of infirmities and destruction of his property and impoverishment by the war, declined to serve. Remaining active in Providence to the day of his death, Williams served on the town council for four years and his party, headed by Fenner, Dexter, and himself, controlled most of the town offices.

Baffled by an adverse majority in Providence, Harris revived his scheme to thwart town meeting democracy by the judicial fiat of an intercolonial court. Harris visited England and, assisted by his connection with Smith and Connecticut,[54] won royal assent. Imperial muddling resulted in creation of a court described by Harris and Massachusetts as "impartial" but actually heavily weighted in his favor, six of the eight commissioners being dignitaries from the United Colonies, two of them, George Denison and Symon Lynde, Atherton partners.[55] Harris in his draft commission for the guidance of crown authorities had specified a jury entirely drawn from the United Colonies,[56] but when the court met at Providence in October and November, 1677, three from Rhode Island sat with the jury. In arguing his case, Harris assailed Williams' party for upholding the cause of "after comers" and declared that under English law the lapse of time since he procured the "confirmatory" deeds of 1659 ruled out the protest of any "pittifull needy flattered Indians."[57] To combat Williams' interpretation of the original boundaries, Harris in his plea to the king contended that Pawtuxet men had made the first purchases from the Indians; to which Fenner, Dexter, and Williams replied with demonstrable accuracy that the Pawtuxet deed showed the land had been bought from Roger Williams, "who is no Indian!"[58] Williams, who in his many years as legislator, judge, and president, had picked up more than a smattering of law, demolished the "upstreams" claim by exposing

---

[54] Updike, *Richard Smith*, p. 47.

[55] *Harris Papers*, nos. 35-37, and p. 249; 5 *Coll. M.H.S.*, IX, 29, 111; *Cal. State Papers, Am. and W. I., 1675-1676*, pp. 214, 261.

[56] *Cal. State Papers, ibid.*, 214.

[57] *Harris Papers*, pp. 198, 202.

[58] *Ibid.*, 129, 198, 214-215, 219-220.

the legal weakness of the basic document in the Pawtuxet case. This, the memorandum of 1639, Williams correctly described as a mere notation of a "courtesy" of Miantonomu which protected the settlers' cattle from becoming the prey of Indians if they grazed up river beyond the town line. The memorandum had no force in law as a grant of the land up river, since it stated no limits and was not a deed but a notation of an oral statement recorded without "the sachem's knowledge," lacking his signature, undated, unwitnessed, and unaccompanied by the passage of any consideration for the pretended grant.[59]

The court, composed, as the Gortonists complained, of "our professed and mortal enemies," "outvoted those of Rhode Island."[60] In effect, the Harris deeds of 1659 were given precedence over the Gortonist deed of 1643 and Williams' deed of 1638. Providence was ordered to run the dividing line between the town and Pawtuxet westward to the mid-point on a thwart line drawn between the heads of the Pawtuxet and Woonasquatucket rivers. Thus, under the aegis of a friendly high court, the Pawtuxet partners circumvented the popular will and like the Yazoo, Arredondo, and other claimants before the Supreme Court in the nineteenth century, succeeding in converting a fraudulent land title into a vested right. Harris, however, was to reap nothing but bitterness and despair and come to a tragic death in his passionate pursuit of a lordship of land. The Williams party ran the western thwart line between the heads of the two rivers in such a way as to cut off Pawtuxet proprietors from virtually all they had hoped to gain.[61] Harris while on ship for England to act as public agent for Connecticut in the Narragansett controversy and to appeal his own case to the king was captured and enslaved by Algerian pirates in 1680, ransomed a year later at an exorbitant figure, reached London a broken old man and died within a week. One of Williams' last acts two years later was the signing of an agreement by which William Carpenter and his Pawtuxet partners forfeited their claim to the lands which Williams purchased for the town by his deeds of 1661.[62] Efforts to revive Pawtuxet claims continued for years after Williams' death, but terminated in failure.

[59] N.C.P., VI, 390, 394.
[60] Backus, The Baptists, I, 446-447.
[61] See map, Richman, Rhode Island, II, 197.
[62] Prov. Recs., IV, 73-76.

Efforts of Fitz-John Winthrop, an Atherton partner, and other Connecticut leaders to wrest the Narragansett country from Rhode Island likewise continued through Williams' last years and into the next century, only to end in failure. Meanwhile evidences multiplied of a profound change in Rhode Island society. Narragansett speculators began to breed horses on a large scale, developing the celebrated Narragansett pacer, and after Williams' death introduced the anomaly of a plantation system with Negro slaves and a fashionable gentry like that of Virginia. Rhode Island land engrossers like Richard Smith and Francis Brinley of the Atherton enterprise and William Brenton and his son Jahleel of the Pettiquamscut company followed the drift of their economic interests and steadily diverged from the social philosophy which had lain at the heart of Rhode Island democracy. William Harris in 1678 described his opponents as "a silly Ignorant yet bold and proud multitude not haveing one Just man of capassety among them."[63] "We are nowe Governed by Mens Wills and most of them Quackers, and of such and worse doe Rode Island consists," wrote Smith in 1679.[64] In the same vein Francis Brinley declared Rhode Island had "a Quaker mob Government" where the "meanest sort rule their betters."[65] Smith and Brinley were soon associated with Richard Wharton of Boston and the disreputable Cranfield, Governor of New Hampshire, in backstairs intrigues in behalf of the Atherton company. Smith, later becoming a member of the Andros council by whose favor he wrested Hog Island from its former possessors, owned at death eight Negro slaves and an estate valued at £1159 not including his widespread holdings of land.[66] Richard Wharton obtained 1712 acres of Narragansett land in 1687 under the friendly auspices of Smith and others of the Andros council.[67] The rising value of fertile Narragansett land may be suggested by the estimate for William Brenton's Pettiquamscut tract in 1674, already rated at £300.[68] In 1678 William Harris satisfied himself of the lawfulness under Rhode Island's charter of aristocratic feudal precedents for the descent of estates and having left his land entailed, expressed the

[63] *Harris Papers*, p. 259.
[64] *Ibid.*, p. 275.
[65] *Pub. R.I.H.S.*, VIII, 94.
[66] Updike, *Richard Smith*, p. 66 and *passim*.
[67] *R. I. Col. Recs.*, III, 225-226.
[68] *Coll. R.I.H.S.*, III, 298.

ardent hope that his great grandchildren would be so "wise" as to entail the land "to theire fourth Genneration also."[69] In the eighteenth century primogeniture appeared in Rhode Island, as English notions of property, class, and family marked the growing division between successful speculators and the common body of small freeholders.

Though Williams won his last struggle with Harris and the Pawtuxet partners, he had cause to doubt that equalitarianism in one colony could survive in the face of an aristocratic world. In 1681 he made the last of his many public appeals to cherish and honor the Rhode Island process of self-government and reminded grumblers against taxes, "There is no man that hath a vote in town or colony, but he hath a hand in making the rates by himself or his deputies."[70] Upon economic opportunity, free access to land, would depend the survival of this freeholders' democracy. In an undated letter Williams urged the town to reserve some of the land for later settlers: "I earnestly pray the town ... that after you have got over the black brook of some soul bondage yourselves, you tear not down the bridge after you, by leaving no small pittance for distressed souls that may come after you."[71] In the years between 1660, when the purchasers in Providence numbered approximately ninety-one, and 1683 when Williams died, only ten new purchase rights were added to the list.[72] Warwick closed the door to after comers in 1677.[73] For a short time the new town of East Greenwich, then Coweset, established by the assembly in 1677 as a patriotic enterprise to head off the Atherton company, gave opportunity to landless young men in older Rhode Island towns to acquire a homestead on the original Providence basis of one hundred acres to each purchaser.[74] In 1682 the purchasers in the various towns, still an overwhelming majority of the whole body of freeholders and voters, consolidated their position with respect to the future by procuring a general statute which vested undivided town lands in the existing holders of purchase rights. Thus, in line with the similar trend in other New England

[69] *Harris Papers*, pp. 249-250; *Prov. Recs.*, VI, 48-56.
[70] *N.C.P.*, VI, 401-402; *Prov. Recs.*, XV, 219-220.
[71] *N.C.P.*, VI, 318.
[72] *Prov. Recs.*, III, 16, 22, 29, 67; VIII, 124; XV, 204. For Providence Williams and John Smith Jamaico, compare *ibid.*, III, 72-74, and XVII, 30-34.
[73] H. R. Curtis, "Warwick Proprietors' Division," *Coll. R.I.H.S.*, XX, 39.
[74] *R. I. Col. Recs.*, II, 588.

colonies, purchasers became "proprietors" and the public domain of each town passed into the hands of a private land company.[75] This discrimination against the common man, tending to identify property and political privileges ever more closely, produced a narrower suffrage in the next century and stunted the growth of a democratic yeomanry.

Williams' great principle of religious liberty remained a rooted article of Rhode Island faith, but the democratic experiment which he, Gorton, and Clarke had so hopefully launched did not long survive them. Last of the three to pass from the scene, Williams died between January 27 and March 15, 1683,[76] leaving the stage to a generation that cherished his name but looked on traffic in slaves and rum, and upon wealth and family position with the worldly eyes of the eighteenth century. On a fragmentary town record appears a reference to "The Venerable remaines of Mr. Roger Williams, the Father of Providence, the Founder of the Colony, and of Liberty of Conscience." He was suitably honored "with all the solemnity the colony was able to shew," the militia firing their guns over his grave.[77]

[75] *Digest of Laws of the Colony of Rhode Island* (Newport, 1730), pp. 30-32; Akagi, *Town Proprietors*, chapter III.

[76] *Coll. R.I.H.S.*, XV, 421; *Prov. Recs.*, VIII, 122.

[77] *Prov. Recs.*, VIII, 17; *Coll. R.I.H.S.*, IV, 147; XXVII, 54.

21

ROGER WILLIAMS AND THE AMERICAN TRADITION

THE HUMANIST AND LIBERTARIAN SPIRIT in Rhode Island represented no wholly indigenous growth on American soil but a transplanted culture finding new vigor in a more favorable clime. Its inspiration and direction sprang from the radical reaction of outcast stepchildren of the Reformation who recoiled from tortures of the body and outward compulsions employed to uphold authoritarian dogmas and who fixed upon the inwardness of spiritual regeneration as the prime essential; conceiving of truth as something not revealed only to scholars but within the comprehension of all men, these sectarians turned to the democratic process of free discussion and free competition among churches as the surest means to awaken the individual conscience and guide man into the way of the good life. Religious equalitarians, proclaiming force both ineffective and irrelevant in determining matters of opinions, making all sects equal in status and all communicants equal with one another, passed readily on to a larger belief in a free society. In Rhode Island these radical dissenters, carrying their logic over into the political sphere, struck at unequal privileges and arbitrary compulsions and framed their laws with an eye to liberation of the human personality, leaving politics open to the free competition of parties and opinions.

This new social psychology was powerfully reinforced by the frontier position of early Rhode Island. The negligible degree of imperial supervision in the generation of the founders of the colony, the absence of a royal governor, official clerical class, or intrenched landed gentry, left the early settlers relatively freed of pressures which normally tended to produce close conformity to the aristocratic English mold. The dynamic factor of open land and the extensive degree to which Rhode Island settlers were recruited from the ranks of common folk combined to validate the radical doctrine of common brotherhood, provided a sound social and economic basis for equalitarianism, and left the deep imprint of a sectarian and frontier humanism upon social legislation touching debtors and sinners, marriage and divorce, military training and slavery.

Rhode Island in the age after Williams' death was to be marked by a more glittering culture, but in the process of change new forces sapped the vitality of the old libertarian values, following the general line of tendency in the seaboard settlements north and south. Although throughout New England as estates were subdivided and new settlements founded, the body of freeholders multiplied its numbers, the genius of the town land system proved increasingly more hospitable to the interests of speculators than of ordinary settlers. While on the later American frontier the presence of free land quickened the democratic impulse, the mode of land disposal in New England tended to retard that impulse. Williams early discovered a fundamental organic weakness in the town system, the allocation to a self-perpetuating corportion of the power of distributing the local public domain. By this system, incongruous in a democracy, admission as a purchaser became a privilege and not a right, and purchase shares descended on the hereditary basis, creating in each town an inner circle of privileged families. Half-way in the seventeenth century when the notion of popular consent in government was still generally limited by the feudal identification of political privileges with landed property, Rhode Island went to the radical extent of enfranchising all freeholders however small their holdings; but not even in Providence where equalitarianism remained a powerful force during the first generation did Williams and the townsmen convert the privilege of an equal right to undivided town land into a universal right open to all comers. Thus long before the available land was actually distributed, the original democratic factor of relative ease of acquiring it began to lose force; and in eighteenth century Rhode Island, as in other colonies, the more successful land jobbers gave stimulus to the movement which narrowed the franchise and concentrated political power in the hands of men of property.

The political peregrinations of Roger Williams represented a distillation of the best in the great English revolutionary movement and a high endeavor to build in the American wilderness a humble experiment in a more generous fellowship. Not a systematic philosopher, Williams wrote tracts to meet the needs of the times and his published works did not survive; nor was the wide sweep of his thought to be found in them, but rather in his whole career, his unpublished letters and public appeals to Rhode Island citizens, and the institutions he founded and struggled to preserve. Like Milton and Locke, he bore an honored part in developing the vision of the rights of man which flowered in the enlightenment of the eighteenth century. His political testament was bred of a virile endeavor to create a democracy and keep it in being. Facing partisan divisions, defiance of authority, and even secession, he never despaired of popular government nor ridiculed the assumption that man is rational and an electorate capable of intelligent judgment; and in times of crisis he devoted his talents to the crucial task of organizing popular consent and rallying the citizens to subordinate their private interests to the larger public interest and keep open the social mechanisms for arbitration and compromise. Forerunner of the eighteenth century enlightenment in America, precursor of Jefferson, he conceived of a reconciliation of property and democracy through a wide distribution of wealth and continuous adjustment of political functions to the great end of "the commonweale" and "peace and welfare of the state." His social outlook was in some respects more inherently democratic than were the ideas of many of the political leaders who framed the American constitution. Disregarding the formalized fiction of the social contract, he conceived of fundamental law in terms of an expanding democratic compact continuously reinterpreted to accord with the actual will of the people. Higher law or judicial finality as a protection of property against democracy found no place in Williams' thought. Governmental form was related to function and power to need. Addressing the rump parliament of Cromwell, he warned bluntly of the folly of setting up fundamental restrictions to bind the will of future generations: "the childrens work hath been to tumble down their fathers buildings. Nor can your most prudent Heads and potent Hands possibly erect that Fabrick which the next Age (it may be the next Parliament) may not tumble down."[1] Though an apostle of the philosophy of the rights of man, rights as he conceived them were generally conditioned by the supreme test of social welfare. Concretely he defended freedom of thought and religious worship as absolute rights; but his political ideas were grounded in a concept of social coöperation rather than atomic individualism. Trusting like the philosophers of the eighteenth century to the free play of reason and the generally sound impulse of the conscience of mankind, Williams envisioned radical liberty for free development of individual personality; but the very

[1] *N.C.P.*, IV, 12.

principles by which the government was obligated to protect the
civil rights to life, liberty, and property, "the safety . . . of a people,"
as he phrased it, "in their bodies and goods," necessarily meant
refusal to protect an acquisitive and arbitrary freedom of action
which infringed the rights of others or became in essence a right
against society.

As in Williams' life, so in death, the spokesmen of the New
England gentry gave little recognition to the founder of Rhode Island.
Though in the eighteenth century Thomas Hollis, the English
benefactor of the Harvard library, presented the college with a
copy of the *Bloudy Tenent*,[2] Thomas Hutchinson and other con-
servators of the aristocratic tradition largely ignored the radical
significance of Williams' challenge to the regnant orders. Stephen
Hopkins, governor of Rhode Island and Revolutionary leader,
proudly acclaimed Williams as the founder of religious liberty
and in 1771 led the first movement in Providence to honor him
with a monument; but historical sketches by Callender, Hopkins,
Morgan Edwards and others, though attesting the local fame of
Williams, were unknown to the outside world.[3] In 1777 Rhode
Island's government drew attention in Germany;[4] but in the years
when the colony of William Penn, intimately associated in the mind
of the *philosophes* with the "legend of the good Quaker," won the
admiration of French intellectuals,[5] Rhode Island went largely
unnoted. In the nineteenth century German, French, and English
scholars were to perceive and publicize the significant relationship
of Williams and Rhode Island to the European intellectual revolution which culminated in the great political upheaval of 1789;[6] but
even in America in the eighteenth century Williams' reputation
remained obscure until the Revolutionary War precipitated the
struggle to overthrow the system of established churches.

Absolute religious liberty had yet to win respectability when
the Baptist, Isaac Backus, under the cold stare of John Adams,

---

2 J. D. Knowles, *Roger Williams* (Boston, 1834), p. 360 n.

3 *Ibid.*, 430-431; *Coll. R.I.H.S.*, VI, 319-320.

4 *Freyheitsbrief den Kolonie Rhode-Island* (Leipzig, 1777).

5 Edith Philips, *The Good Quaker in French Legend* (Philadelphia, 1932),
pp. 91-93.

6 George G. Gervinus, *Einleitung in die Geschichte des Neunzehnten Jahr-
hunderts* (Leipzig, 1853); Jellinek, *Declaration of the Rights of Man and of
Citizens;* Masson, *Milton;* Charles Bourgeaud, *The Rise of Modern Democracy
in Old and New England* (London, 1894).

appeared before the Continental Congress and pleaded the cause of Massachusetts dissenters. In 1777 in his history of the Baptists, Backus struck another blow for a free church system and in his first volume, largely a biography of Williams, called the attention of the new nation to Rhode Island's founder as a great early champion of religious equality and civil liberty. Early in the next century Dr. David Ramsay of Charleston, South Carolina, friend of Benjamin Franklin and pupil of Benjamin Rush, extolled Williams as "more bold, just, and liberal" than any of his predecessors, an apostle of "civil and religious freedom" and peer of Milton and Locke.[7] As dissenters slowly won the struggle against the established church in the three die-hard states, Massachusetts, New Hampshire, and Connecticut, Williams' prestige steadily gained even in the old stronghold of orthodox Puritanism. The Connecticut historian, Benjamin Trumbull, spoke favorably of his "illuminated" views,[8] and Hawthorne in his tales of early Salem seized upon the benevolent personality of Williams to give dramatic contrast to the inhumanity and intolerance of the Puritan fathers.

A scholarly biography by a Baptist professor in a theological school appeared in 1834.[9] But it remained for the son of a Unitarian clergyman, George Bancroft, rebel against conventional training at Harvard and ardent Jacksonian Democrat, to portray Williams with the exuberant spirit of American democracy and single him out as an American immortal, gifted with "one of those clear minds, which sometimes bless the world by their power of receiving moral truth in its purest light."[10] Setting Williams' banishment against the background of intolerance and arbitrary aristocratic rule of New England's founders, the first volume of Bancroft's famous history of the United States brought out for the first time the democratic character of Williams' agitation at Salem, extolled the novel institutions of Rhode Island, and praised and quoted freely from the writings in which Williams undertook to "publish to the world" his defense "of the religious freedom of mankind." "At a time when Germany was the battlefield for all Europe in the implacable wars of religion; . . . when France was still to go through the

---

[7] History of the United States (Philadelphia, 1816), I, 155.
[8] A General History of the United States (Boston, 1810), I, 105.
[9] J. D. Knowles, Roger Williams.
[10] History of the United States (Boston, 1834), I, 397.

fearful struggle with bigotry; when England was gasping under the despotism of intolerance; . . . and two years before Descartes founded modern philosophy on the method of free reflection,— Roger Williams asserted the great doctrine of intellectual liberty. . . . He was the first person in modern Christendom to assert in its plenitude the doctrine of the liberty of conscience, the equality of opinions before the law; and in its defense he was the harbinger of Milton, the precursor and the superior of Jeremy Taylor."[11]

This resounding panegyric found immediate echo in school histories. Embellished with a picture of the banished man in lonely flight from Salem, a textbook of 1836, making acknowledgment to Bancroft, classed Williams "among the most celebrated assertors of intellectual freedom."[12] In illustrated schoolbooks, sketches of Williams' flight and his kindly reception among his Indian friends became a favorite, and the accompanying text continued to reflect the sonorous language of Bancroft: "exiled *to* Massachusetts, and now exiled *by* Massachusetts, he brought to the banks of the Narragansett the great doctrines of perfect religious liberty, and the equal rights of men."[13] At the outset of the Pequot war, declared Lossing's popular "family" history, Williams "saved his persecutors from destruction, yet they had not the Christian manliness to remove the sentence of banishment."[14]

Through the same process by which George Washington and the Revolutionary leaders became figures of legendary proportions, symbols of unity and constitutional rights, Williams emerged on a lesser plane as a national folk hero, celebrated as a friend of the Indians, a colonial founder of "pure democracy," and popular symbol of intellectual freedom and civil liberty. Thus in his comic

---

[11] *Ibid.* (5th ed., 1839), I, 375-377. Bancroft retained his portrait of Williams virtually unchanged; see 24th ed., 1872.

[12] John Frost, *History of the United States for the Use of Schools* (Philadelphia, 1836), p. 93.

[13] John Clark Ridpath, *History of the United States for Schools* (Cincinnati, 1878), pp. 92, 133; Marcius Willson, *History of the United States for Schools* (N. Y., 1847), pp. 112-113; J. Olney, *A History of the United States for Schools and Academies* (rev. ed., New Haven, 1851), pp. 54 n., 90; G. P. Quackenbos, *Illustrated School History of the United States* (N. Y., 1867), p. 85; John J. Anderson, *The United States Reader* (N. Y., 1874), pp. 67-70; Thomas Wentworth Higginson, *Young Folks' History of the United States* (Boston, 1879), pp. 68, 70.

[14] Benson J. Lossing, *A Family History of the United States* (Hartford and Chicago, 1881), p. 91.

history Bill Nye was simply relying upon a firmly established popular conception: Williams, in contrast to Puritans "who had enlarged consciences, and who desired to take in extra work for others who had no consciences," was the first to believe "that a man's own conscience must be his own guide and not that of another"; "too liberal to be kindly received" by the Puritans, he was driven out and took refuge with the Indians who "were less rigid and kept open on Sundays"; so he founded a colony of his own on the idea that "no man should be required to whittle his soul into a shape to fit the religious auger-hole of another."[15]

Invocation of dead heroes to stem the tide of popular reform and condone a rooted abuse was an old and recurrent social phenomenon; but such use of symbolism to lend sanctity to a vested right was an ironical fate which it was Williams' fortune generally to escape. By the very nature of his fame popular appeals in the name of Williams drove toward goals of which he spiritually approved. The eloquent Unitarian leader, William Ellery Channing, pleading the cause of emancipation in 1840, urged Baptists in the South not to be "forgetful of the sainted name of Roger Williams, whose love of the despised Indian, and whose martyr spirit should have taught them fearless sympathy with the negro."[16] So also the German immigrant, Carl Schurz, himself a refugee, speaking in 1859 on "True Americanism" at historic Fanueil Hall, Boston, invoked the magic of Williams' name: attacking the persecuting spirit of Know-Nothing legislation against the Catholics, Schurz demanded "perfect freedom of inquiry . . . what Roger Williams, one of the most luminous stars of the American sky, called the sanctity of conscience."[17] Similarly a generation later Senator Hoar, flinging defiance at the political pressure of the anti-Catholic American Protective Association, affirmed his faith in "the American Spirit . . . especially what Roger Williams called 'Soul Liberty.' "[18] Meanwhile a minor political chieftain, James A. Garfield, indulging his penchant for preaching, went the whole way

---

[15] Bill Nye, *History of the United States,* J. B. Lippincott Co. (Philadelphia, 1894), pp. 50, 52, 68.

[16] "Emancipation," *Works* (Boston, 1899), p. 836.

[17] *Speeches, Correspondence and Political Papers of Carl Schurz* (ed. by Frederic Bancroft, G. P. Putnam's Sons, New York, 1913), I, 62.

[18] George F. Hoar, *Autobiography of Seventy Years,* Charles Scribner's Sons, (New York, 1903), II, 292.

in an address to gentlemen of the press; warning of the difficulties with which freedom had been won, he canonized Roger Williams as "our earliest apostle of the freedom of the press"; the illustrious exile of Rhode Island spoke for "the right to utter his own convictions,—as the inalienable right of every freeman," but it took more than a century for his "great thought" to crystallize at last in the "enduring form of constitutional law."[19]

By the second quarter of the twentieth century the meaning of the living Williams in the American tradition had become more portentous. As savage persecution of Jews reappeared in Europe, thoughtful Americans became troubled by a revitalized anti-Semitism in their own country and with increasing frequency appealed to the spirit of Roger Williams. Meanwhile as the rising tide of anti-intellectualism weakened the faith in the rational capacity of men in the mass and truculent fascism bluntly asserted majority rule an iniquitous sham, students of affairs belatedly recognized a growing crisis in modern thought. As democracy was thrust on the defensive, public spokesmen invoked the names of the nation's heroes and, among others, harked back to Williams as a seventeenth century figure of vital signification for the democratic way of life. Those who feared the impulse to defend democracy in a fascist manner cited Williams in opposition to teachers' oaths, called him in to testify for academic freedom as a prime essential for rational progress, and apotheosized him in declamations against proscription on account of race or creed.

Thus as the fundamental premises of the American faith came increasingly under fire, its defenders linked the warm humanism and virile intellectual insurgency of men like Williams ever more closely with the democratic tradition; and Rhode Island's founder attained full stature, by no means so powerful a symbol as Washington or Lincoln but a folk hero popularly associated with the great heritage of the Bill of Rights. It was clear, however, that Williams' fame stood on no more secure footing than the strength of the premises upon which democracy rested; and that his reputation would conceivably decline unless Americans of the future retained a belief in equalitarianism as purposeful as his and passed through the ordeal of resolving class conflict and social maladjustment by the democratic process.

[19] *Works* (ed. by B. A. Hinsdale, Boston, 1883), II, 578.

INDEX

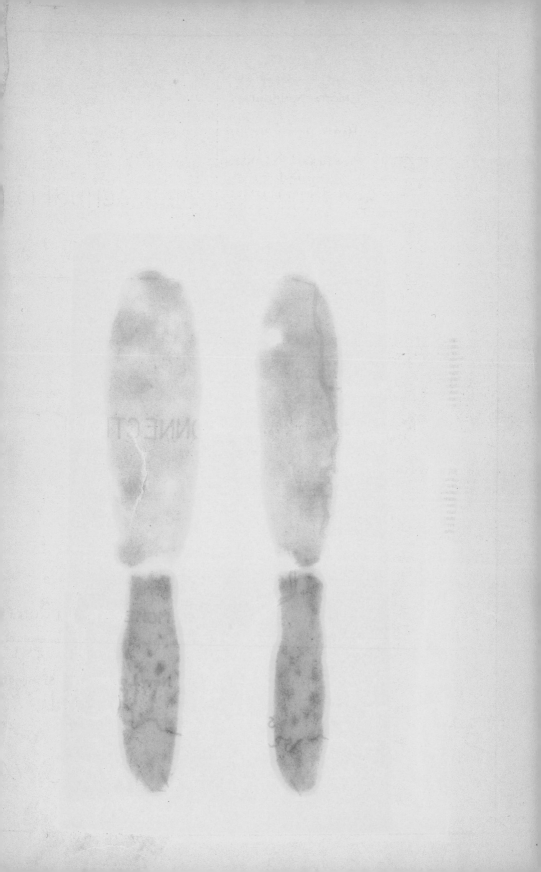

MASSACHUSETTS

COUNTE
Pequot
Fort

Stonington

New Ha

Har

Wethe